Success in Your Project
A Guide to Student System Development Projects

PHILIP WEAVER (Wolverhampton University)

 **Prentice Hall**
FINANCIAL TIMES

An imprint of **Pearson Education**
Harlow, England • London • New York • Boston • San Francisco • Toronto • Sydney • Singapore • Hong Kong
Tokyo • Seoul • Taipei • New Delhi • Cape Town • Madrid • Mexico City • Amsterdam • Munich • Paris • Milan

Pearson Education Limited
Edinburgh Gate
Harlow
Essex CM20 2JE
England

and Associated Companies throughout the world

Visit us on the World Wide Web at:
www.pearsoned.co.uk

ISBN 0 273 67809 4

British Library Cataloguing-in-Publication Data
A catalogue record for this book is available from the British Library

Library of Congress Cataloging-in-Publication Data
Weaver, Philip L.
  Success in your project : a guide to student system development projects / Philip Weaver.
    p. cm.
  Includes bibliographical references and index.
  ISBN 0–273–67809–4 (pbk.)
  1. Computer software—Development.   2. Computer science—Study and teaching.   I. Title.

  QA76.76.D47W39 2004
  005.1—dc22

                                                          2003055632

10 9 8 7 6 5 4 3 2 1
09 08 07 06 05 04

Typeset in 9.5/12.5pt Stone serif by 35
Printed and bound by Bell & Bain Limited, Glasgow

For Anna

Contents

Part Two   **Project execution**

Preface

Projects are an important feature of most undergraduate and postgraduate degrees in the fields of information systems, software engineering and business computing. Indeed, for the majority of computing-related degree courses, projects represent a mandatory double module, undertaken in the final year of study. As such, they make the largest single contribution to the final degree classification of many students.

While a small number of students will undertake pure research projects, most will carry out a system development project that aims to deliver a business system, software component or technical infrastructure. This is usually supplemented with an element of research, and with critical analyses of the execution of their project and of the theory applied. System development projects are largely self-managed by students, with occasional supervision and review by a member of the academic staff.

The problem that confronts students is how to bring together and apply their theoretical knowledge of system development to a real-life situation, in a way that will satisfy both the academic requirements of their university or college, and the business or functional objectives of their system and its sponsor. While students should be equipped with most of the technical skills needed to carry out a successful project, this will be the first time that they have been asked to apply those skills to anything other than carefully constrained academic case studies, and in a situation where they are working without the close scrutiny and guidance of their lecturer or teacher. Many students will also need to use techniques in the areas of research, project management, and report preparation that have either not been covered in their degree course or that require significant adaptation to meet the unique requirements of an academic systems development project (as opposed to a business project).

Before now, there have been no textbooks that address the full range of challenges that students on computing-related degree courses encounter during the setting up, execution and completion of their system development projects.

Aims and scope

This book is the first to provide detailed guidance and support for students in preparing for, conducting and evaluating the outcomes of a system development project, irrespective of the development methodology or technologies used. It also caters for projects that range in scope from feasibility studies, through software prototype development, to development projects that cover the entire system development life cycle.

The book introduces no new formal system development theory or software construction techniques, as it is assumed that students will have acquired these during the course of their other studies. Instead, it provides guidance on how such theory and techniques should be applied to a real-life student project, including the selection, adaptation and application of the major system development approaches, such as rapid application development (RAD), structured methods and object-oriented approaches. It also provides detailed instruction on how to adapt more generic techniques, such as requirements definition and fact finding, to the special requirements of a student project.

For some students, the successful delivery of system development products will be sufficient to meet the assessment criteria of their project module. However, for many computing-related degree students, and certainly for postgraduate students, their project will also involve an element of research. This book therefore introduces the main research techniques (such as literature searches, critical analysis and data presentation) that are appropriate for the completion of a system development project.

In addition to guiding students through system development and research activities, the book provides detailed instruction on how to manage a student project. This includes the critical tasks of selection, planning and initiation of the project, as well as project control, record keeping, time management and progress reporting.

Finally, this book will assist students in the analysis, evaluation, writing-up and presentation of their projects.

Structure and approach of the book

The book is broken into three parts, each of which reflects a key phase in the conduct of a student project:

1. **Project preparation.** Part One defines a number of different types of project, and provides an overview of how each type might be approached and structured. It introduces the academic and business requirements of a systems development project, and discusses the identification and selection of potential project topics. Finally the generation of a project proposal is covered in detail. This includes the activities of objective setting, high-level planning and scoping.

2. **Project execution.** Part Two opens with detailed guidance on how to manage your project. The following chapters cover the core stages of systems analysis, system design, construction and implementation, all of which present unique challenges within the special context of a student project.

3. **Project completion.** The third part of the book covers the preparation, structure and content of the final project report. Guidance is provided on how to write and present the report, including how to conduct a software

demonstration. There is also a discussion of the academic requirements of the final report, with a focus on the important, but all too often neglected, areas of critical analysis and evaluation.

Features of this book include:

- numerous tables of guidelines, tips, and checklists for completing key project activities;
- real-world examples highlighted in boxes;
- samples of project documents, with templates available for commonly used systems analysis and design products available from the companion website;
- tables of common errors, and how to avoid them;
- links to other sources of information and support, both within and outside the book (including Internet resources);
- focus points, highlighting areas and issues that are either academically or technically significant.

Who will use this book?

Virtually all HND, undergraduate and postgraduate students on courses in business computing, information systems and software engineering will be required to undertake a final year project, the majority of which will include a significant element of system development. A substantial number of students on more general business studies courses will also choose to undertake a systems development project. In addition, many students will also carry out project work, including group projects, at other times during their studies.

The self-managed nature of a project, combined with the limited time that even the best academic supervisors can make available to advise individual students, means that students inevitably feel short of day-to-day support. This book is intended to supplement the advice provided by project supervisors, and be an invaluable source of on-hand guidance.

The book will also appeal to project supervisors. Owing to the large number of students undertaking this type of project, many supervisors will come from academic areas outside systems development. For these supervisors this book will act as a valuable back-up resource.

Supplements

There is an accompanying website for this book, providing a comprehensive set of checklists and templates, together with sample documents in Microsoft Word and Excel format. Visit www.booksites.net/weaver.

About the author

Philip Weaver, formerly of Westminster University, is a Senior Lecturer in Information Systems at the University of Wolverhampton, and is an experienced project supervisor. He has also held a number of posts in industry, including Systems Development Controller at B&Q plc, Project Manager at EMI Records and Business Analyst at the John Lewis Partnership.

Philip Weaver is the author of the textbook *Practical Business Systems Development Using SSADM*, published by FT Prentice Hall, and now in its third edition.

Acknowledgements

We are grateful to the following for permission to reproduce copyright material:

Box 1.1 reproduced by permission of Christopher Casey; Figure 3.3 from *Business Information Systems, Technology, Development and Management for the e-Business* (2nd edition), Pearson Education (Bocij *et al.* 2003); Figure 3.7 reproduced by permission of www.dsdm.org

Part

1

Project preparation and set-up

1 Introduction to student projects

1.1 Introduction

The aim of this chapter is to do some scene setting. A student project is very different both from a commercial project and from a standard piece of coursework. So, before dealing with the practical challenges of setting up and executing a project, this chapter introduces the basic concepts that will underpin the rest of the book. It also discusses the factors that distinguish a good project from a bad one, and provides the background for you to begin thinking about what you want your project to deliver.

Learning Outcomes

After reading this chapter, you will be able to:

- Understand what student projects are designed to achieve
- Describe the principal activities of a student development project
- Describe the different types of student project
- Understand the critical success factors in undertaking a student project

1.2 What is a student system development project?

Most computing-related degree courses require students to complete at least one piece of substantial project work. Many courses culminate in an individual project, often equivalent in its contribution to the final degree award to two taught modules. In addition, some courses will require individual or group projects to be undertaken at other times, either as a learning experience or as part of an assessment.

Regardless of the stage at which they are carried out, projects can be used to explore, develop or examine two areas: firstly, your ability to apply skills or knowledge acquired during your studies in a situation that is much closer to the real world than an examination or piece of academic coursework; and secondly, your critical understanding of the work you have carried out during the project itself. What will vary is the balance between these two areas. Early on in a degree course projects will typically be used to develop or test the application of theory, while in the final year the emphasis will shift to include an exploration of your deeper understanding of this theory.

The emphasis placed on critical understanding also varies greatly with the level of the degree course in question. Most HND projects will focus on the application of tools and techniques to a real-world problem, while at the other end of the spectrum the majority of Masters courses will demand a significant element of research, critical analysis and evaluation.

Computing projects come in all shapes and sizes. Some institutions suggest that students spend as little as 100 hours on their final-year projects, while others advise that they will need to allocate anything up to 500 hours. Most final-year projects will be individual pieces of work. However, particularly early on in a degree course, projects may sometimes be undertaken by a group.

The nature of the work undertaken and the types of project that fall into the category of computing projects are discussed in some detail later in this chapter. The requirements of individual courses will often dictate the degree of freedom that students have in selecting a topic or area of study, but projects undertaken by different students within the same course can range from business system development and complex programming to pure research and case studies (although most degree courses require some element of software development).

1.3   Why do a project?

Projects, and in particular final-year projects, are in many ways the most significant part of your degree course. It is important, while selecting and undertaking your project, to bear in mind all of the points listed below, as most will be examined or explored during the assessment of your project.

From an educational perspective a project will enable you to achieve the following:

- Bring together the skills and knowledge you have learnt during your studies. Most of the skills you have acquired to date will have been taught in distinct modules over a period of time. However well integrated your course has been, your project is almost certainly the first opportunity you will have had to use your full range of skills together. For many students it is only when working on their projects that the relationships between what appeared to them to be a disjointed set of skills become apparent.

- Explore an idea, problem or area of study that is of special interest to you.

- Experience the satisfaction of using previously theoretically based skills to solve a real-world problem. It is only during their practical application that the purpose and relevance of some skills will be clarified.
- Gain an insight into the complexities of real-world problems, and the adaptation of theory that is necessary to solve them.
- Develop skills that have not been, or cannot be, taught effectively during your formal studies. Some skills, such as time management, data collection, project management, report writing and teamwork (for group projects), are difficult or impossible to practise or learn in any situation other than a self-managed project. Most courses will allocate a significant number of marks for skills demonstrated in these areas.

From an assessment perspective, projects provide an opportunity to examine your competence in the following areas:

- Application and adaptation of core tools and techniques to a complex problem, in a situation that is not as artificially constrained as an examination or essay, where solutions are of necessity free from ambiguity.
- Investigation and analysis of the problem, its context, and methods for solving it.
- Development and evaluation of potential solutions.
- Implementation and demonstration of the solution.
- Self and time management.
- Teamwork (in group projects).
- Independent learning and the ability to think for yourself.
- Evaluation of your solution and the work you undertook to deliver it.
- Depth of understanding of the problem context and of the theory applied to its solution.

It should be clear from the points covered above that merely implementing a straightforward piece of software (e.g. a simple website) for an external client will be insufficient to meet the requirements of most degree courses. The main thing that sets an academic project apart from an industry project is the need to demonstrate a depth of theoretical understanding and independent thought. The issues involved in selecting a suitable project will be addressed in detail in Chapter 2.

1.4   The main activities and stages of a project

Although every course will have its own timetable of deadlines (often published in a course or project handbook) and its own specific requirements about what must be submitted at each deadline, the main stages and activities of a project remain highly consistent from institution to institution.

Table 1.1 Main project activities

Phase	Activities	Chapter
Preparation	Generate ideas for potential project topics. Select a topic and create a project proposal or brief that outlines its objectives, scope and deliverables.	2
	Identify a member of the academic staff who will act as your project supervisor. Create a Project Initiation Document in agreement with your project supervisor and external client (if you have one).	2
	Identify the research approach and/or development methods that you will adopt during your project (the development method may be an output from your research).	3 and 4
	Create a Project Initiation Document detailing the key aspects of your project, and agree it with your supervisor.	5
Execution	Manage and report on the progress of your project.	6
	Prepare an interim report or presentation mid-way through your project.	11
	Carry out research.	4
	Investigate and analyse system requirements.	7
	Explore potential options for meeting requirements. Produce system design for selected solution.	8
	Build and test your software.	9
	Create user documentation, conduct training and install solution.	9
Completion	Analyse and critically evaluate the execution and outcomes of your project.	10
	Prepare and submit a draft and final reports.	11
	Attend a viva voce examination (interview), which may require you to demonstrate your software.	11

Table 1.1 provides list of the principal activities of a typical computing project, broken down into three phases reflecting the structure of this book. Each item in the list includes a reference to the chapter that deals with it in detail.

1.5   Types of project

Computing projects fall into two main groups. The first, and by far the most popular with students, is the development project, where the ultimate aim is to deliver a piece of software (and/or hardware infrastructure) that satisfies a set

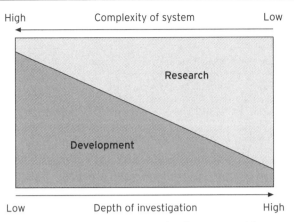

Figure 1.1 Proportion of development and research effort varies with system complexity and the depth of investigation

of defined requirements. It is this group that is the focus of this book, and the different types of development project are explored in some detail below. The second group is the research project, where the aim is to investigate an area of computing, such as a particular technology or a case study, and deliver an original conclusion or insight.

Development and research projects are not however mutually exclusive. Indeed, with the possible exception of HND courses, most development projects will, at the very least, include an investigation of the context of the project and of methods for its delivery. Likewise, most research projects will include an element of development, such as a prototype or software model.

As illustrated in Figure 1.1, the proportion of your total effort that is dedicated to research activities will be low, but not zero, if the complexity of the system or software being developed is high. Conversely, if your project involves a greater depth of research, the proportion of your total effort that is dedicated to development activities will be low, but again not zero.

Development projects

When carrying out a development project, you are likely to use methods, techniques and tools that you have learnt during your course of study, or are familiar with from your workplace or educational background. The research component of your project will need to include an investigation into how these tools and techniques should be adapted for use in your project, as well as demonstrating that they are suitable for solving the problem in the first place. It is not acceptable to state in your project report that you have used techniques 'because they were the ones taught to me on my course', or even 'because I already had a copy of the software on my PC'. While it is undoubtedly the case that existing expertise in a particular technique or the cost of a piece of software is an important factor in selecting tools for a project, you will still need to demonstrate its suitability for the specific project you are undertaking. In doing

Table 1.2   Key development project tasks

Project type	Key development tasks	Key research tasks
Database system	Analyse existing data and processing, including manual systems. Define and model system requirements, with emphasis on data. Develop options for satisfying problem, and select preferred option. Design and develop interfaces and data processing. Map data or object model to relational database tables. Optimise database and interface designs. Populate database with data and implement system.	Research business and application area for common terminology, activities and data. Identify and analyse case studies for successful solutions, lessons learnt, project costs etc. Investigate alternative development methods. Evaluate method used and success of development.
Large business system	Analyse information system (IS) and business strategy, and identify constraints and objectives. Assess feasibility of project and potential solutions. Investigate organisational issues and develop change management plan. Analyse existing data and processing, including manual systems. Define and model system requirements. Develop options for satisfying problem, and select preferred option. Develop prototype partial solutions.	Investigate alternative strategic approaches to business area. Research business and application area for common terminology, activities and data. Identify and analyse case studies for successful solutions, lessons learnt, project costs, etc. Investigate alternative development methods and change management approaches. Evaluate methods used and success of development.
Multimedia	Analyse existing systems, including manual systems. Define and model system requirements, with emphasis on user interfaces. Develop alternative designs for user interface, and select designs for prototyping. Design and implement database and/or database interfaces. Design and implement prototype interfaces.	Research business area and multimedia literature for common terminology, solutions and user interface design approaches. Investigate human/computer interface (HCI) factors and creative design alternatives. Investigate alternative development methods and technical implementation alternatives. Evaluate final designs, prototypes and development method.
Complex programming	Analyse problem and identify key design issues and objectives. Define minimal appropriate user interface. Specify program as series of demonstration prototypes. Develop alternative algorithm designs. Design and implement prototype solutions. Complete development of final solution. Produce supporting program documentation.	Investigate existing or related programs within problem domain. Research algorithms. Investigate alternative programming techniques, languages and tools. Evaluate techniques and tools used, and quality/success of solution.
Technical implementation	Analyse and document existing infrastructure, identifying technical constraints and issues. Confirm functional, performance and data requirements of new infrastructure. Develop options for satisfying problem, and select preferred option. Define and develop any necessary application changes or enhancements. Design and implement test infrastructure. Install production infrastructure.	Identify and analyse case studies for successful solutions, lessons learnt, project costs, etc. Investigate alternative technical implementation and development methods. Evaluate method used and success of implementation.

so, you will inevitably come across alternatives, which you will need to eliminate on the basis of sound analysis and reasoning.

You may find that the tools and techniques that you had intended to use are unsuitable, in which case your research should establish which new skills and techniques you will need to acquire. Alternatively, you could try to modify the project so that it provides a suitable problem for your existing skills.

Several of the most common types of development project are discussed below, with examples. Detailed advice on the tasks that should be carried out in a development project is provided in Part Two of this book, while a summary of the key tasks that differentiate each type of project is given in Table 1.2.

Database system project

The database system project is the most common type of project carried out by computing students. Its main aim is to deliver a system consisting of a relatively complex database, together with a reasonably straightforward (in algorithmic terms) set of programs and interfaces. The emphasis of the project will be on the modelling of data, and the construction of a database along with its associated data manipulation and interface programs, rather than on the design and programming of sophisticated algorithms or state-of-the-art multimedia components.

Database system projects are frequently designed to support the activities of a 'client', who may be a representative of an external organisation or less commonly a member of the academic staff (see Section 6.3 for advice on working with clients). The activities of virtually all types of business, organisation, club or society are candidates for a database system project, given sufficient complexity in their data requirements. To give you a flavour of this diversity, the following list is a small sample of the types of organisation selected by students of the University of Westminster for database system projects:

- advertising agency;
- car breakdown services;
- childminding and nanny services;
- computer sales and services;
- conference organisers;
- electrical suppliers and installers;
- estate agents;
- garage services;
- leisure centre;
- local newspaper;
- tool hire;
- playgroups and nurseries;
- printers;
- restaurant chains;
- sports clubs;
- travel agent;
- vehicle hire business;
- video library.

Large business system project

If your project concerns the development of a system for a large organisation, or if its scope is particularly wide, then you will probably need to target the completion of a small subset of the System Development Life Cycle (SDLC). Of necessity, student projects are relatively short in duration and have extremely limited resources (usually a single person, or at best a small group).

Projects for large organisations will invariably require significant time and resources to be spent in addressing organisational and change management concerns. This means that even if system requirements appear to be relatively straightforward (which would be unusual for a large and complex organisation), a student project will rarely be able to cover the entire life cycle of the project. Likewise, if the organisation is relatively small but the functional scope is very wide, then the amount of effort needed to complete all of the necessary development activity will be beyond the limited resources of your project.

To overcome the problems of scale in a large business system project you will need to identify one or more self-contained pieces of the overall project that together will constitute a meaningful, complete and individual project. One approach might be to take responsibility for the development of a small functional area of a larger project. However, this can lead to difficulties in distinguishing between those products that have been delivered by you and those that have been delivered by the rest of the project team. More significantly perhaps, this approach carries a high risk that any slippage elsewhere in the project will create delays in your project, possibly taking you beyond the project submission deadline.

A more successful approach can be to take on a complete phase of the project. This will usually be an early phase, such as a strategy study, feasibility study or requirements analysis, as the resources required will be less than for the later phases of a large project. More importantly, in the earlier phases you will be able to demonstrate a greater degree of independent work and thinking than you would towards the end of the project. For example, if you were to undertake a project during the design phase you would be constrained by the output of the analysis phase.

Note that if you do choose to carry out a phase from early in the life cycle, you may still need to deliver some software in order to satisfy the academic requirements of your course. For example, if your project consists of a feasibility study you could develop a prototype in order to illustrate potential system solutions to a business problem. Even if not strictly necessary to fulfil the needs of your client, the delivery of software will often prove useful to them.

The topics for large business systems are similar to those of database system projects, but concern the activities of bigger and more complex organisations, such as:

- major high-street retailer;

- international airline;

- news organisation;

- mining company;

- international shipping or freight operator.

Multimedia project

A multimedia project involves the development of a system that has an emphasis on interaction with the user through a variety of media, such as graphics, sound and video. The main development activities will be concerned with the development of the user interface, and research activities will centre on the investigation of interface design, components and technology. In most cases the system will access and manipulate an underlying database, although the complexity of the data will be somewhat less than for a database system project.

An increasing number of students are choosing to undertake multimedia projects that aim to deliver a website for an external client, mainly because of the availability of external clients willing to sponsor such projects. Sadly, many of these projects fail to meet the academic requirements of their courses, as they are too straightforward to provide sufficient technical or intellectual challenge. In order to meet the academic requirements of your course, you will need to ensure that website projects for external clients involve one or more of the following:

- A significant element of underlying complexity, e.g. in the database that the website will connect to (in which case the project is in reality a database project).
- A significant piece of research (in which case your project might in reality be looked upon as a research project).
- An innovative and complex user interface design, which makes advanced use of multimedia technology or design techniques.

Other topics for a multimedia project might include:

- an interactive computer-based training (CBT) system;
- a multimedia product catalogue or kiosk, incorporating graphics, sound and video;
- an on-line manual, again incorporating graphics, sound and video.

Complex programming project

A complex programming project will involve the design and implementation of complex algorithms. The requirements of the project will often be relatively straightforward to define, and the data involved may be trivial, but the programming required will be both intellectually challenging and make sophisticated use of development software and components, and possibly of hardware. In addition, many complex programming projects will involve a relatively significant element of research into potential solutions and software capabilities.

Complex programming projects may involve the complete production and implementation of a commercially useful program for an external client. More often they will be concerned with demonstrating that a specific academic problem can be solved and be programmed.

Examples of complex programming projects undertaken at the University of Westminster include:

- optimisation of vehicle usage;
- game-playing software, such as chess and poker;
- trajectory mapping;
- animal movement tracking and plotting;
- data pattern recognition;
- vehicle movement simulation.

Technical implementation

Technical implementation projects are concerned with the delivery of significant infrastructure components, such as complex hardware devices, operating systems or database management systems.

Projects that involve upgrading or installing a straightforward piece of infra-structure, such as installing a PC or upgrading a server, will not be sufficiently challenging to meet the academic requirements of many courses. Simple technical implementations can be used to demonstrate the outcome of a technology research project, and may form part of a broader development project, but they are unlikely to provide a sound basis for an entire project in their own right.

As with other development projects, there will usually be a research element to even the most substantial of technical implementations. As a minimum you will need to investigate the capabilities of different types of infrastructure components, and to investigate appropriate development and implementation methods.

It is common to find that what you might at first have considered to be a pure infrastructure project also has implications for the systems that utilise the infrastructure. This might arise because constraints on the systems have been removed, or because the new technology has enhanced capabilities that the systems could or should utilise. It is also possible that some rework will be necessitated by the implementation of new or upgraded technical components (for example, a new database management system may require database changes to be made), and this in turn may provide an opportunity to make some enhancements to the systems at the same time.

Some examples of technical infrastructure projects are:

- a local area network implementation;
- WAP (wireless application protocol) installation;
- database migration.

Research-oriented projects

The focus of this book is firmly on the needs of development projects. However, as most development projects will include a research component, it is worth pausing to consider what constitutes a research project.

Many computing students are frightened by the term research. They tend to view it as something that only the most learned of scholars should undertake. This is far from the truth, however. Research is a process that all students will almost certainly have engaged in at some level during their studies, without ever calling it that.

Research, at a basic level, consists of a systematic investigation of some sort, leading to an insight or conclusion that can be backed up by the results of the investigation. This is a process that you will probably have applied to numerous pieces of coursework during your studies, usually in order to answer a question posed by a lecturer.

A good research project will make in-depth use of the research process to add to the body of knowledge in a specific area. Many computing research projects will do this by recommending how or when to do something using a particular methodology, tool or technique. Alternatively, they may provide insights into what or why things are happening in industry, often through the exploration of a case study.

Computing research projects will usually need to be backed up by a limited practical implementation, in order to demonstrate your full understanding of the subject matter, and in order to validate your findings. Before undertaking a research-type project it is essential that you have in place one or more clearly stated objectives: it is not good enough to investigate an area in the hope that you will happen upon something of interest. Research objectives can take many forms, such as a question to be answered, a hypothesis to be tested, or a set of events to be analysed. Another essential prerequisite for the success of a research project is the selection and justification of your research approach (i.e. your method for collecting and analysing data). Some of the more commonly used research approaches are outlined in Chapter 4.

There are many more types of research project within the field of computing, for example in the fields of theoretical computer science or artificial intelligence, or into the sociological effects of computing. The project types discussed below have been chosen for inclusion in this book because they will frequently form the basis of the research element of a development project, albeit in a cut-down form.

Methodology investigation project

The objective of a methodology investigation is to evaluate the effectiveness of different methodologies in solving a given problem or problem type. The problem to be solved will usually be outside the standard scope of the methodologies in question, as this will usually be well documented and understood already. In this case the investigation should aim to provide original insights into the shortcomings of the methodologies, and to propose ways in which methodologies could be adapted or used in combination.

A methodology investigation is often carried out as part of a development project. The investigation will tend to focus on research into standard methodologies, and an evaluation of the application and adaptation of a single methodology to the development problem concerned. The products delivered by methodology investigation projects will usually include the models and design components of each methodology, together with simple software implementations or prototypes that demonstrate the capabilities and outcomes of each methodology.

The focus of the investigation will determine the extent of any software implementations. For example, if the investigation is centred on user interface design, the software element of the project may comprise a number of alternative interface designs, while if the focus is on database design, the project is likely to implement a number of database designs.

If your investigation is directed at the early stages of the SDLC, and the requirements of your course will allow it, then there may not be any software implementation at all. An example of this type of project would be an evaluation of the effectiveness of different methodologies in capturing and communicating user requirements (and even in this example it could be argued that one way to test this effectiveness would be through the evaluation of software prototypes).

Technology investigation project

The objective of a technology investigation is to evaluate the application of one or more infrastructure components (hardware or software) to a given problem. The investigation may focus on the application and adaptation of a standard infrastructure component to a problem that is particularly complex or original. Alternatively, the investigation may take a standard problem and research new solutions from an emerging set of technologies. In either case the project should aim to make original recommendations as to how the technology in question should or can be used in a specific scenario. In addition, the project will also need to deliver a simple implementation of the technology, in order to demonstrate that the solution will actually work in practice.

Many development projects will include an element of technology investigation, but the focus will tend to be more on the standard use of established infrastructure components than on the innovative application of new components.

Case study

The objective of a case study project is to investigate and evaluate how computing is being used in a real-life situation. The area under investigation should ideally be one which is not well understood and documented currently, so that original descriptions can be made and conclusions be drawn. The investigation may range from an examination of a company's information systems strategy to the study of how a specific technology is being used in a particular situation.

The outcomes of the study will need to be compared with published research in the area, and any disparities discussed. The key to success in a case study project is to recommend how your conclusions can be adapted to a wider context.

Within a development project, a case study may be used to develop a strategy for the solution of a specific problem. For example, you could adapt your conclusions regarding the application of groupware within one organisation to the development of a specific workflow application in another organisation.

1.6 Critical success factors

Before we get started on the tasks involved in setting up and then executing your project, it is worth pausing to reflect on some of the things that make a real difference to whether your project will succeed or fail, regardless of the type of project you are thinking of taking on. We will come back to all of these issues later in the book, but the sooner you start thinking about them, even if they appear obvious to you, the better.

- **Start early.** If you are already late, then don't panic (yet). With good planning and time-management you can still recover the situation, but you may find it an uphill struggle. If you have not started yet and think you still have plenty of time, then grasp the opportunity to start early, as it really will make a difference. In most cases those students who start late will not enjoy their project, will need to make sacrifices elsewhere, will not gain full educational value from the experience, will have to cut corners, and most importantly will usually fail to do themselves justice. The main problem for students is that they have little experience of project work, and will find that everything takes longer than they thought. They will also find that their assessment schedule has an uncanny knack of coinciding with the latter stages of their project, and if they have started late they will not have the opportunity to make up for lost time. Finally, supervisors are likely to be extremely busy towards the end of the project (not least in dealing with all the other late starters) and will not be able to offer the support needed. So the message is: do yourself a favour and **start early**.

- **Choose a topic that interests you.** It may sound obvious, but many students choose the first topic that occurs to them, and then struggle to maintain their interest and commitment throughout the life of the project. In most cases, you will be living with your project for a long time, and if you get bored you will fall behind schedule, start skimming key issues and generally under-perform.

- **Identify your other commitments.** Do not fool yourself. You will not be able to plan everything in your life around your project, nor will you be able to fit your project into the 'spare' bits of time left in your normal life. Not only will you have other academic commitments, you will have personal commitments that will constrain the time you have available for your project. All too many projects fail because students have not taken full account of the time they have available. In an ideal world, you would be able to give everything as much time as it needs. In the real world you need to compromise. This is a two-way process, so firstly you should identify other activities that will be compromised by your project work, and secondly you will need to be realistic and scope your project work to fit in with your other commitments.

- **Carry out a self-assessment.** Before selecting the topic for your project, you should spend some time thinking about your personal strengths and weaknesses. As well as taking into account your technical skills and the tools that you have available, you should also consider your personal traits. For example, do you prefer studying the literature and theory surrounding a problem area, or do you prefer producing something practical, such as a piece of software? There is little point in undertaking a project with a research bias if your strength is in programming. It is also vital to identify missing skills, so that you can acquire them before they are needed in your project (yet another reason to start early).

- **Create and maintain a plan.** Many students regard the project plan as an optional extra, or just a way of keeping their supervisor happy (although this is not a bad idea in itself). This is a big mistake, and well-planned and monitored projects are invariably more successful than those where the plan is nothing more than a gesture. A good plan is an invaluable aid, and the time spent producing and maintaining it is often less than expected, and is always time well spent. A plan will help in establishing the initial project scope and provides an excellent ongoing aid for discussions with your supervisor. It also acts as an early-warning system for identifying when your project is falling behind or deviating from its schedule and scope, and is crucial in establishing the tasks and activities that you will need to carry out during your project. A plan is even more important for group projects, where the coordination of activities and the scheduling of meetings can be a real challenge.

- **Do plenty of background reading.** Yet more things that you will have time for if you start early are background reading and discussions. Many good project ideas come from reading abstracts of past projects in your institution's library or intranet. Few subject areas are wholly untouched by past projects. While merely re-running a past project is not acceptable, you will find that many of their topics can be adapted to form the basis of new and highly original projects.

- **Start a project diary and project file now.** It is never too early to start a project diary. When it comes time to write up your project you will not be able to remember why or when you did what without one. Along with your project plan a diary will provide some of the most informative input into the evaluation of your project. You should use the diary to record such things as what you have done, decisions you need to make, things you need to include in your final report, and questions that you need to ask your supervisor.

- **Create a set of contingency plans.** This is not as complicated as it sounds. In any project you need to have an idea of what you will do if things start to fall behind schedule or things emerge that you had not expected. In the early stages you should have one or two other projects that you could switch to if you are unable to find a supervisor for your project, or if your project turns out to be unworkable for any reason. Later on you will need to have a fall-back position in case your project overruns. It is risky to have a single objective for a project. It is much better to have a set of prioritised objectives, some of which you could drop if your project goes astray. Finally, you should always have some time in your plan with no activities scheduled for it. This will act as contingency time to be used when tasks overrun (which some of them will inevitably do).

■ **Use your supervisor properly.** Your project supervisor will probably be the most important person (after yourself) on your project. Supervisors are essential sources of information, support and guidance. They are both your mentor and ally (do not forget that in most institutions the supervisor will be one of the most important assessors of your project). In many institutions you will need to find a supervisor yourself, in which case, the earlier you have a well-formed idea (or set of ideas) for a project topic, the better the choice of supervisors you will have. In some institutions you will be allocated a supervisor, and in others you may be given a list of supervisors and topics they have on offer as projects. In all these cases it is essential to meet potential supervisors as soon as possible. It will also help to set up your regular meetings as early as possible, as appointments made early are more likely to happen. No supervisor will appreciate last-minute requests for meetings.

For an alternative view on how to succeed in your project, read the following extract from the computing project handbook of the University of Central Lancashire (Casey, 1999) on how to fail your project, and then plan to do the opposite. While a lot of the advice is tongue-in-cheek, and some of it is really only directly relevant to their institution, most should provide you with some food for thought.

Box 1.1

How to fail your project

A good project is smoothly run and provides high quality results on time and with a minimum of fuss. There are no crises or panics and everyone's blood pressure stays low. In fact, it's all pretty boring. The following guidelines will help you spice things up and ensure a memorable disaster.

1. Don't plan
Resist all pressures from whatever quarter. If the pressures become intolerable, produce an unattainable plan. This is easy: don't talk to your client or supervisor about the necessary tasks; ensure that the plan loads you to seven full days per week; use lots of diagrams drawn using a PC package that requires several weeks to become familiar with; be as vague and ambiguous as possible; forget about any inter-dependencies between the tasks.

2. Don't produce specifications or designs
Coding is the most important task. It is best started before the project is selected. Specifications and designs are best produced several weeks (preferably months) after the code has been written especially if they can be cobbled together in two hours the day before your last 3 assignments are due in.

3. Schedule meetings carefully
There are two systematic strategies: arrange meetings at 10.30pm in the bar of your choice or arrange for all participants to turn up at different places or times. If, by chance, you do arrive at the same point

▶

in the space–time continuum, ensure either that no one has any idea why the meeting is to be held or that everyone has a different idea.

4. Avoid your supervisor

Try not to make initial contact with your supervisor until at least Christmas. (If possible avoid having a supervisor at all.) Aim to turn up without notice in their office when they are likely to be busy or about to leave (5.10pm or two minutes before a lecture are good initial ploys). An alternative strategy is to lurk near your supervisor's office until they leave for lunch, then queue ostentatiously for 20–30 minutes. Having repeated this process for several days, you can lodge a formal complaint about the supervisor's unavailability. Under no circumstances leave a message to arrange an appointment and do not use email which would allow the supervisor time to give you a reasoned response to your query.

If meeting with a supervisor as part of a group, ensure that no more than 70% of the group is present at any meeting and that it is never the same 70%. When a scheduled meeting is unavoidable, turn up late and unprepared. Always have two excuses for lack of progress (e.g. blame the rest of the team).

5. Start as late as possible

You can always find an excuse for deferring the start of the project: the need to settle into the third year, the weight of other coursework, looking for a job, preparing for Christmas, recovering from Christmas, the impending inter-semester week . . . A careful selection of friends will provide mutual support for these delays.

6. Don't prepare for the oral presentations

Your thoughts and opinions are more valuable if spontaneous. If members of a group working in related areas make contradictory statements, proclaim that your presentation is to take the form of a debate. If possible, let the seminar degenerate to open warfare.

Imply that staff present, particularly any External Assessors, are totally unfit to assess your work.

Overhead slides are best written as you talk, at an angle, and in a worn out red pen. If you must print them prior to the meeting, ensure that you use the smallest font available.

7. Prepare for the oral presentations

Ensure that you are both hung-over and drunk from the previous night. Don't wash or shave for several days beforehand. Practise delivering your presentation in a whisper. Ensure that you arrive three minutes late in a state of panic.

8. Ensure your project report is unreadable

Do not discuss your planned chapter headings with your supervisor.

Write in the style of your favourite pop star/footballer/alternative comedian.

Select three of the following:

- Start a new paragraph every 4 lines.
- Intersperse paragraphs on a variety of different topics.
- Shuffle the pages after printing.
- Avoid a logical ordering of chapters.
- Write the project report by hand.
- Lose the printed report and re-format any discs containing sections.
- Include pages of uncommented code in the main body of the report.
- See how few words you can spell correctly.
- Ensure that the final report is identical to the draft report that the supervisor spent a week making suggestions on.
- Only submit a draft report when it is 200 pages long.

- Send the report to the printer 10 minutes before the project deadline.

- Inject water into your printer's ink to get that subtle pale grey text. The artistic effect can be augmented by pushing and pulling on the paper as it moves through the printer to create random distortion of the characters.

9. Try to use undocumented/notoriously bug-ridden packages/hardware
This works especially well when the supervisor is unaware of this.

10. Aim for an all or nothing target
It is particularly important that it be impossible to decide if you are going to achieve the target until the week that the project is due. Preferably, the system should be constructed without testing. The final week can then be used for testing and completing the project write-up.

11. Pick a trivial task
Use strategies 4, 5 and 9 to ensure your supervisor can't spot this until the poster presentation.

12. Pick an impossible task
Justify this with the phrase 'An Honours project must have considerable academic depth'.

13. Dump the diary
Keeping a diary, like housekeeping, is a drag. So don't bother to complete it regularly. When commenting in your report on your project management, explain that you left it under a pile of unwashed clothes for the sock-pixies to update. Since the clothes and the diary are untouched, you are taking the lot home for your mum to sort out.

14. Base your mini-paper or literature review on a comic
Find a couple of trivial articles from a computing magazine, and combine bits with ill-informed speculation of your own. Alternatively, take a computer system from a popular science-fiction programme and analyse it in depth.

A similar recipe for disaster is to base your paper on a ranting conversation from one or more obscure newsgroups on the fringes of computing.

Source: Casey (1999), reproduced by permission

1.7 Assessment criteria

It may appear that assessment criteria are something that should concern you only as you produce each deliverable, such as your proposal or project report. However, it is worth considering them now at a high level, even before you start planning your activities or researching potential topics, as they will provide a valuable input into how you conduct your project from the outset. We will be returning to the subject of assessment criteria a number of times throughout the book, as we discuss the specific products and activities that criteria may be applied to.

Each institution and course of study will have its own specific set of assessment criteria. These will set out the percentage of marks to be allocated to each stage or major deliverable of your project, as shown in Table 1.3. The allocation of marks will help to guide you in assigning your time and effort to each stage,

Table 1.3   Example of mark allocation by deliverable

Deliverable	%
Project proposal	10
Interim report/presentation	10
Final report	15
The deliverables (e.g. software and models)	50
Project diary/project management	5
Viva/demo	10

Table 1.4   Example of mark allocation by activity/product

Activity/product	Marks
Analysis	12
Design	12
Testing	5
Implementation	8
User guide	3
Evaluation	10

and may prompt you to start some activities earlier than you might have thought necessary. For instance, if your course allocates some marks specifically to your project diary, then it will be essential to set it up immediately, as the more complete it is, the more marks you will receive.

In addition, many courses will describe in detail how marks will be allocated to specific products or activities within the development process (others may determine the precise allocation of marks for each activity through negotiation between students and supervisors). For example, Table 1.4 illustrates how marks might be allocated to the principal activities and products of a software development project. Together these activities and products would make up the final deliverable of Table 1.3.

The way in which marks are allocated to activities will reflect the underlying academic objectives of your course or institution. This allocation should help you in thinking about the nature of the project that you want to carry out. For instance, in the example shown in Table 1.4 there is an emphasis on the analysis and design activities of the project. In this case you will need to ensure that the

Table 1.5   Examples of project execution questions/quality criteria

Question	Quality criteria	Marks
How challenging was the project?	Trivial	1
	Complex problem, but limited in scope	5
	Complex problem, and ambitious in scope	9
How deep was the understanding of the problem domain?	Superficial	1
	Understands main concepts as covered by lectures	4
	Understands advanced concepts covering entire problem domain	7
How creative was the solution?	Substandard and limited	1
	Straightforward and fit for purpose	4
	Highly original and convincing	7
How thoroughly were alternative approaches to the problem researched?	Superficially	1
	Some alternatives considered, with acceptable conclusions	5
	Convincingly, covering all main alternatives, with well-reasoned conclusions	9
Have appropriate records been kept of the work carried out?	No records	0
	Logical set of notes, covering main issues	2
	Full set of notes and complete diary, with all issues concluded	4

project you undertake has a significant element of analysis and design complexity, and that you plan your time in order to focus your effort in these areas. In other cases there will be an emphasis on the programming or implementation activities, so your project will need to tackle a problem with a significant technical or algorithmic challenge.

Some institutions take an approach to assessment criteria that is not aligned to any particular project life cycle, largely because the projects they will accept vary so greatly in nature that allocating marks to specific activities or products is close to impossible. In these cases they will often produce a set of questions and/or quality criteria covering the overall execution of the project, such as those in Table 1.5. Once again, such criteria can be used to direct your project effort and selection.

1.8 Summary

1. Early on in a degree course projects will typically be used to develop or test the application of theory, while in the final year the emphasis will shift to include an exploration of your deeper understanding of this theory.

2. The emphasis placed on critical understanding varies greatly with the level of the degree course in question. Most HND projects will focus on the application of tools and techniques to a real-world problem, while Masters courses will demand a significant element of research, critical analysis and evaluation.

3. The main thing that sets an academic project apart from an industry project is the need to demonstrate a depth of theoretical understanding and independent thought.

4. The most popular type of computing project is the system development project, where the ultimate aim is to deliver of piece of software that satisfies a set of defined requirements. There are five main types of development project: database system project, large business system project, multimedia project, complex programming project and technical implementation.

5. Research projects aim to investigate an area of computing, such as a particular technology or a case study, and deliver an original conclusion or insight. There are three main types of computing research project: methodology investigation project, technology investigation project and case study.

6. Most development projects will, at the very least, include an investigation of the context of the project and of potential methods for its delivery. Most research projects will include an element of development, such as a prototype or software model.

7. Assessment criteria will provide a valuable input into how you conduct your project from the outset.

2 Identifying and selecting a project

2.1 ## Introduction

This chapter provides guidance on finding and selecting a topic for your project, a process that many students find difficult and stressful.

> ### Learning Outcomes
>
> After reading this chapter, you will be able to:
>
> - Describe the process of identifying and selecting a project
> - Understand how to generate ideas for project topics
> - Apply techniques for testing and short-listing ideas for project topics
> - Understand the key features of a good project topic
> - Make and document the final selection of a project topic

2.2 ## The project selection process

Students often panic when faced with the task of identifying a suitable project topic; so much so that they put it off for as long as possible, and then run the danger of making a last-minute and ill-advised choice. This is not altogether surprising. Even if their course has involved a lot of coursework, the topics covered will have been selected or suggested by their lecturers. So for many students the project will be their first experience of a self-initiated piece of work.

While the selection of a suitable topic is a factor in the success of your project, it is secondary to its execution. There really is no need to worry if you are not brimming with brilliant ideas. As long as you follow a reasonably logical selection process, it is unlikely that you will fail your project purely because of a poor topic. Few students come up with truly original or exciting project ideas

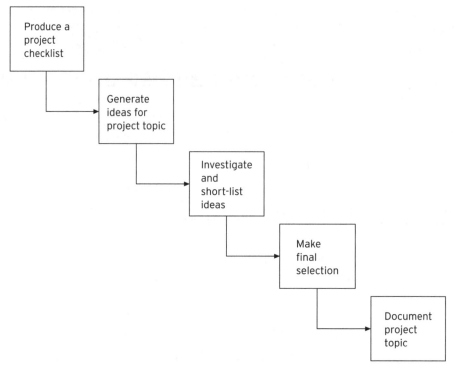

Figure 2.1   Identifying and selecting a project

off the top of their heads, but with a little thought and research even the most seemingly unambitious of ideas can give rise to highly suitable topics.

The basic steps in identifying and selecting a project topic are shown in Figure 2.1, and discussed in Sections 2.3 to 2.7.

2.3   Producing a project checklist

Before you start to work on your ideas for project topics, it is useful to review the requirements of your course, and to reflect on what you want to gain from the project. This will not only help in guiding your thoughts when generating ideas for your project later on, but may itself lead directly to ideas for potential topics.

Your review could involve little more than a brief read-through of your institution's project handbook or syllabus. However, it is better to do it in a slightly more formal manner, by creating a project checklist that summarises your project requirements, and against which you can test potential topics. In practice, creating a project checklist should not take much time, and the process itself will help you to structure your thoughts and provide input to your proposal. A requirements checklist will also demonstrate to your assessors that your proposal is well thought through (an essential factor in attracting marks for your proposal).

Table 2.1 Course document contents to be reviewed

Document section	Example checklist inputs
Assessment criteria	Proportion of effort to be spent on certain activities, e.g. design, programming, research
Project parameters	Deadlines, size of project (suggested number of hours of work)
Academic objectives	Use or development of particular skills and tools
Scope restrictions	Areas that are off limits, or that should be included
Deliverables	Products that should be produced during your project, e.g. Requirements Catalogues, data models, software implementations
Essential activities	Literature review, software demonstration
Institution/course guidelines	Preferred types of project, things to avoid
Special features	Group work, client-based

For a 300-hour project, I recommend that students spend no more than one hour on the production of their checklists. This will not allow any time for elaborate formatting of your checklist, but the reality is that it is the content that matters, and not its appearance.

Reviewing your course requirements

The main sources of input to your checklist will be your course handbook or project syllabus, and your institution's project handbook. While the contents of course documents vary greatly, the things that you will need to review should include some, but probably not all, of the items in Table 2.1.

If you already have a project supervisor, or if your course has an overall project coordinator, you should also try to get their views on what to look for, and what to avoid, when selecting a project topic.

Reflecting on your needs

Just as important as the requirements of your course are the things that you want to achieve through your project. A project provides you with a unique opportunity to develop and demonstrate a deeper understanding of an area that is of particular interest to you. If you do not take proper account of your needs in selecting a project topic, you run the risk of wasting this opportunity. You are also less likely to perform well on your project, as it is difficult to remain committed to a subject that does not really interest you.

You should review the things that have really grabbed your attention during your studies. Reviewing your lecture notes and past coursework will help to

Table 2.2   Reflections on your personal needs

Question	Example checklist inputs
What parts of my course have really interested me?	Technologies, topics, or industries you would like to investigate further
What are my strengths?	Skills that you would like to develop further Competencies that you would like to demonstrate
What are my weaknesses?	Areas to avoid or minimise Weaknesses that you would like to address
What types of academic activity do I enjoy most?	The types activities you would like to undertake, e.g. practical or theoretical Your preferred balance of research and development The environment you would like to work in, e.g. academic or commercial
What things might potential or existing employers regard as important?	Experience of particular types of workplace, exposure to specific tools, techniques or technologies Hard and soft skills you need to develop
What new skills or knowledge would I like to acquire?	Specific languages, hardware, or theory you would like to make use of
What personal constraints do I have?	Restrictions on your time and the locations you can work in (e.g. you may not be able to travel far to an external client because of family commitments) The facilities you have at your disposal Financial constraints

remind you about general subject areas that you would like to investigate and understand further. More importantly, it may also give you specific ideas that can be expanded or modified into project topics.

In selecting a project topic, you need to be honest about your strengths and weaknesses. You could choose to play to your strengths. You could also attempt to address areas that you regard as current weaknesses, but which you believe are important to develop further skills in. In either case you should record your preferences in your project checklist.

Finally, you will also need to make a note of any personal constraints that need to be taken into account when considering potential topics. If you ignore personal constraints, such as the time you have available, or the facilities that you have at your disposal, then you will soon run into problems as your project progresses (or, as is more likely, fails to make progress).

Table 2.2 summarises some of the questions you need to ask of yourself in formulating your project checklist. The result of reviewing your course require-ments and your personal needs will be a set of selection criteria that can be used to help you investigate potential project topics. It is helpful to distinguish between those requirements that are essential or mandatory, and those that are just desirable. You are unlikely to find a project that meets perfectly all of your preferences, but it is important that it meets at least your essential requirements.

The example in Box 2.1 shows a fairly short, but representative, checklist of requirements.

Box 2.1

Example of a project checklist

Project checklist: essential requirements

Project must be completed by 20 April.

Project effort should be between 250 and 300 hours.

Must be an individual piece of work (not a part of a team project).

Must include use of data modelling (5% of marks).

Must include a software implementation (even if just a prototype).

Must include a literature search.

Project must be outside the airline and video shop business areas (covered in detail in lectures).

Desirable features

Requirements analysis should be at least 20% of total development effort.

Final report should include between 20% and 40% research content.

Would like to acquire Java programming skills.

Should make use of Structured Systems Analysis and Design Method (SSADM) methodology.

Project must not include significant hardware configuration component.

Any website development should include a significant database implementation.

Should be able to carry out the software development using freely available tools (preferably on home PC).

Any external client should allow at least 20 hours of access time.

Any external client should be within 1-hour travel time.

Would like to develop graphical user interface (GUI) design skills.

2.4 Generating ideas

If you have produced a properly thought-through project checklist you will now have a good idea of the features that you would like your project to have. If you are lucky, you may even have thought of some potential topics as you were producing the checklist. For most students, however, the next step is to generate ideas for specific project topics.

While your choice of topic is important to the success of your project, there is no such thing as the perfect topic. Some students become obsessed with finding an exciting-looking topic, in the mistaken belief that this is the key to a high mark. This really is missing the point. What attracts high marks is not an impressive-sounding project, but one that has a topic that meets the essential requirements and has been properly planned and well executed. An obsessive search for the perfect project topic inevitably leads to dithering and last-minute choices that are rarely well thought through.

At the other extreme are those students who panic and grasp the first idea that occurs to them. This is extremely risky because, while you may be fortunate, it is more likely that a little more time spent thinking about your needs and opportunities would have yielded a more satisfying topic.

Coming up with topics

The following section deals with some of the many ways in which students generate ideas for their project. There is no foolproof method, as the needs of every university and every student are different. However, the vast majority of topics, including group projects, will come from one (or a combination) of the methods discussed below.

Workplace

Some students, most notably those on part-time, postgraduate or professional courses, may be able to find or be asked to do a project at their place of work. This has a number of clear benefits for the student, and most workplace projects are highly successful.

Many workplace projects are reasonably challenging or complex, giving the student every opportunity to demonstrate or develop a depth of practical competency. They are by their nature grounded in the real world, and as the student is an organisational 'insider' they may have access to people and knowledge that would be impossible for an outsider.

There are, however, a number of pitfalls that anyone contemplating a workplace project needs to be aware of. The most significant issue is the understandable tendency within an organisation to treat the project needs of employees differently from those of outsiders. People from outside an organisation are there for one purpose only: to complete a project. While outsiders may experience problems with gaining access to staff and to confidential information, it is unlikely that the organisation will ask them to do anything other than their project. An employee on the other hand can be diverted at any time, according to the changing priorities of the organisation.

If you undertake a workplace project you may also need to defend the academic objectives of your project. If your project is in your normal area of work, your line manager may well expect you to perform in the same way as normal, rather than to adopt the more reflective approach required by your university. You may also need to persuade your employer that you should be allowed to use techniques and tools that are different from those it would normally use.

The bottom line with a workplace project is that you must ensure that you have not adopted it purely because it is presented to you 'on a plate'. It must, as a minimum, meet your mandatory project requirements.

Notebook of ideas

Saunders *et al.* (2003) suggest keeping a *notebook of ideas*, in which you make an immediate note of any ideas as they occur to you, together with what prompted them. This is a useful technique for capturing ideas that you can then consider further at a later date. As many of you will know from experience, it is all too easy to have fleeting ideas that you are entirely unable to recall later if you fail to write them down.

Conversation

When discussing with students how they found their topics, the most common answer, at least for system development projects, is through conversations with friends, family, lecturers or colleagues. Discussing your project needs with people will often prompt an idea, either from yourself or from others. You may also discover that fellow students have had ideas that they have decided not to take forward, but that might suit your needs or which you think you may be able to develop further.

Discussions with friends and family are a particularly good source of client-based projects. This is especially so if you or your contacts are actively involved with clubs, charities or special interest groups, as such organisations are frequently in need of small-scale system developments.

Brainstorming

For any type of project, one of most effective techniques for generating project ideas is *brainstorming*. Brainstorming can be applied in a wide range of situations, particularly in a business context where it is frequently used as a way of generating solutions to problems.

Brainstorming sessions are especially useful for group projects. They are an excellent way to encourage participation by all group members and to instil a sense of ownership in the project at an early stage.

Although brainstorming sessions can be carried out by an individual, they are far better conducted within a group. While a group could consist of a pair of fellow students, the optimum number of participants is probably between three and five. In some universities tutors will act as facilitators and secretaries to the brainstorming sessions, in which case the number of students could rise to around eight with careful management (any more and the process becomes too

Box 2.2

The brainstorming process

1. Use the project checklist to define rough scope. Add personal interest areas (e.g. leisure, sports, community action).

2. All participants should suggest as many ideas as possible. Be as creative and 'off the wall' as possible.

3. Record **all** ideas, using one of the following mechanisms:

   Removable 'Post-it™' notes. This is the best mechanism for most situations, and is particularly useful if members of the group do not know each other well. It is far easier for people to quickly jot their ideas down on bits of paper and post them up on a wall, than to speak out in an unfamiliar group. Removable notes can also be used in any room, without any special facilities. With removable notes, all participants can write at once, rather than waiting their turn to speak (as can happen when one person has to do all the writing). The best brainstorming sessions rely on people throwing out ideas quickly and spontaneously. If participants need to wait for their idea to be noted, they may decide against making the suggestion as they have too much time to reflect upon it. Once ideas are ready to be discussed and amended, notes can easily be moved around, grouped or added to. At the end of the session notes can be removed and taken away as a record of the session, rather than being transcribed onto paper (as with whiteboards).

   Whiteboard. Whiteboards make a reasonable second choice if removable notes are unavailable for any reason, or the group is a small one that includes participants who know each other well. They have the advantage of being visible to all participants and easily amended or erased. At the end of the session the contents will have to be transcribed onto paper if the whiteboard is not a self-printing model.

   Pen and paper. If brainstorming is being undertaken by an individual student or by a pair of students, then a notebook will be perfectly adequate for supporting the session.

4. Only call a halt to the process when the ideas really start to dry up, or when the ideas being suggested are all clearly duplicates of previous suggestions.

5. Each idea should be examined briefly in order to clarify its meaning, and any duplicates should be eliminated.

6. If there are a large number of ideas, it can be useful to group the suggestions by subject area or type. Each idea should then be discussed and a decision made on whether to discard it, or perhaps to combine it with one of the other suggestions. The remaining ideas should then be expanded with any suggestions on how to take it further (in a small group this can form the basis of another short brainstorming exercise).

difficult to manage, with people less willing to speak up). Brainstorming sessions can be used to generate ideas for just one of the participants, but in most cases each student's project needs will be considered in turn.

The brainstorming process is set out in Box 2.2. There are also a few rules and tips that will make brainstorming more effective:

■ All ideas are valid.

   – Do not criticise any suggestion, however absurd it might appear. The whole point of brainstorming is to encourage participants to be as creative as possible. This will be severely compromised if boundaries are placed around the ideas that are 'acceptable', or participants feel undermined, and therefore unprepared to risk suggesting particularly imaginative ideas.

- Do not attempt to filter ideas as they are suggested, even if they appear to be duplicates. Often even the subtlest of differences between apparently similar suggestions can be important in highlighting potential new ideas.

- Try to draw out as many suggestions as possible.

- The process should be fairly rapid. This encourages a free flow of ideas, rather than withdrawal into reflection.

The Internet

The Internet is an increasingly useful source of ideas for system development projects. Not only can it be used as part of your initial literature search, but it can also provide a virtually limitless number of topics in its own right.

The main advantage that the Internet has over most other sources of project topics is its immediate accessibility to real-world business systems and technology applications. Anyone with a connection to the Internet can view and interact with the systems and technology of countless businesses, in almost any sector of industry, commerce or the public sector.

The Internet can provide you with examples of real-world business scenarios that you can adapt to demonstrate the application of various tools or techniques. You can also use the Internet to identify practical business or technology problems, which can form the basis of a wide range of projects (see Table 2.3).

Never be tempted to use the Internet to buy or copy a past project, or to hire a dissertation writer. You will always be discovered, either because the style and content of your final report arouse suspicion or through questioning at your viva voce examination (this type of plagiarism is easy to spot).

Background reading

If you are considering a project that includes a substantial piece of research or complex programming, an initial search of the literature (see Sections 4.3 to 4.7 for more on literature searches) in the areas in which you are particularly interested can be an effective way of identifying potential topics. The best sources of ideas are journals and periodicals, as they provide up-to-date reports on emerging trends in technology and practice, academic theories and problems, and innovative applications of technology or software engineering.

Even if you feel that you are unlikely to find your project topic by searching the literature, you should always carry out a high-level search of your areas of interest, as you will often pick up ideas for modifying or adding to topics uncovered elsewhere.

Table 2.3 Internet project opportunities

Opportunity	
Business and system modelling	Projects that are centred on the modelling of business activities or systems can be based on Internet businesses. Many of the key processes and data of businesses are visible over the Internet.
Case studies	As well as documented case study reports that can be researched over the Internet, the websites of many leading businesses can provide the start point for case study-based projects.
Requirements analysis	Internet sites can be a rich source of requirements for input into system development projects, and can be used to demonstrate and explore the application of analysis techniques.
Re-engineering and improvements	Many Internet-based businesses have flawed or non-standard user interfaces or processes. These can be used to demonstrate the application of analysis and design techniques, by engineering improved (albeit experimental) business systems and sites.
New portal designs/ business opportunities	The Internet presents opportunities for new business models and systems, either based on models already present on the Internet, or based on new models that take advantage of the Internet as a delivery medium (e.g. portals). These opportunities can take the form of real-world business ventures or academic exercises.
New or modified algorithms	Many Internet sites make use of relatively sophisticated algorithms. Complex programming projects can be set up that use these algorithms to provide ideas for new ones, or that aim to improve on them or adapt them for different purposes.
Technology issues and problems	Internet forums are a good way of identifying problems and issues with emerging technologies and with development techniques and tools. Projects that address such issues and problems, and that illustrate their solution can be highly original.
Innovative design and technology	The Internet is a rich source of ideas for projects that illustrate and explore the innovative use of technology, design techniques and development methods, particularly for multimedia projects.
Technology evaluations	Comparative studies that investigate and analyse the use of technology, business models and user interfaces of businesses on the Internet can make good projects. Such projects should aim to identify industry standards and illustrate the application of standards through small-scale demonstrator applications.
Research questions	Examination of papers and reports on the Internet can throw up research questions and objectives that can be modified to provide new research questions as part of a systems development project.

Past projects

Another good source of ideas is your university's collection of past projects. By looking through the project reports of previous students you may be able to identify a topic that could be adapted to form the basis of your project. Past projects can also be useful in providing pointers as to how a successful project might be structured.

The thing that you must avoid at all costs is the temptation to re-run or copy a past project (this is easily detected by the university). Taking a topic and using it without modification for your project will inevitably result in work that is a repetition of the previous student's work. Re-running a project will therefore be treated as a form of plagiarism, as it will be impossible for the university to determine if your work is original or has been copied from the previous execution of the project.

Because of the danger of plagiarism, or at best the lack of originality and innovation that can arise from barely modified project topics, some universities are reluctant to share past projects with students.

If you do decide to adapt an idea from a past project, you must highlight the source of your idea with your supervisor, in order to confirm that your idea is sufficiently original. You will also need to take care that you are not unduly influenced by the structure and methods used in the past project, as they may not be suitable for your project.

Clients or local businesses

If you intend to carry out a project that involves the solution of a business problem for an external client, *and you are clear on the nature of the project you wish to undertake*, the fine detail of your project topic can be greatly influenced by your choice of client.

Note that you *must* be clear on the broader details of your project, such as what techniques and tools you wish to use and what your research objectives are, in advance of securing a client, and not wait for those details to be determined by your client. Otherwise you may have a project that meets the objectives of your client, but does not meet your personal requirements or those of your university. Section 6.3 discusses some of the other issues that can arise when working with clients.

Far too many students focus all of their energy and time on the search for the perfect external client, with no more than the vague objective of wanting to solve a real-world system development problem, in the hope that their client will present them with a perfect project. This approach rarely succeeds.

In some universities and colleges, an external client may appear to be an essential feature of a good project. This is rarely the case in reality, but even if it is true the actual identity of the client and the nature of their business problem are secondary to the way in which the project is conducted. For most courses an external client is not a necessary feature of a project, and many students would be better advised to concentrate on a more academic problem, a fictional client (physical clients are not necessary to demonstrate most system development skills) or research, if acceptable.

If you are clear on the objectives of your project, then identifying an external client will provide the detail of the business problem you will be attempting to solve or demonstrate your skills and theories on. If the problem is fairly trivial in nature, you will need to place the emphasis of your project on its research and academic elements, and use the software development as a means of illustrating theory. If the business problem is fairly complex, the software development element may provide you with an opportunity to focus on the exploration and demonstration of your skills and techniques, and your project is likely to have a smaller research component.

Lecturers' lists

In a few universities students can (or are expected to) apply to undertake a project from lists supplied by project supervisors. While this has the obvious attraction that students do not have to spend much time searching for and formulating a project for themselves, they may well find that the project they end up with does not match their personal objectives, and that they soon lose motivation.

In most universities lecturers' lists are a last resort measure for students who have failed to identify a project. They do not have a track record of great success, often because the failure to identify a project topic is an indicator that the student is not fully engaged in their project. There are exceptions, of course, particularly when students have not been able to devote time to selection of a project through extenuating circumstances, such as illness.

2.5 Investigating and short-listing ideas

Once you have completed your investigations into potential project topics, you need to explore your ideas in a little more depth, and select one of them as your proposed project. You may feel that one of your ideas looks like a clear winner. Even so, it is worth spending some time examining it closely before diving in, to ensure that it really does satisfy your project requirements, or can be made to do so. It is all too easy to be blinded by one especially attractive feature of a topic, so that you fail to recognise that there are serious flaws with the idea.

Alternatively, you may have been given a project to do by your employer. In this case you will probably feel a great deal of pressure to keep your employer happy. If the project is the right one, it will indeed provide you with an ideal opportunity to demonstrate your skills and to further your career. However, you will not be able to do this unless you ensure that the project will meet the requirements of your course, and is feasible within the time available. Workplace projects can sometimes be too large and complex for adoption as a student project. By investigating and testing the project you have been given, you should be able to uncover its weaknesses, and identify what measures you can take to address them. Fortunately, most workplace projects can be modified or added to in such a way that they continue to satisfy the needs of your employers, while meeting your personal objectives and the requirements of your university.

Expanding your ideas

The first step is to make a few notes that help to describe exactly what your project ideas are all about. The intention here is to flesh out potential project topics with just enough detail to be able to test them against a range of selection criteria, not to produce a first draft of your project proposal, or to win any prizes for presentation or grammar.

Taking a single sheet of paper for each of your potential topics, you should attempt to jot down the following:

- A *single paragraph* describing the topic. The detail should be just sufficient enough to allow a fellow student to understand the essence of your proposed topic.

- A *list* of the key objectives, tasks and deliverables of the project.

- A *list* of the main skills and resources that would be needed for the project.

- A *list* of any risks and issues that you are already aware of. For example, you may have some concerns that an external client may not be able to provide you with as much of their time as your project would need.

- A *list* of any alternatives or choices that you have still to consider fully. For example, you may have thought of more than one research question that could be applied to your topic, and have still to decide which is the more appropriate.

The result will be a one-page topic outline that can then be used to decide which idea to adopt, and which can also be used as the start point for your project proposal. Box 2.3 provides an example of a one-page topic outline. This example will be used as the basis for a formal Project Brief later in this chapter.

If you are unable to complete a one-page outline, even in bullet-point form, then you will need to do a little more investigation. Many computing students find that the most difficult part of this process is listing their research objective. Discussions with your project supervisor (if you have one at this stage) or course tutors will help you in this.

It is important to give each idea at least some serious consideration, even if it requires some time and effort, as many good ideas are eliminated too early. Remember too that you will need to come up with all of this information anyway for at least one of your ideas, as part of preparing your project proposal. However, if you find yourself unable to put together just a single sheet of notes on an idea, it is extremely unlikely that this idea will have sufficient depth to sustain a substantial project. You may still be able to use the idea in combination with another potential topic, so do not be too quick to dismiss it too early.

Box 2.3

Example of a one-page topic outline

Title
Development of a system to support the work of a language translation business (Borders).
The main aim of this project would be to develop a system to support the management of translation assignments for Borders. The solution is likely to be an extranet. A secondary aim would be to investigate best practice for implementing an extranet in businesses of similar size to Borders.

Objectives
- To identify best practice, as used in industry, for designing an extranet
- To design target technical architecture for Borders
- To produce requirements specification for translation services management system
- To design entire system for management of translation services
- To implement a prototype covering the core functions of the system
- To acquire and demonstrate Java programming skills

Tasks and deliverables
The project will cover the entire Systems Development Life Cycle (with the exception of the maintenance phase) using SSADM notation. The deliverables of the project will include:

- Requirements Catalogue.
- Business system options (alternative outline solutions).
- Functional specification.
- Data model, database design and implementation.
- Prototype application, covering subset of total functionality.
- Test infrastructure.
- Test plans, implementation plans and user guide.
- Literature review (plus analysis of limited secondary data – no primary data will be collected).

Resources
The project should make use of hardware and software that is freely available to me at home, at Borders or at the university.
Borders may be prepared to pay for any additional developer licences.

Risks
Availability of the self-employed translators – may need to concentrate on the requirements of internal staff.

If the system design requires new skills in addition to Java, then the scope of the implementation will need to be restricted.

Alternative/supplementary objectives
To evaluate the suitability of structured methods for designing extranets.

Apply selection criteria

Once you have expanded your idea or ideas, you should examine each one carefully to establish its suitability as a project topic. One way of doing this is to apply the series of tests suggested below. As with many of the processes discussed in this chapter, it should not take long to test your ideas in this way, and the result will be a much better understanding of your potential topics.

1. Test your ideas against your project checklist

If you have used your project checklist while generating your ideas, most of them should meet at least your essential requirements. Even so, it is still essential to carry out a formal check against your checklist for two reasons:

■ While drawing up your one-page outlines, you may have uncovered some issues or features that do not meet, or carry a risk of not meeting, an essential requirement. You will need to modify any ideas that fail to meet your mandatory requirements or dismiss them outright if the requirements cannot be met.

■ Each idea is likely to meet a different subset of your desirable requirements. These differences will be key factors in deciding which idea to adopt.

As you test each of your ideas you should make any modifications that are necessary, and record the requirements that are not met against the list of issues in your one-page outlines.

2. Test your ideas against assessment criteria

Next, you will need to reflect carefully on the deliverables and tasks of each of your ideas, to ensure that you are confident that the final product of your project has the potential to score well against your course's assessment criteria.

Again, you should record any concerns that you have against the issues in your one-page outlines. After following up on your concerns, you may find that the issue can be resolved by negotiating a different set of assessment criteria or by adjusting your project idea (see example in Box 2.4).

Box 2.4

Example of use of assessment criteria

Isla has a project idea centred on testing different data capture devices and interface designs for consumer surveys. The assessment criteria for her course suggest that 10% of the final project mark will be allocated to requirements analysis.

In Isla's original idea, she had intended to take an existing paper-based survey and concentrate on developing alternative interface designs and mechanisms.

After confirming with her project coordinator that the marks allocated for requirements analysis cannot be adjusted, Isla reshapes the idea to incorporate an analysis of requirements for an annual student satisfaction survey at her university.

Table 2.4   Features of a good project (killer questions)

☑   Does the topic really captivate you?

☑   Does the project enable you to *explore*, *develop* and *demonstrate* skills and knowledge relevant to your course, and to a level that exceeds previous coursework?

☑   Can the project be achieved in 80% of the available time (leaving 20% contingency)?

☑   Does the topic enable you to be creative, and to produce original or innovative work?

☑   Do you have the necessary skills, facilities and tools readily to hand?

☑   Do you have the finances available to purchase tools or materials, if needed?

☑   Do you have the time and facilities to acquire any missing skills?

☑   Does your topic have a fall-back position, should you fall behind schedule?

☑   Are your research objectives *directly* relevant to your system development objectives?

☑   Does your proposed system development provide the opportunity to illustrate your research findings?

☑   Are you confident that you will have sufficient access to external clients and facilities?

☑   Is your project consistent with your career goals?

☑   Does the topic meet the requirements of your course; in particular does it have sufficient depth or complexity?

☑   Are you sure that the scope of the project is manageable, and will not 'creep' wider?

☑   Does your topic enable you to look deeply into a narrow area, rather than superficially into a wide area?

☑   Is your idea original, and *not* a near duplicate of a past project?

☑   Does your topic involve *substantially* more than a straightforward programming task?

☑   Are all of the activities of your proposed project self-consistent, and consistent with the objectives of your topic?

☑   Are all team members committed to the topic (group project)?

☑   Are all team members confident that there would be a clear role for them, and that there is enough work to go round (group project)?

☑   Can you visualise yourself justifying the project to a supervisor (or fellow student)?

☑   Do you know enough about the subject area to feel confident about your ability to complete the project?

☑   Is the project big enough to keep you busy for the suggested amount of time?

☑   Does the topic deal with subject matter that is within the scope of your course?

☑   Do you feel that the risk of your failing to complete the project is acceptable?

3. Test your ideas against killer questions

Some universities provide a list of *killer questions* or desirable features that you should use to test the potential of your project ideas. Once you have applied your university's list of questions, or if your university is among those that do not provide such a list, you should apply the killer questions in Table 2.4 (there will inevitably be some duplication with your university's list).

Some of the killer questions will not be applicable to all of your project ideas, as each topic will have a different set of desirable or necessary features, and the list is not exhaustive. However, most of these questions will be relevant to most projects, so you should consider each question carefully before dismissing it.

You may find yourself unable to answer all of these questions with complete conviction for all of your ideas without a little more investigation. Indeed, you may not be able to give a fully informed answer to every question until you have fully defined your project. However, you should be able to give at least a provisional answer to every relevant question. If you are unable to do so for a particular idea, or, worse, cannot decide which questions are relevant, then it is probable that you do not have sufficient knowledge of the area to be confident of undertaking the project.

The final question (i.e. do you feel that the risk of your failing to complete the project is acceptable?) is a difficult one to answer. One way to go about this is to weigh up all the outstanding concerns on your one-page outline, and ask yourself 'if someone else was doing this project, am I sure they would complete it?' Again, if you still cannot answer it, then it is likely that you do not know enough about the topic to undertake it with any confidence.

Table 2.5 lists some examples of the types of topics that would fail the killer question test if proposed at final-year degree level.

Feasibility assessment

In some circumstances you may find that the number or complexity of the issues you have documented in your one-page outline makes it difficult to assess the topic properly. It may be that the volume of issues is an indicator that the idea is too far removed from your knowledge base to be a viable topic for your project. However, it could also be that the idea is a sound one, but that the complexity of the topic is such that the issues cannot be addressed without carrying out an initial study or feasibility assessment.

An initial study should aim to do no more than is necessary to address the key outstanding issues. What you must avoid is the obvious temptation to start delving into the substance of the project. While the idea of getting a head start on your project might appear attractive, there is a real danger that your efforts could escalate out of control, and on an idea that may turn out to be infeasible, or unacceptable to your supervisor.

The issues that are most often difficult to address without some sort of preliminary study are time, complexity or depth, and access to clients.

Table 2.5   Examples of topics failing the killer question test

Project type	Common features	Killer question issues
Simple website	Little substantive research. Trivial database implementation. Standard GUI. Project report padded out with simplistic analysis and design models.	Unlikely to be innovative or original in design. Straightforward programming task. Insufficient depth or complexity. Does not enable demonstration or development of skills beyond coursework level. Not all activities are self-consistent (inappropriate models and methodologies used).
Large-scale business system	Functionally wide area of study. Complex system, data and organisational issues. Substantial technical implementation. External client.	Not achievable in timescales (even for group project). Unlikely to have sufficient access to clients. Skills and facilities often not available, or acquirable in timescales. Often no fall-back position (half-completed analysis does not tend to impress). Tends to result in superficial examination of too wide an area. Risk of failure high (due complexity of issues).
Collection of loosely related tasks	Project plan has several distinct threads. Objectives and activities fall into a number of separate groups. Project title or one-sentence description contains the word 'and'. Attempts to include all main areas covered by course.	Activities and objectives are not self-consistent. Research and development components not of direct relevance to each other. Tends to result in superficial examination of several areas. Will have problems justifying the topic to a supervisor as a single, substantial piece of work. Unmanageable scope.
Virtual re-run of coursework	Business area coincides with coursework case study. Techniques and tools are similar and applied at same level as coursework. Poor research element.	By definition, does not enable demonstration or development of skills beyond coursework level. Insufficient depth and complexity. Not an original idea, and work unlikely to be viewed as original or innovative. Too small to fill time.

Time

The thing that causes students most problems is estimating how long a project might take. Time constraints are usually very tight for student projects, and so in most cases the issue is one of ensuring that you can complete the project in time, rather than checking that the project is big enough to fill the expected time commitments. Without the benefit of experience, producing even a ballpark estimate of project effort and duration can be extremely challenging. Section 5.4 deals with the planning of projects, so if you have serious concerns about timings you should read this before conducting your feasibility study. At the short-listing stage we are more concerned with ensuring that a potential project

Table 2.6 Project effort guidelines

Project phase	Percentage of total project effort
Project set-up	10%
Research	15%
Requirements analysis	10%
System design	20%
System construction and testing	30%
Final report	10%
Project management	5%

is a good *rough* fit for the time available than we are with the scheduling of activities and tasks. So if you are just seeking confirmation of your view that the project is the right sort of size, you could look at similar past projects or discuss it with one of your tutors. Alternatively, you could think about first phase in some detail and then apply the guidelines in Table 2.6 to estimate overall project effort. Table 2.6 must be used with some caution, as it is based on an examination of past projects where the aim has been to deliver a complete system solution, using a mix of programming and code generation tools, to a self-contained business problem. If your project does not fit this broad description, you will need to adjust the percentages in Table 2.6. For example, if your topic has more emphasis on programming, then you will need to assign more of the total effort to the construction phase (possibly up to 50 per cent), and reduce the other system development phases accordingly.

If you find that your project does not fit the time available, then do not fool yourself: projects rarely take *less* time than expected. If you are still interested in pursuing the idea you will need either to reduce the scope of the business problem you are attempting to solve, or aim to implement a subset of the design or requirements. Note that contingency should not be less than 20 per cent of each phase.

Complexity or depth

It can be difficult to assess the complexity or depth of a topic until you start to get into the detail of the project. This is especially so for client-based projects. Many seemingly promising-sounding ideas turn out on closer examination to be rather superficial. Conversely, some ideas that sound manageable on the surface have unexpected complexities hidden in their detail. If you have doubts as to the depth of your project idea, then the only the only way to remove the uncertainty is to carry out an initial requirements analysis. This may take the form of an interview or two, or perhaps a high-level examination of company documents. You may also need to carry out a review of the literature (see Chapter 4) if your project is more academically or research based. At this stage, you should aim to do no more than capture requirements and objectives in text form. Producing analysis or design models as part of your short-listing process would almost certainly represent overkill.

Access to clients

The best way to reassure yourself that you will be able to gain sufficient access to clients is to set up some appointments, or better still request some office space. There is no guarantee that appointments will be kept when your client's first flush of enthusiasm is over. However, one thing is certain: if your client is reluctant to set up or keep appointments at the beginning of your project, things will only get worse.

2.6 Making the final selection

By the time you have applied the tests suggested above you will almost certainly have a clear view on which topic you want to take forward as the basis for your project. Occasionally students are still left in something of a dilemma, with more than one idea that they really want to pursue. If you are lucky enough to be in this position you could apply the following selection techniques to help you decide which topic to adopt.

Requirements scoring

1. For each entry in your project checklist decide whether the requirement is essential, desirable or just 'nice to have'.
2. Against each checklist entry assign your topics a score out of ten that indicates how well the requirement is met.
3. Multiply all of the scores for essential entries by 5 and the scores for desirable entries by 3, leaving 'nice to have' entries as they are.
4. Add up the total scores for each topic.

The total scores are an indication of how well each topic fits your requirements. However, this is not the only factor that you need to consider when measuring one topic against another. The other factors can be assessed using pros and cons.

Pros and cons

For each of your topics make a list of pros (features in favour of the topic, including the requirements score) and cons (outstanding issues that suggest you should not do the topic). Again you could score each entry in the list out of a total of ten, to indicate how strongly it counts for or against the topic. However, this is rarely helpful, as just one or two big issues will usually dominate the list, with the remainder being of minor concern.

By examining your list of pros and cons, and discussing it with your tutors or project supervisor, you should be able to identify which topic is most likely to result in a successful project (see example in Box 2.5).

Box 2.5

Example of requirements scoring and pros and cons

Molly has narrowed her search down to two equally suitable topics. The first is a project for an external client. It involves the development of a system to support the operations and management of a catering services business. The second is a more academic project, involving the development of an Internet portal that will enable her to explore the application of discussion group technologies and designs.

To help her decide which of the ideas she should pursue, Molly decides to conduct a requirements scoring exercise:

Requirement	Value	Project 1 Score	Total	Value	Project 2 Score	Total
Project completed by 20 April	3	10	30	3	10	30
Data modelling	3	8	24	3	6	18
Literature search	3	7	21	3	9	27
20–40% research content	2	7	14	2	9	18
SSADM applicability	2	9	18	2	7	14
GUI design skills development	2	7	14	2	8	16
etc.						
Total score:		**Project 1:**	**343**	**Project 2:**		**329**

Molly also makes a list of the pros and cons of each topic:

	Pros	Cons
Project 1	Fairly complex	Large project – scope could drift
	Real-world development	Business located some distance away
	Good fit with requirements (score 343)	May require hardware upgrade
	Interesting business problem	Heavily reliant on client access
	Enthusiastic client	
	Requires application of core skills	

▶

Project 2	Fairly deep understanding required	Technical skills currently lacking
	Enables demonstration of innovation	Not a real-world problem
	Good fit with requirements (score 329)	Requirement analysis fairly trivial
	Interesting technical problem	
	Not reliant on external client	
	Requires acquisition of key skills	
	Scope can be controlled	
	Good research potential	

Both of Molly's project ideas score well against her project checklist, with the external client project coming out marginally ahead. Both projects also have a positive balance of pros against cons. After discussing the topics with her tutors Molly decides to adopt the more academic portal project. Despite its slightly lower requirements score, Molly is attracted by the potential to explore new technical areas. She is also keen to avoid over-dependence on an external client, whose initial enthusiasm may not be sustained. Molly's greatest concern with the portal project was its trivial requirements analysis component. However, her tutors are happy to accept this, given the depth in the other areas of her project.

The reality is that you could run with any of the ideas that you are still actively considering at this stage, as they have all passed your suitability and feasibility tests. So, if you are still undecided you should adopt the idea that scores highest against your *personal* interests. Alternatively, you could use a technique suggested by Dawson (2000) and flip a coin. The idea is not to let chance decide for you, but to see which side you really want to land face up.

2.7 Documenting your project topic

If you have done all of the things suggested above, then your idea is probably a winner. It should also be relatively easy to agree your project with a sponsor, as the work you have done will provide evidence of a good level of initial understanding, organisation and motivation.

The process for documenting and agreeing your project will vary according to the requirements of your course. In many instances you will begin with an informal discussion with a sponsor or tutor, followed by written proposal in the form of a Project Initiation Document (PID). In other universities the process may be more formal, and consist of two stages, in which you will submit a short Project Brief (or outline) for approval by your supervisor or tutor, followed later by a more detailed PID.

In some cases, a Project Brief may be all that your university requires you to submit, but while a Project Brief is sufficient for the suitability of your project proposal to be assessed, it is not a suitable document on which to base the management of your project. This is the function of a PID, which you will need to produce as your earliest project deliverable.

The actual names of the documents you submit will depend on the university concerned, but their contents will remain fairly consistent. The production of a PID requires a reasonably detailed level of planning, and is covered in Chapter 5, following a discussion of development and research approaches, which are both important inputs to the planning process.

Project Brief

Table 2.7 summarises the contents of a typical Project Brief. The contents are similar to those suggested by the project management methodology PRINCE,

Table 2.7   Project Brief contents for a student project

	Description	Examples
Essential items		
Title	Your title should convey the flavour of your project, without turning into a multi-sentence description. Your own understanding of your project is likely to change as you develop your PID, so you should regard your title as a working title until the PID is complete.	Development of a system to support translation services. Investigation into the application of innovative discussion group technologies. The future of teleworking in the UK.
Background	A few paragraphs should be sufficient to cover the background to your project. Try to explain the overall aims of your project, its type and the work you have done to date. You should also describe your external client, if you have one.	
Key objectives	Objective setting is covered in some detail in Section 4.2, in the context of research objectives. Students often struggle to appreciate what an objective is, and how it differs from a deliverable or aim. If this confuses you, it is probably best to look at Section 4.2, and in particular at Box 4.1 before completing your Project Brief. While Box 4.1 deals specifically with research objectives, the same principles can be applied to any type of aim or objective. It is necessary to list only the primary academic, personal and business objectives in your Project Brief. More minor objectives will be added when you produce your PID. Take care to ensure that the objectives are phrased so that your success or failure in meeting them can be tested or measured. Research objectives are discussed in more detail in Chapter 4.	To acquire and demonstrate Java programming skills. To identify GUI design approaches for the development of a discussion group interface. To evaluate the suitability of structured methods for analysing and designing web portals. To develop and implement a web portal. To identify and evaluate discussion group technologies. To demonstrate the application of one or more innovative discussion group technologies. To establish and recommend best practice for the design of discussion group interfaces.

Table 2.7   (*Cont'd*)

	Description	Examples
Justification	You should justify your choice of project by explaining how the project will meet the requirements of your course, why the topic interests you, and what you will gain from the project.	
Scope and deliverables	The scope of a project is a description of what activities you plan to carry out, and of the functional or academic boundaries of your project. In order to clarify the scope it can be helpful to list what you are not going to be doing. Functional boundaries will help to define which parts of a problem or business you will be addressing.	If you know which development and research methods you are planning to use, you can be fairly specific about your activities and deliverables, if not you should include general phase and output descriptions. Activities could include things such as business analysis, data modelling, data collection, critical analysis. The list of deliverables could include such items as requirements specifications, programs, algorithms, research reports, models, test plans. Functional scope might be limited to, say, the marketing and sales parts of a business, but exclude accounts and human resources.
Major milestones	Rough timings for your main deliverables and activities. You must ensure that they are aligned with your university's project submission timetable.	

Optional items

Constraints and assumptions	Any project-specific constraints and assumptions should be noted for review by your supervisor. Avoid bland statements that apply to all projects, such as the constraint that 'the project must be completed on time'.	Constraints often cover time and cost restrictions. Assumptions might include things that you believe will happen or be in place, such as the availability of lab space at your university at specific times.
Resources	An optional item, but it is worth documenting at an early stage any special resources that you will need to complete your project. It will reassure supervisors that you have not overlooked the need for specific hardware or software. Your supervisor may also be able to assist in identifying where you can access them.	Software, such as programming environments, network management tools, databases, computer aided software engineering (CASE) tools and graphics packages. Hardware, such as communications hardware, servers, multimedia work stations and printing facilities.
Risks	Risks are the things that you aware of that might happen, and if they do will have an effect on your project. For each risk you should have a fall-back position in case they do occur. If you have produced the one-page outlines suggested earlier in this chapter, than you should have this information ready to hand.	Risk: Java may take longer to learn than anticipated. Fall-back: Reduce implementation element of project, and re-focus effort on research and GUI design activities.

with a number of adjustments reflecting the needs and nature of a student project. The items listed in Table 2.7 as optional are required for a PID, but would usually be omitted from your Project Brief unless they are of particular significance for your project.

The purpose of a Project Brief is to provide a good understanding of what your project is all about, without getting into the detail of how you will deliver it. Your Project Brief should present all of the essential information needed by your supervisor or tutors to review your outline proposal. They will then be able to verify that your project is acceptable, and to advise on any changes that are required, before you undertake too much detailed planning work.

Even if your university does not require you to submit a Project Brief, it is still a useful exercise to complete one, as it will help to remove any ambiguity, and can be lifted virtually intact to form part of your PID. As you can see, a lot of the information that you need to complete a Project Brief will be contained in your one-page project outline.

A good Project Brief is one that presents the information needed to enable your supervisor to understand the purpose, scope and deliverables of your project in a concise and easy to read format. You do not want to obscure that understanding with unnecessary clutter and detail. It is all too tempting to try to include all the work that you have done in exploring the topic so far. Vital though this work may be in taking the project forward, it will serve only to confuse the reader at this stage. It is far better to present a well-targeted brief, and have the additional work to hand when discussing your proposal with a potential supervisor. Conversely, you must avoid producing a proposal that either misses vital information or is rendered unreadable through too great a level of summarisation (often characterised by the inclusion of bullet points with no accompanying explanation).

The example in Box 2.6 illustrates what a Project Brief might contain. Each section has been kept fairly brief in the interests of space, but it should give you an indication of the level of detail that you will need to include.

Box 2.7 is for the same project, but shows how the real worth of a topic can be undermined by over-summarisation. There is nothing incorrect in this Brief, but a lot of important information is overlooked or hidden inside a general statement. The overall impression is of a project that lacks depth and clarity of thinking. Sadly, it is all too representative of the Project Briefs submitted by many students.

Box 2.6

Example of a Project Brief for a student development project

Title
Development of a system to support the work of a language translation business.

Background
Borders is a firm offering a wide range of language translation services to private and commercial customers. Most of their clients are small to medium enterprises (SMEs), requiring the translation of documents between different, mainly European, languages. They also provide translators for business trips, conferences and meetings. They have a permanent staff of eight translators, but supplement these with a network of self-employed translators to cover as many languages as possible. The self-employed translators carry out over 50% of Borders' assignments.

The main aim of this project is to develop a system to support the management of translation assignments for Borders. A secondary aim is to investigate best practice for implementing an extranet in businesses of similar size to Borders.

Investigations carried out so far suggest that the solution is likely to be an extranet, consisting of a central database of clients, translators and assignments, with an Internet-based interface to enable the self-employed translators to access the system.

Objectives
- To identify best practice, as used in industry, for designing an extranet
- To identify appropriate implementation technologies for small-scale extranets
- To design target technical architecture for Borders
- To produce requirements specification for translation services management system
- To design entire system for management of translation services
- To implement a prototype covering the core functions of the system
- To evaluate the suitability of structured methods for designing extranets
- To acquire and demonstrate Java programming skills

Justification
This project will enable me to explore analysis and design techniques in depth, and in a real-world environment. It will also enable me to develop an understanding of how the skills acquired during my studies fit together over the full system development life cycle (excluding maintenance). The topic also offers an opportunity to investigate how extranets are designed and implemented in SMEs, which is an under-researched area at present. The external clients are happy for me to take a prototyping approach to the implementation of the user interfaces, which should allow me the flexibility to meet project deadlines, by selecting an appropriately sized first implementation.

The topic also offers me an opportunity to acquire some further technical skills in web development, and on a project that has sufficient depth to provide some real challenges.

Scope and deliverables
The functional scope of the project is limited to Borders' core business activities, namely:

- the assigning and distribution of written translation assignments to translators;
- the booking of verbal translation assignments;
- the tracking of assignments;
- customer management (excluding those activities related to payment processing);
- the maintenance of a translator skills database.

The project will cover the entire Systems Development Life Cycle using SSADM notation, with the exception of the maintenance phase. The software implemented will consist of a prototype system with limited functionality, but it will be delivered alongside user training materials.

The project will include a literature review and limited secondary data collection, in order to identify best practice in implementing an extranet in an SME. No primary data collection will be carried out.

The deliverables of the project will include:

- Requirements Catalogue;
- business system options (alternative outline solutions);
- functional specification;
- data model, database design and implementation;
- prototype application, covering subset of total functionality;
- test infrastructure;
- test plans, implementation plans and user guide.

Major milestones
Detailed plans will be produced as part of the Project Initiation Document, but the following milestones appear achievable from initial planning:

- Project Initiation Document | 20 October
- Requirements analysis complete | 12 December
- Interim project report | 11 January
- Functional specification complete | 20 February
- Technical design | 17 March
- Test infrastructure set up | 2 April
- Prototypes and database delivered | 22 May
- Final report | 10 June

Constraints and assumptions
The requirements analysis phase must be completed by mid-December, as the staff at Borders will be unavailable to me in the run-up to the end of their financial year.

The project assumes that my only missing skills are the area of Java programming.

As stated in the course handbook, the project must be completed by 10 June.

Resources
The project is expected to make use of hardware and software that is freely available to me at home, at Borders or at the university. In any event, Borders are prepared to pay for any additional developer licences if they can be justified.

Risks
The main risk to the project is the availability of the self-employed translators. They do not work exclusively for Borders and therefore their time cannot be allocated to the project in the same way as for internal staff. The fall-back position, should their availability cause issues, will be to concentrate on the requirements of internal staff.

The other significant risk is that the project assumes that the only skills that I will need to acquire are in Java programming. If the system design requires additional new skills, then the scope of the implementation will need to be restricted.

Box 2.7

Example of an over-summarised Project Brief

Title
Development of a system to support the work of a language translation business.

Background
The main aim of this project is to develop a system for Borders, a translation services company.

Objectives

- To analyse and design a system for management of translation services
- To implement a prototype system
- To investigate the business use of extranets
- To learn Java

Justification
This project will enable me to explore analysis and design techniques in depth, and in a real-world environment.
   The topic also offers me an opportunity to acquire some further technical skills in web development.

Scope and deliverables

- The functional scope of the project is limited to Borders' core business activities.
- The project will use SSADM.
- The implemented software will consist of a prototype system.
- The project will include a literature review.

The deliverables of the project will include:

- Requirements Catalogue;
- functional specification;
- data model, database design and implementation;
- prototype application.

Major milestones

- Project Initiation Document   10 November
- Interim project report   11 January
- Prototypes and database delivered   22 May
- Final report   10 June

2.8   Summary

1. While the selection of a suitable topic is a factor in the success of your project, it is very much secondary to its execution. If you follow a logical selection process, it is extremely unlikely that you will fail your project because of a poor topic. With a little thought and

research even the most seemingly unambitious of ideas can give rise to highly suitable topics.

2. A project checklist summarises your project requirements, against which you can test potential topics. The process of creating a project checklist will help you to structure your thoughts and provide input to your project proposal.

3. Ideas for project topics can come from a number of sources: workplace, notebook of ideas, conversation, brainstorming, the Internet, background reading, past projects, clients or local businesses, and lecturers' lists.

4. It is all too easy to be blinded by one especially attractive feature of a topic, so that you fail to recognise that there are serious flaws with the idea. By investigating and testing the topic you should be able to uncover any weaknesses, and identify what measures you could take to address them.

5. Project topics can be tested against your project checklist, your assessment criteria and the features of a good project.

6. Complex topics can be explored by carrying out an initial study or feasibility assessment.

7. Final topic selection may require the application of requirements scoring or lists of pros and cons.

8. The purpose of a Project Brief is to provide a good understanding of what your project is all about, without getting into the detail of how you will deliver it.

3 System development approaches

Introduction

The main aims of this chapter are to discuss the application of system development approaches in the context of a student project, which is very different from their application in a commercial context, and to establish common terminology for the remainder of this book. This chapter does not attempt to teach system development methods from scratch, as it is assumed that you have already covered this during your previous studies.

Learning Outcomes

After reading this chapter, you will be able to:

- Describe the suitability of standard life cycle models to different types of student project

- Understand how development methods can be applied and adapted to the needs of individual projects

3.2 The System Development Life Cycle

The stages that all development projects go through are very similar, regardless of the methodology, techniques or tools that are used. What changes greatly from project to project is the way that we approach each of the stages, the precise tasks that we choose to carry out and how we sequence them.

For any system development project, the basic stages are:

1. decide that we need a new system;
2. find out what the system should do;
3. decide how the system will work and look;
4. build and test the system;

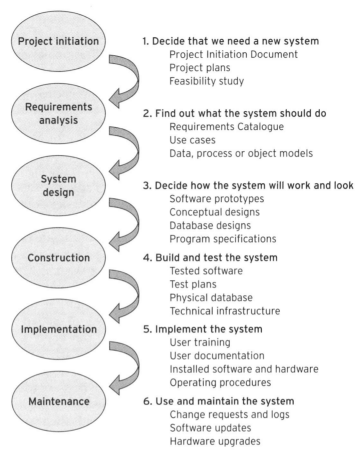

Figure 3.1   The System Development Life Cycle (SDLC)

5. implement the system;

6. use and maintain the system.

Of course, we traditionally use rather more formal terms for each stage or phase and its outputs. Figure 3.1 shows one version of the System Development Life Cycle (SDLC), along with examples of typical outputs of each stage.

Within any individual project we can loop back through stages a number of times, and apply numerous different techniques, tools and methods. We could try to deliver as much of the required system at one time as is possible, or to deliver the system in a sequence of chunks, or we could even develop a number of chunks in parallel.

Even if some of the stages appear relatively trivial or straightforward in your project, you will still need to go through them, however briefly. But before that you will need to make decisions about how you are going to approach them. For instance:

■ Are you going to apply a structured methodology such as SSADM or information engineering?

- Are you going to use object-oriented techniques such as the Unified Modelling Language (UML)?
- Are you going to follow rapid application development (RAD) principles?
- Are you going to use a CASE tool?
- How are you going to adapt techniques, structures and approaches to suit your project?

There are several models or strategies for navigating our way through the stages of the SDLC, such as the waterfall, iterative or incremental models. Life cycle models provide us with a framework or route map for planning the project, but do not in themselves present us with any specific tools or techniques for developing the system. This is the function of development methods or approaches, such as SSADM, UML and RAD, most of which can be adapted or supplemented to fit the framework provided by any of the life cycle models.

No development method should be taken as a recipe book that, if followed step by step, will churn out a perfect system. Rather, each method should be seen as providing a toolkit of techniques, notations and project structures that can be used in any number of ways to suit the needs of a given project.

While some methods are definitely more suited to particular life cycle models than others, it is also true that you can apply the principles and techniques of any of the system development approaches mentioned above to any of the life cycle models. They can even be used in combination with each other, and the best projects often do adopt a hybrid approach. For example, a common approach in student projects is to use a structured method for the requirements analysis and specification stages, and then switch to a more RAD-based approach, using prototyping, for the incremental delivery of the software.

Why adopt a formal approach?

It is important to recognise that one of the academic objectives for any student development project must include *clear and convincing* demonstrations of the following:

- A logical process of selecting and adapting your development approach.
- A deepened understanding of the development life cycle.
- A deepened understanding of system development techniques and products, and how they can be used in the context of a substantial piece of work.

It is critical, therefore, that you give proper thought to how you will approach your system development, and that you then apply your chosen approach with some rigour. No supervisor or assessor will be convinced by the all too common approach of knocking out a piece of ill-thought-through software, followed by an attempt to put together some formal models in order to create the illusion of having applied a method.

By applying techniques in a proper and considered manner, you have the opportunity within your project to gain a valuable insight into the effectiveness and purpose of the techniques within your chosen approach. Even on the best taught of courses, you will not have been able to practise the techniques of system development in a way that enables you to understand fully how they fit together and support each other in a realistic context.

3.3   Development life cycle models

Life cycle models provide a framework for managing and structuring a project, while approaches and methods provide the activities, tasks and deliverables used within that framework. The three models that are used or, more realistically, adapted for use on student projects are the waterfall model, the spiral model and, to a lesser extent, the incremental model. These are outlined below, and then summarised in Table 3.1. There are other models that could be used, but the three discussed here cover the vast majority of student projects.

Waterfall model

The waterfall model dates back to the 1970s, where it was introduced in order to impose some control over the informal and somewhat chaotic system development process that existed previously. The waterfall model is illustrated in Figure 3.2, and while it shows a typical breakdown of stages, the make-up and naming of each stage can be varied from project to project.

In a strict interpretation of the waterfall model, the products of each stage are subjected to quality assurance (QA) inspections, and only if the products are acceptable is the stage signed off as being complete, and the next stage allowed to start. In this way each new stage starts from an agreed baseline established at the end of the preceding stage. In reality, stages will often overlap, with work progressing on some of the more easily agreed upon elements of the previous stage, while other more involved or contentious elements are still being subject to review.

If any errors are detected in the course of a stage, then corrections are made to the affected products, and the stage continues. No stage is repeated, unless there is a radical change of project scope.

The waterfall model, or variants of it (see discussion of hybrid models below), is still used extensively in industry, particularly on large or multi-agency projects. It is well suited to formal project planning and control, and its insistence on QA reviews and sign-offs makes it relatively easy to build into contractual projects. For projects where requirements are complex and/or well understood, or where the system will be mission or safety critical, the waterfall model may well be the most appropriate.

For more volatile projects, where requirements are likely to change or cannot be tightly specified in advance, there are probably more effective models for structuring the development. The waterfall model has also been undermined by mismanagement, where an over-insistence on rigid interpretations of the model have led to unnecessary bureaucracy and project delays.

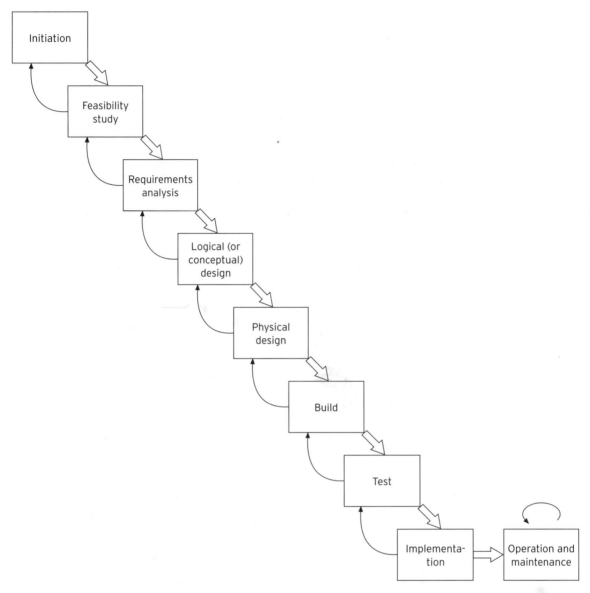

Figure 3.2   The waterfall model

On student developments the waterfall model may provide a good start point for structuring the project. Although it is unusual in industry to find small projects that use the waterfall model in anything close to its 'pure' form, the model can be useful for inexperienced practitioners, such as students. The ready-made structure is easy to build a simple plan around, and even if some of the individual stages turn out to be fairly trivial in nature, the sign-off process at the end of each stage gives the student and their supervisor some confidence that the project is progressing to plan. Nevertheless, for most students a hybrid structure is likely to prove more appropriate, unless the objectives of the project require you to demonstrate or experiment with the strict application of a specific step-by-step development method.

Spiral model

Where requirements are not well known in advance, or the shape of the solution is difficult to establish, the spiral model developed by Boehm (1988) may provide an alternative to the waterfall model. This model, illustrated in Figure 3.3, takes an iterative approach to developing a system. In the first instance a high-level requirements specification is drawn up, which is then tested by building a prototype solution. The prototype is reviewed, requirements are clarified or changed as a result, and an amended requirements specification is issued. The cycle is then repeated until the requirements are stable and users approve the design. As each iteration is completed the prototype gets nearer to the final solution, and the issues that arise from the review process become more detailed and design oriented. So at the beginning of the spiral the issues will tend to focus on requirements, while at the end the issues will be largely concerned with technical design issues.

The spiral model is often associated with the use of RAD techniques, largely because of its emphasis on prototyping. However, the model is also well suited

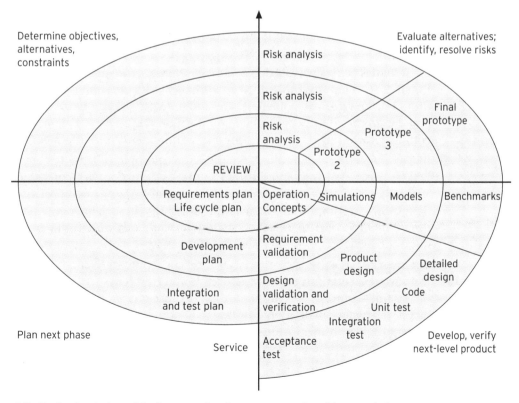

Figure 3.3 Boehm's spiral model of systems development, reproduced by permission
Source: Bocij *et al.* (2003)

to the application of more structured modelling techniques, particularly in the drawing up of the requirements specification, where each iteration can be viewed as a cut-down SDLC.

The spiral model can be applied to an entire system development, or to just one part it (see hybrid models later in this section), such as the development of the user interface, where requirements tend to be hard to express and to capture without a physical model to work on.

As with any life cycle model, the spiral model has a number of issues and drawbacks associated with it that need careful handling:

- The iterations can spiral out of control if they are not tightly managed. Because each iteration, however close it is to an acceptable solution, will inevitably throw up some requests for change, it can be difficult to call a halt to the process, resulting in projects than run late and over budget.

- It is also possible for the process to take on a life of its own, and move away from some of the high-level objectives and scope of the project.

- The final solution can be inadequately documented and poorly structured unless the development of the prototypes is well disciplined. It is all too easy to view the prototypes as the primary vehicle for capturing requirements and creating the system design, thereby cutting out the need for formal documentation and design. While this *may* deliver the software more quickly (if the iterations are relatively quick and the same individuals are present throughout), the result will be a system that is difficult and expensive to maintain, in much the same way that legacy systems that have been maintained in a piecemeal fashion are.

- If a system is being developed in a number of pieces, the spiral model, if adopted for all of the pieces, is difficult to coordinate across the subprojects. Each subproject will progress at a different rate, and unless the revisions to requirements and designs are tightly controlled and documented there is a real risk of miscommunication of changes to common requirements and interface designs.

- In a commercial system of any significant scale much of the system design will be concerned with interfacing to other systems, or with core processing that will make use of standard algorithms that require careful analysis and design. Attempting to impose a spiral model on these elements of a system, even if it is appropriate for other, less stable, elements, will disrupt and undermine the development process rather than assist it.

- The delivery of early user interface prototypes, however superficial they are, can raise expectations within the user community that the implementation of the final solution is imminent. This is especially dangerous if the system has a relatively small user interface component when compared with its underlying (or 'hidden') functionality. If users believe that a system is near completion, and there is then a delay in its delivery, they can rapidly become disillusioned with the entire development and their support and engagement will be lost.

Many of the problems associated with the spiral model are more acute on large projects. For this reason the model is probably more suited to smaller systems.

While the benefits of the spiral model for projects with unclear or emerging requirements might appear attractive, it has not gained widespread acceptance in industry, largely because of the drawbacks outlined above. For student projects, where system scope, scale and complexity will be significantly smaller than in industry, the spiral model has a lot to recommend it if, as is often the case, there is a significant proportion of user interface development within the project. However, the use of the spiral model and the accompanying prototypes should not be seen as an excuse to avoid the systematic production of formal development products, as these will almost certainly be key academic objectives. If the system requirements of your project are relatively straightforward and stable, the spiral model will not be appropriate, as multiple iterations of the SDLC will not deliver any real benefits, while eating into your already limited time.

Incremental model

In the incremental model a system is delivered in a succession of self-contained pieces or phases. Each phase is run as a mini-project in its own right, but all phases are built upon a common set of requirements and high-level design. As later phases are delivered they will inevitably cause some rework in the software delivered by earlier phases, not least in the interfaces that will be required to the new pieces of software.

Each increment could conceivably make use of either the waterfall or spiral model. The version illustrated in Figure 3.4 shows a subset of the waterfall model in each of the increments, as this is the most common scenario. The incremental model works best when system requirements are clear for the entire system and are relatively stable. If requirements are unclear or volatile then each increment will lead to significant (and potentially expensive) rework of the earlier increments.

A project can be broken into phases that deliver distinct sets of functionality. For example, a project could begin by delivering the transaction management functionality of a system, followed by a phase that delivers management reporting. In another example, a project could start with the delivery of a website that offers marketing information, followed by a phase that delivers on-line ordering, and concluding with the implementation of discussion groups.

Alternatively, a project can be broken into delivery phases along organisational lines; for example, by developing system support for the accounts department, followed by support for human resources, etc.

The incremental model can be very effective on large projects, where development of the entire system could take a long time. By delivering the system in phases the interest of users within the business can be more easily maintained, benefits can be taken early in some high-priority areas (by delivering them first), and change can be introduced into a business more gradually. Managing large projects can prove extremely cumbersome and challenging. Smaller phases are easier to manage, but overall will take longer. This is because of rework to earlier phases and the retesting of the entire system that may be needed after each phase.

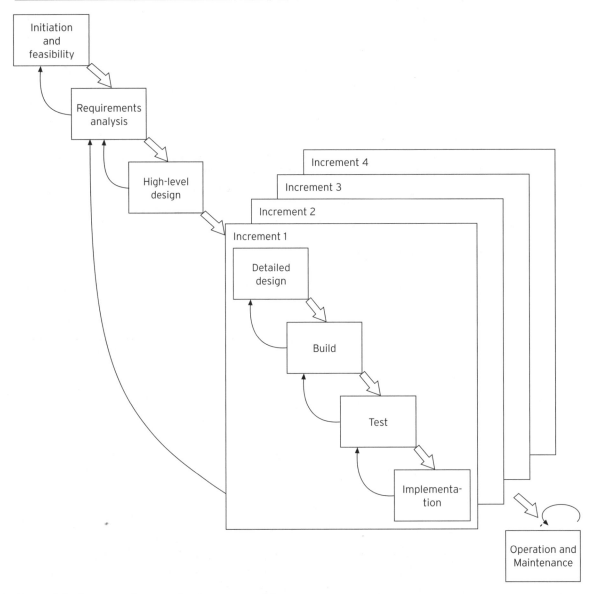

Figure 3.4   Incremental system development model

   The biggest issues with the incremental models are the identification of suitably self-contained pieces of system functionality, and the impact on overall timescales and budgets of the rework and retesting necessary with each phase. While incremental delivery is common in large businesses, the later phases of a project are frequently downgraded in business priority and subsequently cancelled, as the major benefits of the system tend to be delivered in the earlier increments. This has led to a deep suspicion of incremental delivery in some organisations.

   The incremental model may sometimes be appropriate in a student project where the overall system scope is too large to be completed in time, but where one or more increments might well be feasible.

Hybrid models

In reality a great many student projects will be hybrids of the waterfall and spiral models. Two of the most widely applicable hybrid models for use on student projects are outlined below. Both work well in practice, and both strike an effective balance between meeting academic objectives involving the evaluation and demonstration of formal life cycle models and efficient system development in the context of a small project.

Spiral design model

In the spiral design model a waterfall structure is adopted for the early stages of the project culminating in a detailed requirements specification. The spiral model is then applied to the physical design and construction stages, as illustrated in Figure 3.5. In a project where the requirements are reasonably well understood and/or complex, or where an existing system is being replaced without significant functional change, *and* where the system will be largely GUI-based the spiral design model may be appropriate.

In many ways the spiral design model brings together the best aspects of the waterfall and spiral models. It ensures that requirements are rigorously analysed and well documented, thus providing a firm base on which to build and test the software, while at the same time taking full advantage of the power of GUI development tools, thus enabling rapid user-driven software delivery.

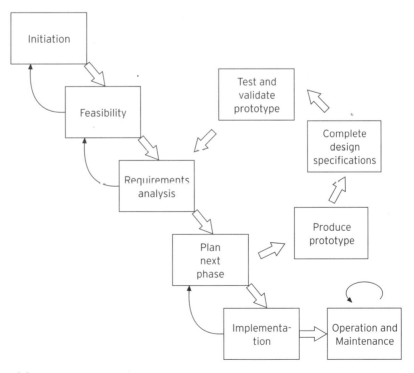

Figure 3.5 Spiral design model

The spiral design model can also be useful in a wide range of student projects, where the business problem is frequently too large for a complete solution to be delivered in time, but where the implementation of at least an initial prototype is essential to meet the requirements of the university. Using the spiral design model, the student is able to develop and demonstrate a deeper understanding of formal system development techniques, most notably in the modelling of requirements. At the same time they are able to demonstrate their ability to deliver a working piece of software that meets those requirements.

Without careful planning based on the structures provided by the waterfall model during the analysis and conceptual design stages, and by the spiral model during the physical design stage, projects that address large business problems can fall into two traps. The first is a hurried and uncontrolled rush to produce a piece of software at the last moment, which then fails to deliver against the formal requirements specification. The second is to develop some software early on, to make sure that the most 'visible' of deliverables is in place, and then try to reverse engineer the formal specification products to fit the software. Both of these approaches will be exposed in a viva voce examination, and will not be acceptable to your university.

Spiral GUI model

The spiral GUI model adopts a waterfall structure throughout the project life cycle, with the addition of a spiral structure for the delivery of just the GUI component, as shown in Figure 3.6. The projects that are most suited to the spiral GUI model are similar to those that are suited to the waterfall model. The key refinement is that the spiral GUI model is applicable only to systems that have a significant, but not dominant, GUI component. The main advantage in adopting the spiral GUI model is that the GUI can be developed rapidly and with maximum user involvement, while a more formal and rigorous approach is applied to the database, off-line and algorithmic system components.

One area that needs careful management with the spiral GUI model is the coordination of changes to requirements that may arise in either the spiral or the waterfall strand of the design process. Effective management procedures are required to ensure that any changes to requirements that arise during the design stage (and in particular the GUI design process) are documented and reflected in all design components.

The benefit of the spiral GUI model for student projects is the ability to demonstrate the application of formal techniques to the core of the development, while in parallel providing an opportunity to explore the application of prototyping as a development tool.

Table 3.1 provides a summary of the models discussed above.

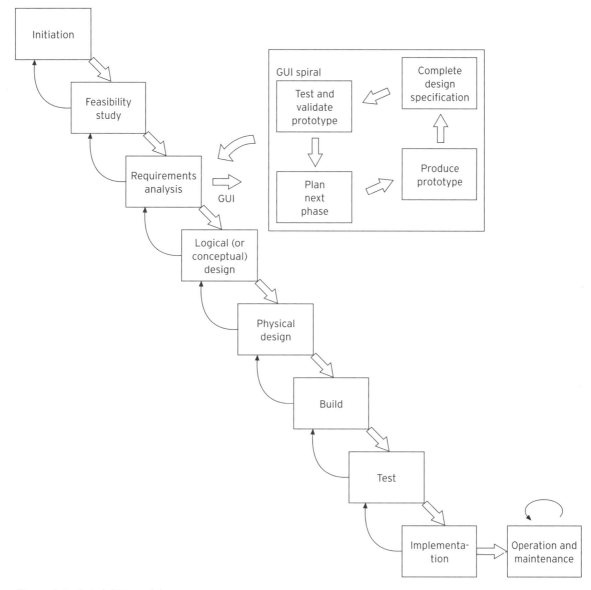

Figure 3.6 Spiral GUI model

3.4   Development approaches and methods

The methods that students apply to their development projects may be mandated by the requirements of their course. More often, the time constraints of a project leave little time for students to learn new techniques, so the method that they adopt will be the one they have been taught during their course. In both of these situations you will already know which method you are going to use, so the main decisions that you need to make are how to customise, adapt and supplement the method to meet the needs of your project.

Table 3.1 Summary of life cycle models

Model	Features	Appropriate projects
Waterfall	Characterised by a series of stages that are carried out in sequence. In reality, stages will often overlap. The products of each stage are subjected to quality assurance (QA) inspections. Each new stage starts from an agreed baseline. No stage is repeated, unless there is a radical change of project scope. Has been undermined by mismanagement leading to unnecessary bureaucracy.	Variants of the waterfall method are used extensively in industry, particularly on large or multi-agency projects. The model is well suited to formal project planning and control. Appropriate for projects where requirements are complex and/or well understood, or where the system will be mission or safety critical.
Spiral	An iterative approach to developing a system. Often associated with the use of RAD techniques. Also well suited to the application of more structured modelling techniques. Iterations can spiral out of control if they are not tightly managed. The final solution can be inadequately documented and poorly structured. Can lead to false user expectations.	Where requirements are not well known in advance, or the shape of the solution is difficult to establish, the spiral model may provide an alternative to the waterfall model. Probably more suited to smaller systems. Difficult to coordinate across a large project broken into subprojects.
Incremental	System is delivered in a succession of self-contained 'chunks' or phases. Each phase is run as a mini-project in its own right built upon a common set of requirements and high-level design. As later phases are delivered rework will be needed to earlier phases. Can be difficult to identify self-contained chunks of system functionality. Project timescales and budgets can be impacted by rework and retesting.	Works best when system requirements are clear for the entire system and are relatively stable. If requirements are volatile then each increment may lead to significant rework of earlier increments. Most effective on large projects. May be appropriate in a student project where overall system scope is too large to be completed in time, but where one or more increments might be feasible.
Spiral design	Waterfall structure is adopted for the early stages of the project. Spiral model is applied to the physical design and construction stages. Ensures that requirements are rigorously analysed and well documented. Takes full advantage of graphical development tools, thus enabling rapid user-driven software delivery.	In a project where the requirements are reasonably well understood and/or complex, or where an existing system is being replaced without significant functional change, *and* where the system will be largely GUI-based, the spiral design model may be appropriate. Useful in a wide range of student projects, where the business problem is frequently too large for a complete solution to be delivered in time.
Spiral GUI	Adopts a waterfall structure throughout the project life cycle, with the addition of a spiral structure for the delivery of just the GUI component.	Suited to similar projects to the waterfall model. Key refinement is that the spiral GUI model is only applicable to systems that have a significant, but not dominant, GUI component.

If, however, you are taking the opportunity within your project to explore a new approach, or if you have knowledge of more than one approach, you will need to decide which approach is most appropriate to your project, and within that approach, which specific notation or method you are going to adopt. You may also decide to take elements of more than one method or approach and combine them in an innovative way.

The following section discusses the applicability of the major system development approaches to student projects, together with some of their features, benefits and drawbacks. Individual techniques will not be discussed here in any detail, but will be covered in context in Part Two. There are many other development approaches, but few are used widely in student projects.

Structured methods

Most students undertaking a system development project will use at least some of the techniques from a structured method, such as SSADM or Information Engineering. This is partly because the majority of student projects will involve the development of a data-centric system that requires the implementation of a relational database, and it is this type of system for which structured methods are most suited. It is also because structured methods are widely taught in universities and colleges, not least because they are common in industry and mandatory in large parts of the public sector.

Where a system is concerned more with complex processing rather than data manipulation and retrieval, especially where the target system will be not implemented using a relational database, other types of method may be more appropriate.

Structured methods are most frequently associated with the waterfall model, but can also be used effectively with the spiral models, especially the spiral design or spiral GUI models, in conjunction with prototyping (some structured methods, such as SSADM, include prototyping as a formal part of requirements specification).

Structured methods typically consist of three main elements: a set of integrated techniques; a set of products that are created or modified by the techniques; and a planning framework that provides structures for use of the techniques within a project. Underpinning most structured methods are the following concepts:

- **Logical and physical views of the system.** By separating the analysis and design of the underlying requirements of a system (the logical view) from the constraints of the technology that will be used to construct the system (the physical view), developers are free to concentrate on what the system will deliver for a business, rather than how it will be built. The resulting specification can then be implemented in a wide range of environments, using a number of different technical design approaches.

- **Data-driven system design.** In structured methods, the data model lies at the heart of the system design. As most information systems provide relatively simple processing, designed to manipulate and report on relatively complex data structures, this is a sensible approach. The data model also remains fairly stable within a system, whereas processing tends to change on a regular basis in response to new working practices.

■ **User involvement.** Most structured methods build acceptance and sign-off procedures into their structures. Users are also encouraged to be involved in the production of analysis and design products, rather than merely providing input to and reviews of the products. In order to assist in this, most structured methods use notations and products that are relatively non-technical and narrowly focused in nature, particularly in the early stages of the SDLC where user involvement is at its most critical. While users will not have to be experienced in systems development in order to take an active role in using structured techniques, they will need some formal training.

Most products of structured methods are diagrammatic and designed to capture a particular aspect of a system's specification requirements. The diagrammatic nature of many products reduces the ambiguity inherent in textual specifications, and also enables a lot of information to be captured in a readily accessible and compact form.

A system specification is created by identifying the products within the method which, when taken in combination with each other, will describe what the system is to deliver and how it will be structured. Structured methods have been undermined in the past by inexperienced practitioners adopting a recipe book approach, where they apply every technique at their disposal, regardless of whether it is relevant to the project or not. Within most structured methods is a set of flexible techniques, products and project structures, which can be adapted to a range of different project types. It is not intended that any single project should make use of all the available products, but that those that are applicable to the type of project being undertaken are selected and developed as needed. The recipe book approach will inevitably lead to wasted time and unnecessary bureaucracy.

There have also been arguments that the way in which structured methods make use of techniques and products that focus on one particular aspect of a system, such as data, processing or the user interface, leads to disjointed designs that do not map cleanly onto some specific programming technologies, and that can be difficult to coordinate. While there may be some truth in this if products are developed in isolation without rigorous cross-checking, the reality is that many users and systems professionals find the techniques easy to learn and to apply (compared with those of other methods) due in part to their focused nature.

The open nature of some structured methods (such as SSADM), where the system specification is deliberately created so that it can be implemented in a wide range of technical environments, means that design products will need to be mapped and translated into environment-specific technical specifications, using techniques such as structured English, Jackson Structured Programming or object-oriented modelling when the project moves into physical design. This is only a problem of any significance where the system is not going to be built

Box 3.1

SSADM

SSADM (Structured Systems Analysis and Design Method) is the most widely used structured method in industry and in student projects. The Central Computer and Telecommunications Agency (CCTA) originally developed SSADM in 1981 for use across industry and the public sector, with the most recent version (SSADM 4+) being issued in 1996. SSADM is based on best practice, and is available for use by any company or individual without the payment of fees.

SSADM provides a number of tried and tested techniques and products covering the SDLC up to the early part of physical design. The techniques include:

- logical data modelling;
- business activity modelling;
- data flow modelling;
- requirements definition;
- entity life histories;
- relational data analysis.

All these techniques are based on best practice, and are similar to those used in many other methods. The techniques and products can be used in combination with each other to create a complete system specification, ready for technical design, or separately to investigate or refine one or more aspects of a system design. Few, if any, projects will need to make use of the full range of techniques, and in many projects they will be substituted with techniques from other types of method, such as object-oriented design. At the centre of the method are the logical data model and the Requirements Catalogue. Both of these products are developed at an early stage and gradually refined as the project progresses.

This customisation and substitution approach to the techniques and products is encouraged within the guidelines of the method. SSADM also provides a default structure *suggesting* how all of the techniques can be used together within a project, but again it is expected that the structure will be heavily adapted to the needs of an individual project. The default structure consists of the stages listed below, although the physical design stage is more concerned with preparation of the logical system specification for technical design and construction than with the techniques of physical design themselves:

- Feasibility.
- Requirements analysis.
- Requirements specification.
- Logical system specification.
- Physical design.

SSADM is a highly suitable method for any data-centric student project, regardless of the implementation environment. It produces an unambiguous specification that can be mapped efficiently and effectively to virtually any programming environment, as long as care is taken with customising the method. The techniques of SSADM are also widely understood in industry, where structured methods are prevalent. Most mature structured methods are built around the same core techniques. So even where diagrammatic notations differ, the skills acquired in carrying out an SSADM-based project will be easily transferred to most industry projects.

around a relational database, which is rarely the case in a student project. Issues can also be encountered if your system involves a relatively trivial database coupled with complex programming. In these projects it may be more appropriate to use methods that are designed from the outset to meet the specific needs of the physical programming environment. Alternatively, techniques that are specific to the programming environment may be substituted for the generalist techniques of the structured method (see Section 3.5 on customising methods).

RAD

Rapid application development (RAD) came into being in the early 1990s in response to the ever-increasing speed of change within businesses. The key enabler for RAD approaches was the availability of tools that were capable of generating software quickly, thus allowing developers to use prototyping in order to confirm user requirements and in the right circumstances to reduce overall development times.

There are many definitions of RAD, and many proprietary models of how tools and techniques can be used to accelerate development. RAD is less a method than an approach to software development, in that it does not itself provide a complete set of techniques or products that can be applied to system development. Instead most definitions of RAD offer a number of guiding principles and recommendations that if adopted in the right circumstances should deliver an application more rapidly.

Most RAD approaches have a number of features in common:

- **User involvement.** Users of the system must be actively involved throughout the life of the project. This is particularly important at the beginning of the project, where users from all the groups affected by the system should participate in establishing high-level requirements. It is important that the users who work on the project team are well respected and empowered by the organisation. By involving users in a central way within the project team itself, it is more likely that the wider user community will accept the final system and that the implementation will be smoother, as training and change management procedures will have been defined by business users rather than by systems developers.
- **Prototyping.** While prototyping is a feature of any RAD project that is not implementing an unmodified package, it can be used in virtually all types of approach. In a RAD project prototyping is often used to iteratively develop the software, but it can also be used as an investigative tool to define requirements or test certain design approaches.
- **Acceptance of imperfection.** At all stages of a RAD project imperfections should be treated as acceptable. This means that dead ends, where experimentation or assumptions have led to designs or software that need to be reworked, should be acceptable, and to an extent expected. It also means that the finished software may not be as slick as users would ideally like, but should still meet the essential requirements.

- **The 80/20 rule.** If a RAD project is to be implemented in a truly rapid fashion, it is important to identify and stick to the most important requirements that together will deliver the majority of the system's benefits. A well-worn rule of thumb is that 80 per cent of the benefits of a system can be delivered by just 20 per cent of the functionality. RAD projects that fail to adopt the 80/20 rule run a real risk of becoming drawn out. The remaining 80 per cent of requirements may still be critical to the long-term acceptability of the system, in which case they may be delivered by subsequent projects or phases, either using a RAD approach or some other more formal method.

- **Timeboxing.** Many RAD projects use the concept of timeboxes, in which the system is delivered within strict time constraints. The presence of a well-publicised timebox acts as a focus to all of the project team, and assists in ensuring that all team members concentrate on the aspects of the system that really matter. Without timeboxing there is a tendency for people to lose sight of the need to channel their efforts and to revert to the practice of attempting to deliver perfection.

- **Workshops.** Workshops are a very effective way to accelerate the processes of requirements definition and of design. Many RAD projects will begin with cross-functional workshops that define requirements at a high level, which are then refined through a process of prototyping and further, more focused workshops, and users who are drafted into the project team.

RAD projects are good candidates for the spiral and spiral design models, but in practice many will adopt a less formal model. One approach is to use a version of the spiral design model, where formal system models are produced in the analysis phase (data models, use cases, activity models, etc.), followed by just two iterations of a combined design and build phase. The first iteration will lead to a rapid implementation of a pilot application. The pilot is then tested, either in a limited live environment or an intensive testing environment. Necessary modifications are made to the pilot in the second design and build iteration, which is then implemented fully. This approach is more common where a package is being implemented with minimum modification.

A real danger with RAD projects, particularly in the hands of an inexperienced practitioner, is that the rush to implement the system will lead to poorly structured software, lacking in flexibility for the future, with almost no design documentation. While such projects may succeed in delivering a system rapidly, they do so at the expense of ongoing maintainability and high running costs.

The tendency of early RAD projects to deliver poorly constructed systems led to the RAD approach being labelled 'Really Awful Developments' or 'Rapidly Achieved Disasters'. This is largely unfair, as the problems were often due to misunderstandings about how RAD projects should be constructed, and about which projects are suitable for the RAD approach.

It cannot be over-emphasised that even in the most time-constrained of projects it is essential that the system is properly documented, and that the critical components of the system are correctly modelled and structured. Use of a RAD approach does not mean that formal models can be dispensed with entirely. Some of the later specification or design models are indeed replaced by physical

Table 3.2 RAD project characteristics

- The project team must be genuinely empowered to make decisions, and should include fully committed user involvement from all affected groups for the duration of the development.
- The system should not be computationally complex.
- The system should not be safety or mission critical (where perfection is the goal).
- Requirements should not be rigidly defined up front.
- The system should have a significant GUI element, and not be dominated by system-to-system interfaces.
- The environment should be stable, both technically and organisationally.
- The project must not be too large or must be able to be delivered in small sequential increments. Many RAD approaches have maximum timebox sizes, such as 90 days, within which it should be possible to deliver the system or its first increment. The Dynamic Systems Development Method (DSDM) suggests 6 months as the absolute maximum.

prototypes, but the earlier analysis models (such as the data model) are vital to ensure that the system is built on solid foundations.

Likewise, the detailed technical documentation that renders a system maintainable cannot be overlooked. In some cases this will entail retrospectively created documentation, completed by the people who have built the system. The paradox here is that in businesses where time pressures make the RAD approach attractive, there is often little opportunity for project teams to find the time necessary to clear up after themselves.

RAD approaches can be extremely effective if managed carefully, but they are not a panacea. As a general rule RAD approaches are best applied to projects that have the characteristics shown in Table 3.2. An alternative view of RAD is that it can be used for any application or project, even if none of the characteristics in Table 3.2 apply, as long as the team has sufficient experience and expertise in RAD, the tools being used, and in the business area under examination.

RAD is also used by some businesses as a way of exploring the potential of a new development, or to provide a stopgap solution to an urgent problem. In these cases the resulting system could be regarded as a live prototype or pilot, in which a level of support for the business is provided, while a fully functional solution is developed which will make use of the lessons learnt from the RAD implementation.

Students are sometimes attracted to RAD as a development approach as it appears to be tailor made for the timeboxed nature of a student project. However, it is important to look at the other characteristics and principles of a RAD project. The area that most often rules out a full RAD approach for a student project is that of user involvement (which DSDM cites as its number one principle). Student projects, even if conducted as a group exercise, rarely have appropriate levels of user involvement, much less users within their team.

Box 3.2

The Dynamic Systems Development Method (DSDM) was created in 1994 by a not-for-profit consortium of leading companies in order to identify and promote best practice in RAD.

DSDM is not a method in the usual sense of the word, in that it does not define any specific techniques and products. It does define a number of high-level products, together with a framework for managing and controlling their development. DSDM does not, however, define how products should be created or what their detailed contents should be. This is a deliberate strategy, in order to ensure that DSDM can be applied to a wide range of projects and environments. It is possible to create the system development products of DSDM using techniques from a number of different approaches, such as structured methods or object-oriented methods.

DSDM aims to address the three fundamental aspects of any project, namely people, business processes and technology. Its emphasis is firmly on assisting people to work effectively together in a RAD environment, as this is the aspect that lies behind most failed projects.

Underpinning DSDM is a set of nine guiding principles, as described by DSDM Consortium (2002):

I. **Active user involvement is imperative.** Users are active participants in the development process. If users are not closely involved throughout the development life cycle, delays will occur and users may feel that the final solution is imposed by the developers and/or management.

II. **The team must be empowered to make decisions.** DSDM teams consist of both developers and users. They must be able to make decisions as requirements are refined and possibly changed. They must be able to agree that certain levels of functionality, usability, etc. are acceptable without frequent recourse to higher-level management.

III. **The focus is on frequent delivery of products.** A product-based approach is more flexible than an activity-based one. The work of a DSDM team is concentrated on products that can be delivered in an agreed period of time. By keeping each period of time short, the team can easily decide which activities are necessary and sufficient to achieve the right products. Note: Products include interim development products, not just delivered systems.

IV. **Fitness for business purpose is the essential criterion for acceptance of deliverables.** The focus of DSDM is on delivering the essential business requirements within the required time. Allowance is made for changing business needs within that timeframe.

V. **Iterative and incremental development is necessary to converge on an accurate business solution.** DSDM allows systems to grow incrementally. Therefore the developers can make full use of feedback from the users. Moreover partial solutions can be delivered to satisfy immediate business needs. Rework is built into the DSDM process; thus, the development can proceed more quickly during iteration.

VI. **All changes during development are reversible.** To control the evolution of all products, everything must be in a known state at all times. Backtracking is a feature of DSDM. However in some circumstances it may be easier to reconstruct than to backtrack. This depends on the nature of the change and the environment in which it was made.

VII. **Requirements are baselined at a high level.** Baselining high-level requirements means 'freezing' and agreeing the purpose and scope of the system at a level that allows for detailed investigation of what the requirements imply. Further, more detailed baselines can be established later in the development, although the scope should not change significantly.

VIII. **Testing is integrated throughout the lifecycle.** Testing is not treated as a separate activity. As the system is developed incrementally, it is also tested and reviewed by both developers and users incrementally to ensure that the development is moving forward not only in the right business direction but is technically sound.

▶

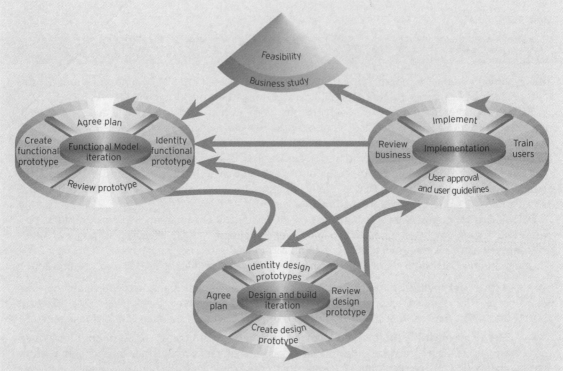

Figure 3.7 DSDM life cycle model, reproduced by permission
Source: www.dsdm.org

IX. **Collaboration and cooperation between all stakeholders is essential.** The nature of DSDM projects means that low-level requirements are not necessarily fixed when the project is begun. The short-term direction that a project takes must be quickly decided without recourse to restrictive change control procedures. The stakeholders include not only the business and development staff within the project, but also other staff such as service delivery or resource managers.

DSDM has its own life cycle model, known affectionately as 'three pizzas and a piece of cheese', as illustrated in Figure 3.7.

The Feasibility and Business studies happen before the project gets fully under way. The aim of the Feasibility study is to establish the viability of the project in business terms and as a candidate for DSDM. The Business study will confirm the scope and users of the system, and identify the high-level system requirements that the remainder of the project will deliver.

The three iterative stages will overlap or merge, according to the needs of the project. The Functional Model will fully define the requirements of the system and develop functioning prototypes. These prototypes are then evolved into a robust fully featured and tested solution during the Design and build iteration. The Implementation stage will be iterated if there is to be a phased roll-out to a physically distributed user base, or if the roll-out process is itself to be prototyped or piloted in the field.

DSDM will not be suitable for all projects or for all organisations. For example, those organisations that are hierarchical in nature, with a culture of command and control rather than empowerment, will not find the collaborative approach of DSDM easy to introduce or manage. Likewise, organisations that demand perfection in their system solutions will not find themselves able to truly buy into the 80/20 rule that is an essential part of the DSDM philosophy.

In addition, even where the organisation finds the DSDM approach culturally acceptable, the individual project itself should also be tested against the characteristics listed in Table 3.2. The failure of a project to match with all of these characteristics does not rule DSDM out as an approach, but will make it more difficult to apply to the whole project. However, as quoted by the DSDM Consortium (2003), 'You can use ALL of DSDM some of the time, and SOME of DSDM all of the time'.

All too often students make the mistake of seeing RAD as an excuse to avoid formal modelling, or to jump straight into programming. The pity is that this then leads to a scenario in which a small project, which might have been an ideal vehicle for testing and experimenting with development theory, is reduced to a trivial prototyping exercise.

A much more effective approach for most student projects is to introduce certain RAD techniques, such as workshops and prototyping, into a structured or object-oriented method.

Object-oriented methods

Object-oriented analysis and design techniques first came to prominence in the early 1990s, following the publication of works by, among others, Coad and Yourdon (1990 and 1991), Booch (1991), Rumbaugh *et al.* (1991) and Jacobson *et al.* (1992). These techniques used the same underlying principles as object-oriented programming languages, such as Smalltalk and, later on, C++ and Java.

Central to all object-oriented approaches is the concept of an object, which is defined by Coad and Yourdon (1991) as:

An abstraction of something in the domain of a problem or its implementation, reflecting the capabilities of a system to keep information about it, interact with it, or both.

In simpler terms an object represents, in a self-contained package, the data and processes (known as methods) associated with a real-world object. Objects then communicate with each other via messages. The claim is that objects provide a more natural way of representing the world in software terms.

The number of object-oriented methods, all using different notations, grew rapidly in the mid-1990s. Many of the methods used superficially similar notation to mean different things, leading to confusion and destructive competition between methods. This state of affairs persisted until the development of the UML by Booch, Rumbaugh and Jacobson (known as 'the three amigos') in 1997. UML is rapidly becoming the *de facto* standard notation for object-oriented design methods.

In a similar way to structured methods, object-oriented methods combine a set of techniques and products with a framework for their application in a project environment. Some methods are tied closely to a specific technical environment, while others are more open in nature. What most object-oriented methods have in common is an assumption that the system will be constructed using an object-oriented language and an object-oriented database.

The programming heritage of object-oriented methods is evident in their theoretical underpinning and in their emphasis on system design. Many of the core object-oriented analysis and design products (such as class diagrams) are based on technical design products. Such products are created at a high level during early stages of the life cycle and gradually added to as the project progresses, thus avoiding issues associated with the mapping or translating of models into a technical design.

Box 3.3

UML (Unified Modelling Language)

UML was developed during the mid-1990s in an attempt to establish an industry standard, based on best practice, for object-oriented techniques and notation. The industry-leading object-oriented methods at this time were the Booch method created by Grady Booch, Ivar Jacobson's Object-Oriented Software Engineering (OOSE) and James Rumbaugh's Object Modelling Technique (OMT). There had been some convergence between these methods leading up to the mid-1990s, but in 1996 the three method leaders (with contributions from around the industry) completed this process by releasing the Unified Modelling Language (UML). In 1997 UML version 1.1 was adopted by the standards body, the Object Management Group (OMG), as the standard object-oriented modelling language. Version 1.4, released in 2000, is by far the most widely adopted object modelling language.

UML, as its name suggests, is a modelling language and not a software development method or process. What this means is that it presents notation for modelling and specifying different aspects of a system. It does not, however, provide a process for creating models, or a framework for organising and controlling that process. In order to apply UML successfully, it must be used in conjunction with a software development process, such as Rational's Unified Process.

The UML notation is largely diagrammatic and consists of nine core diagrams:

■ Use Case diagram. Describes at a high level what the system will do for its users. Use Case diagrams are technology independent, and contain no object-specific notation. They are easy to understand, and provide a view of the system's functionality from the perspective of different users (or 'actors').

■ Class diagram. Models the attributes, associations and operations of classes (a generalised description of a group of real-world objects sharing the same set of attributes and behaviours). The most important UML diagram, which ties together all other diagrams.

■ Object diagram. Illustrates the structure, attributes and association between real-world instances (objects) of classes in a class diagram.

■ Sequence diagram. Shows the flow of messages in time sequence between objects, in order to achieve a meaningful piece of work for the system/user.

■ Collaboration diagram. Complements the Sequence diagram, but without the time dimension. Provides a more structural view of how objects interact to achieve the same meaningful pieces of work.

■ State diagram. Models the life cycle of a class, illustrating how the state of an object will respond to events.

■ Activity diagram. Models the step-by-step flow of internal processing within a complex operation.

■ Component diagram. Provides a static view of the software components (such as programs and tables) of the physical system and how they relate to each other.

■ Deployment diagram. Models the hardware configuration of the system.

Taken together the nine diagrams (along with other supporting documentation) constitute a comprehensive specification and internal design for a system. There are some aspects of the full design that UML does not provide, such as the design of the GUI. It is expected therefore that the UML products will be supplemented with other products to complete the design process.

Few projects are of sufficient complexity to require the use of all-UML diagrams. UML-based methods will provide guidance on which products should be used for different types of project, but all UML projects should use the Class diagram, along with Sequence and Use Case diagrams.

Most of the UML products are intended for use in an object-oriented environment, but one in particular is finding wide use in other environments. Use Cases are entirely free from any mention of objects and are applicable to any technology. In a highly accessible fashion that requires little training to interpret, Use Case diagrams provide an excellent vehicle for representing a user view of the functionality of a system. Use Case diagrams are supported by Behaviour Specifications that can be used to capture user interaction requirements at an early stage of a project.

The benefits of this approach are obvious if the system is to be implemented in a truly object-oriented environment (as opposed to one that is merely marketed as such). However, there are also a number of drawbacks to this approach:

- Object-oriented design products are closely tailored for use in an object-oriented development environment. The necessary conversion of products for implementation in other environments (such as relational database management systems) can be difficult, negating any benefits achieved in the transition from analysis to design.

- Some of the products, while ideally suited to capturing elements of physical design, are far less suited to requirements analysis or specification. For those who are not from a programming background, the creation of models such as the Class diagram can be challenging, even after undertaking significant training. This is, of course, not the case for all products, particularly those that do not have a programming or design heritage. For example, the Use Case diagram (see Box 3.3) is a powerful analysis tool, which is easy to learn and apply, and which can also be used equally well in any implementation environment.

For these reasons, object-oriented methods are widely regarded as design methods, rather than whole life cycle methods, particularly where the system is concerned more with information than processing. In many instances object-oriented design is used in conjunction with other approaches, such as structured methods or RAD, either for the entire physical design or for certain object-oriented components.

Many of the benefits claimed for object-oriented methods come from greater reuse of program code. Because objects capture both the processing and data aspects of a real-world object in a self-contained package that is to an extent context-independent, they can be used in a range of business applications, where they will respond to communications (messages) from different objects to support different business needs. An individual object can also be developed and modified quickly without affecting other objects, which need to know nothing of their underlying structure, as long as they can exchange messages with them.

There are undoubted benefits to reuse in businesses that are in a constant state of change over short timescales, or that produce software that will be implemented in a range of different contexts (such as package manufacturers, whose main aim is to develop flexible software that is reused in a number of client applications). However, most businesses are not in the software industry, and few are dynamic enough to see real benefits of reuse before a system requires major overhaul, often in a new environment that will not allow reuse of objects developed in earlier environments.

The use of object-oriented methods in student projects is growing, owing to the increase in courses offering object-oriented modelling modules (usually in UML). Their use is most common in software engineering projects where the emphasis is on technical design and programming, often using a language such as Java, for which object-oriented techniques are well suited.

Information system and business computing projects on the other hand tend to be data-centric and involve the construction of a system around a relational database management system. Such projects also frequently stress the early analysis and specification stages of the SDLC, with technical design and programming being driven by a prototyping approach. In these circumstances you should not dismiss object-oriented techniques, particularly if they are the only techniques that you have been taught during your studies. However, you will need to think carefully about how to apply them effectively, and how you can supplement them with techniques from other approaches (such as normalisation and prototyping).

Packages

Increasingly in industry, and to some extent in student projects, systems are being implemented using a package. Their use is especially common for standard applications such as accounting, and in small businesses where development resources are often limited.

Most packages offer a set of functionality, which can be configured using table settings and parameters to fit a range of business practices. Unless the package is to be used in a stand-alone mode, some development work will be needed to build interfaces with other systems (unless all of the systems are provided by the same vendor and have not been modified, which is a rare situation).

Organisations may choose to implement a package without modification (i.e. without the addition of new or amended program code), either because it fits their requirements very closely, or because they do not have the financial or technical resources to make and maintain the changes. In this scenario business processes will almost certainly need to be modified to match the functionality of the package. This may be acceptable for some applications, but is rarely the case for systems that support the core business of an organisation, where even small variations in business processes will often be perceived as contributing to the competitive advantage of the organisation. It is extremely common for projects that set out with the intention of implementing an unmodified package to be de-railed by concerns over the constraints imposed by the package, and for modifications to start creeping into the project.

More often, a package will form the basis of the solution, but modifications will then be made to the system in order to fit business requirements, or to enable the package to interface with existing systems. In this scenario the package-based solution will be more closely tailored to the needs of the business, but the development costs will be much greater than for a standard package implementation. There will also be an additional ongoing cost associated with continued maintenance of the modified code.

Regardless of whether a package is to be modified or not, it is essential that user requirements are analysed and modelled fully in order to provide a basis for selecting the package. Even in cases where the package has been 'pre-selected' by an earlier study, requirements will need to be modelled fully in order to drive configuration and/or modification of the package. In package implementation projects special attention should be paid to the analysis of system-to-system interfacing requirements, as well as the modelling of existing system data, in order to identify data compatibility and conversion issues.

If the package is to be modified, then a full requirements specification and system design will need to be produced, using whatever method and approach is acceptable both to the client organisation and to the package vendor (both will need to be able to work with it).

Most information system packages will be implemented using a relational database management system, so the core products for the requirements analysis exercise will usually consist of a data model, Requirements Catalogue and high-level process model, as used by many structured methods. This set of products is the one that is most widely understood by package vendors.

A package implementation approach can be effective for a student project, particularly if being undertaken for an external client, as long as there is enough scope and complexity to meet the requirements of your course. If your project covers the whole development life cycle, the analysis and package selection stages can be challenging and require as much rigour and depth as in a bespoke development project. The implementation of the first increment of the package will then provide you with an opportunity to demonstrate technical configuration skills and to experience change management issues. If the package requires modification then you may also get the opportunity to develop a partial requirements specification and system design. Finally, you may be able to undertake some programming of system interfaces, while the package vendor carries out modifications to the package itself.

The advantage of the package approach for students is that the relatively rapid implementation stage (assuming that extensive modifications are not required) of at least an initial prototype may allow you to experience the full development life cycle for a system that is of a larger scale than normal for a student project. There are, however, some significant disadvantages for a student project:

- Package selection frequently takes a long time, and cannot be fitted into the short timeframe of a student project. Identifying potential packages, inviting tenders from vendors, assessing the functionality of the packages and investigating hardware and interfacing requirements are all time-consuming exercises. Once a package is selected there is often a further delay while contractual and financial discussions take place.

- If an external client has already undertaken package selection, the project will need to focus on the configuration, modification and implementation of the package, as much of the requirements analysis will already have been completed. In many instances this will be insufficiently challenging to meet the academic requirements of your course, unless extensive modifications are required.

- If the package is to be implemented with minimal modification, then the technical aspects of the project may lack sufficient depth. If your course demands a substantial design and construction element, this will almost certainly be lacking in the development work associated with system interfacing.

Package implementations will not be covered in any detail during Part Two of this book, as most of the system development techniques used will be lifted from structured, object-oriented or RAD approaches.

Table 3.3 Development approach suitability

Approach	Features of ideally suited projects	Life cycle models	Pros and cons
Structured methods	Requirements relatively stable. Data-centric projects. System to be built using relational database management system. Suited to all project sizes. Very strong in large projects. Industry-based development.	Waterfall. Incremental. Spiral design. Spiral GUI.	Widely used and understood. Mature and stable. Large degree of technology independence. Can be too bureaucratic if poorly managed. Well adapted to project management.
Object-oriented methods	Requirements reasonably stable. Applications with significant processing. System to be built using object-oriented tools and database. Suited to all project sizes. Strong in projects with large development teams. Academically based projects, or projects with large object reuse potential.	Waterfall. Incremental. Spiral design. Spiral GUI.	Very strong design pedigree. *De facto* standard notation (UML) in place. Not widely understood in industry (outside software houses). Requires high level of training and technical competence. Enables reuse.
RAD	Volatile requirements. Systems with large GUI component. Suited to small projects, or projects that can be broken into increments. Time-constrained projects. Stable technical environment. Relatively non-complex processing.	Spiral. Incremental.	Short development times. User-driven development. Can be seen as excuse for poor system modelling and cutting corners. Committed user involvement is essential.
Package	Stable requirements, well known in advance. Standard business applications. Non-unique business processes. Projects with limited development resource.	Waterfall. Incremental.	If unmodified can be cost effective and rapid. Extensive modification can be costly and time consuming. Can lack sufficient depth to satisfy academic objectives.

Selecting an approach

Table 3.3 summarises the kinds of project for which each of the approaches discussed above are *ideally* suited. This is not meant to suggest that each approach should be used only on projects that have all of the features mentioned, or even that an approach cannot be used with great success for an entirely different type of project. The truth is that some of the most interesting projects involve the examination and exploration of techniques or approaches in non-standard situations. Most student projects will adopt a hybrid or heavily customised development method, and many will choose to apply an approach to a problem that is outside its normal application. The final report of such projects will normally include a critical evaluation of the development approach as one of its most prominent academic deliverables.

However, if you are able to exercise choice in your selection of a project approach and your project fits well with features listed against one of the approaches in Table 3.3, then you should certainly give that approach, or a close adaptation of that approach, serious consideration.

Your project is unlikely to fall neatly into any of the broad categories given in Table 3.3, so you will need to carry out some investigation in order to confirm the approach you should adopt. Most universities will expect your system development project to include a research element of some sort (unless your course is at HND level), even if it consists just of a brief review of the literature. In many instances one of the most appropriate topics for research will be an investigation into the approaches and methods that have been, or could be, applied to the type of development concerned. Chapter 4 provides some guidance on the specific questions you might wish to answer, and on how to conduct the research. At the very least your project should include a brief literature review in order to establish which approaches are appropriate for your sort of project, and to identify any specific issues that might arise from applying a given approach to your project topic.

The type of project you are undertaking is only one consideration (albeit a fairly significant one) in selecting your development approach. There are a number of other equally important things that you need to take into account before making your selection:

- **Techniques and tools available to you.** You may have a strong desire to explore and test the skills that you have already acquired during your studies, even if they do not appear to be a perfect match for the project you are planning to undertake. Alternatively, you may have access to a limited number of tools at your university or workplace, which may restrict you in your choice of development approach.

- **Time available to learn new techniques.** The timescales for your project will place strict limits on the amount of time you can spend on learning and becoming competent in new techniques. Not many students will have the time to learn a new method or approach in its entirety, but most should have the time to learn some new techniques that can be used to customise or supplement a method they are already familiar with.

- **University or course standards.** Your course or university may require you to use a standard approach or method (although this is not common). There may also be a limited number of methods that its lecturers are prepared or able to fully support as project supervisors. In all projects the experience of your supervisor will be a factor in determining your approach, as you will clearly get more direct support if you select an approach with which they are familiar.

- **Client policy.** If your project has an external client they may insist that you use their standard development methodology, or at least adopt an approach with which they are familiar.

- **Your career objectives.** If there are particular techniques or approaches that you feel may enhance your CV, then you may view your project as an opportunity to demonstrate or acquire appropriate skills.

- **Personal interest.** During your studies you may have identified specific techniques or tools that you would like to explore further. Your project provides an ideal opportunity to develop a deeper understanding of techniques and tools, even if you propose to apply them slightly out of their normal context.

- **Other team members.** In a group project, the wishes and experience of all team members will need to be considered in deciding upon a development approach. If consensus cannot be reached, and if there is no really obvious choice, your supervisor or tutor may need to advise or even dictate the approach you take.

3.5 Selecting and customising your approach

Customising methods

Most methods are designed to cope with levels of complexity that are far greater than you will encounter within an academic environment. So, once you have a clear idea of which method or approach is the most appropriate for your kind of project, you will need to consider how you will adapt or customise it to meet the needs of your particular development.

At the start of your project the emphasis of your customisation will be on establishing the techniques that you plan to use, and on how they will complement each other. Once your project is under way you will need to make more detailed decisions about how to adapt the individual techniques themselves.

There are two basic types of method customisation:

- **Method adaptation.** Virtually all system development methods come with a framework and set of products that are designed to cope with a range of project types, sizes and team structures. The project manager is expected to select the products that are appropriate to the project they are undertaking, and to use the flexible framework to create a project-specific plan. Most methods provide guidance on customisation, and some will also have suggestions on how techniques from outside the method can be used to support the core techniques. For example, fact-finding techniques are called on by all methods, but are defined in detail in very few. Where fact-finding techniques are not defined as a core part of the method itself, guidance will be given on where they should be used and how they feed into the method. It is also expected that projects will supplement the method with other techniques where the application has features that require special treatment not covered in depth within the method.

■ **Method modification.** The second type of customisation involves modifying a method, by introducing replacement techniques into the project, or combining one method with another to create a hybrid method. For example, you could use the structured analysis techniques of SSADM for the early part of the life cycle, and then produce the system design using the object-oriented notation of UML if the target environment is object-oriented. Another example would be the adoption of a structured or object-oriented method for the development of the off-line components of an application, alongside the application of DSDM to the development of the GUI-based component (in a spiral GUI life cycle model).

There can be no hard and fast rules for customisation, as every project will have different needs and resources. Indeed for any given project it is possible to identify a number of customisations, all of which may be equally capable of delivering a solid system solution. In essence there is no single 'correct' customisation. However, your chances of succeeding in your project and of optimising your resources will be greatly enhanced if you have taken the care and time to make rational and informed decisions on how to customise your chosen method or methods. In many cases the customisation of your development method will be a key objective of your project, as will the subsequent evaluation of its success.

Table 3.4 lists the main activities that you need to complete when customising a method. Once the process of customising your method is complete, it is essential that you properly document your approach. This should take the form of a list of activities, products and resource requirements, all backed up with a convincing rationale for the approach you are adopting. Remember that if you want a good mark, it is not good enough just to blindly follow an approach covered in your lectures. A lot of what you produce by adopting a 'recipe book' approach would be irrelevant and time wasting. You will get much more credit for a thoughtfully constructed approach. The exception to this would be a project in which your objective is to explore the use of techniques specified by your course in the context of a real-world project, in order to test your ability to apply those techniques.

Whichever development approach or method customisation you decide to adopt, the key questions that your supervisor is likely to ask are the following:

■ Does the application of your chosen method to the problem concerned represent a good academic test, i.e. will it prove to be intellectually and technically challenging?

■ Does the chosen approach meet with the requirements of your course?

■ Is the chosen approach capable of supporting the kind of development you are undertaking?

■ If you are proposing a novel application of a method, have you considered fully the research implications for your project?

■ Do you have the time and resources required to acquire and apply the skills and tools necessary to use your chosen approach?

Table 3.4 Method customisation

Activity	Comment
Review the literature	Literature reviews are covered later in Chapters 4 and 10. At the planning stage, in addition to researching appropriate methods for your type of project, you should also try to establish how these methods have been customised or supplemented. In particular you should look for innovative adaptations of your proposed method.
Look at past projects	Past projects are a good source of information on how methods have been customised across a range of project types. Be aware, though, that while past projects from your university library may give you some ideas of how to approach your project, they do not generally carry any indication of how successful they were.
Identify constraints	The tools and skills that you have available to you, or that you have the resources to acquire, may restrict your capabilities to execute some of the techniques of your chosen method. This should not be the case for the core techniques; otherwise you should look again at the method you are proposing to use. You will need to examine the 'missing' techniques to establish whether there are ways round them within the method, or whether you can substitute other techniques that you are better placed to use.
Analyse application-specific features	The features of your application may mean that some techniques are unnecessary or should be substituted with more appropriate techniques, e.g. if your application has a minimal user interface you are unlikely to require the use of sophisticated GUI design techniques; a simple prototype should be sufficient. Alternatively your application may require the development of specialist components that are not catered for within your method, in which case you will need to supplement your method with appropriate techniques.
Assess method guidelines	Your chosen method will usually provide some guidelines on customisation, although they may be rather general and high level in nature.
Identify method weaknesses and omissions	Every method has key strengths and weaknesses within it, or even (in some cases deliberate) omissions. For example, most methods deliberately omit specific guidance on fact-finding, while others are targeted at specific stages of the SDLC. In all cases you will need to identify the gaps (by reviewing the literature) and find techniques for filling them.
Identify key needs and products of each stage	You should check each stage of your project against the features of your application and project. All methods have a minimum set of techniques and products for each stage of the SDLC, plus a range of optional techniques to cater for different circumstances. You need to consider each of the optional techniques to establish if it is required for your project, and establish what the implications are if you decide not to use it. You may also conclude that different stages of your project require the application of techniques from entirely different methods, particularly in the technical design stage where environment-specific needs may dictate a specific set of techniques.
Check that deliverables required by course are in place	You will need to double check that the products and deliverables of your customised method still meet the requirements of your course.
Draw up skeleton plan	The planning of your project is covered in Chapters 5 and 6. As an input to this process you should check now that you have identified all the dependencies between your set of techniques and products, in order to ensure that you are not planning to use any techniques that require input from other techniques that you have not yet identified.
Verify training and resource needs	Once you have settled on a customised method, which by now should consist of a set of techniques and products, together with a framework of dependencies (skeleton plan), you should check that you have identified all necessary training and resources (such as software tools).

3.6	Summary

1. The stages that all development projects go through are very similar, regardless of the methodology, techniques or tools that are used. What changes is the way that we approach each of the stages, the precise tasks that we choose to carry out and how we sequence them.

2. Life cycle models provide a framework for managing and structuring a project, while approaches and methods provide the activities, tasks and deliverables that are used within that framework.

3. The three life cycle models that are used or adapted for use on student projects are the waterfall model, the spiral model and, to a lesser extent, the incremental model.

4. No development method should be taken as a recipe book that, if followed step by step, will churn out a perfect system.

5. Some methods are more suited to particular life cycle models than others, but the principles and techniques of any of the system development approaches can be adapted for any of the life cycle models.

6. Many student projects will use hybrids of the waterfall and spiral life cycle models. The spiral design model uses a waterfall structure for the early stages of the project and the spiral model for the physical design and construction stages. The spiral GUI model adopts a waterfall structure throughout the project life cycle, with the addition of a spiral structure for the delivery of just the GUI component.

7. Some of the most interesting projects involve the examination and exploration of techniques or approaches in non-standard situations. There are two basic types of method customisation: method adaptation and method modification.

4 Research issues

4.1 Introduction

The aim of this chapter is to introduce some of the basic research techniques, such as literature searches and the setting of research objectives, that are used within system development projects. As these techniques are frequently applied during the setting up of a project they are presented here in Part One. System development projects also make use of standard research techniques such as interviewing and questionnaires in the execution of a project, and these techniques will be covered in Part Two.

Learning Outcomes

After reading this chapter, you will be able to:

- Write research objectives for your project
- Understand the purpose of literature reviews
- Conduct a search of the literature
- Evaluate and record the results of your literature search

4.2 Research objectives

As discussed in Chapter 1, research at its most basic consists of a systematic investigation of some sort, leading to a novel insight or conclusion that can be backed up by the results of the investigation. Your conclusions may do no more than confirm previous findings or existing theory, perhaps in a context that has not been addressed specifically before, such as your place of employment. This is entirely acceptable, as long as you demonstrate that you have investigated existing theory as part of your literature search, and have come to positive conclusions in the light of that theory. What you must avoid at all costs is setting research objectives that ignore the literature, and suggest for example that you are doing something highly original, when in fact you are merely replicating previous work, or that you are planning to undertake your project without a full understanding of its wider context.

As part of a system development project, research activity typically falls into one of the following broad categories:

1. **Critical evaluation.** Even the most development-oriented of projects should include a critical evaluation of its outcome and execution. This should consist of more than just a brief statement of whether the project's objectives have been met (although this is sadly what students all too often present), or how well you personally have performed the various project tasks. It is important that your evaluation considers such things as the effectiveness of your development method and tools in addressing the problem at hand, the acceptability of your final system, and suggestions for how your conclusions might be applied in a wider context to other projects. Critical evaluation is covered in detail in Chapter 10.

   Many development projects will have explicit evaluation objectives, linked to an investigation of suitable methodologies for the type of development concerned. Such projects usually include an evaluation of one of the following:

   - The application of a particular method, technique, language or tool to a specific system problem, industry sector or organisational type. The research objective in this case may be to clarify or confirm previous findings from similar projects. Alternatively, it may be to reveal unique insights into the use of a technique in solving a type of problem that has not been well documented previously in the literature.

   - The application of a number of alternative techniques or tools to the same problem. In this case the project will be more research focused, and the system development will need to be relatively simple, as project activities will need to be repeated for each technique or tool under evaluation. For example, you might propose to test different ways of capturing system requirements in a workshop setting, for a particular type of user.

2. **Theory development.** A few development projects are designed as vehicles for developing and testing new theories. The research element of these projects will be significantly larger than in projects that involve an evaluation. In some cases they could legitimately be regarded not as development projects at all, but as research projects that have a substantial development element. The number of development projects that involve an element of theory development is small compared with those that are confined to a critical evaluation, even at MSc level.

   There are two types of theory development that are most commonly undertaken in system development projects:

   - Innovative application of existing tools or techniques. This may, for example, consist of a new way of using a tool, perhaps for a purpose or type of problem for which it was not intended, or a novel method of customisation, involving the application of techniques that are rarely used together.

■ Development of new techniques or approaches. In a student project, even at postgraduate level, the development of radical new techniques or system development approaches is very unlikely indeed. This is the stuff of long-term research exercises. However, it is not unknown for students to experiment with minor modifications to existing techniques or with supporting an existing technique with new tools (see example in Box 4.1).

Box 4.1

Example of minor technique modification

Javed was interesting in how he might use a new screen-painting tool to accelerate and accurately capture the design for the user interface for a browser-based stock enquiry system at a local carpet retailer.

During the planning stage of his project, his literature review had suggested that for his type of application a screen painter would be an efficient way of producing rapid user interface prototypes. Further analysis of the literature had also suggested that brainstorming workshops could be used to generate and refine ideas quickly and to achieve rapid consensus.

Javed developed a theory that the two approaches could be used in tandem, with end users of the system being trained to use simple screen-painting tools to 'draw' their ideas for user interface designs in real time within a carefully facilitated workshop. He theorised that by encouraging individuals to contribute and develop their ideas in a concrete form in parallel with each other, the final interface designs would be developed more quickly, with fewer iterations than a conventional sequential prototyping approach.

There are many other types of research that could be carried out for a computing project, some of which may involve an element of system development in order to demonstrate their conclusions. However, these are first and foremost research projects, and are therefore outside the scope of this text.

Writing research objectives

Regardless of the type of research you are proposing to undertake, you need to define precisely the objectives that you wish your research to meet. You also need to express your objectives in terms that enable you to identify exactly how you can answer them. This means that your objectives must be phrased carefully in order to eliminate ambiguity, and narrowly focused so that you will be able to answer them within the time constraints of your project. The requirements of your course will determine how ambitious your objectives should be, but in general the research objectives of your project will tend to be secondary, in terms of the amount of time you will spend on them, to the system development objectives.

The main aims in conducting research within a development project are to deepen and demonstrate your understanding of the system development process and associated techniques. In many HND courses research objectives are strictly optional or even discouraged, whereas on Masters-level courses they will be an essential part of your project.

It is not good enough to investigate an area in the hope that you will happen upon something of interest (a process commonly referred to as 'fishing'); the odds are against you finding something by chance. Your research objectives should help you avoid this trap by defining precisely what it is that you will be investigating and analysing as you carry out your system development work.

As well as being specific about your research, it is important to define your research objectives early on in your project, and to work on them consistently throughout. Failure to do so inevitably leads to a belated and usually panic-ridden realisation that you should have been recording data and analysing events alongside your development activities, followed by a half-hearted attempt to recall something of significance.

During the process of deciding on your project topic you should have been thinking about research areas, and you may have already established your objectives as part of your Project Brief. It might even be the case that your system development objectives are based on a research idea that occurred to you first. Alternatively, you may have little idea as to what form your research will take. Whatever is the case for you, the steps in defining or refining your research objectives are summarised in Box 4.2.

4.3 Introduction to literature reviews

The literature review is an essential part of any project, with the exception of HND projects. In many universities a literature search and review, often at a high level, is a required part of the initiation of a project, where its primary purpose is to demonstrate that the problem domain has been properly explored and understood. The problem domain in this context will consist both of system development aspects, such as the development method and programming environment, and the commercial environment of the external client, if applicable. For projects with a more significant research element, a more detailed literature review will also form part of the project proper.

A literature review consists of two main parts: a search of the literature for relevant data, followed by a critical review of the data. Literature in this context consists of any published data, such as books, journals, reports and newspapers. The format of such material is often paper-based, but may also be electronic. Literature sources are discussed in more detail in Section 4.5.

For development projects the literature review will be less extensive and more time-constrained than would be expected in pure research projects, but must

Box 4.2

Defining research objectives

Identify constraints

You should begin the process of defining and refining your research objectives by establishing the constraints that you will need to impose on your research activities. If your project topic is based around a research idea, you should have addressed constraints in detail already, while investigating your project topic. It is more likely, however, that you have concentrated your effort to date on the development activities of your project. The main constraints are likely to be the following:

■ The **time** that you have available for research activities.

■ **Existing skills.** It is unlikely that you will have the time to acquire many new research skills (in areas such as interviewing, data collection and analysis, and questionnaire design) while undertaking your project, particularly if your project involves a substantial system development.

■ **Resources.** Within a development project the main resource that you might need access to is people. For example, you may want to interview or survey people to establish the effectiveness of your development. If you have already secured access to people for development activities, such as requirements analysis, it may prove difficult to gain additional access to the right people for research purposes. You may also need software resources such as statistical analysis tools, in which case you should investigate the availability of such tools for use in your project.

■ **Data availability.** If your research ideas require the collection of significant amounts of data then you must establish whether you can realistically access and then make full use of the data. This is not only a question of whether you can identify and then access the right people and data sources, but also of whether you will be able to publish any company data that you acquire.

Define your aims

You may have more than one research idea. For each of your ideas you should define one or two key aims. At this stage the aims will not necessarily be precise, but should capture the essence of what you would like your project to address.

In phrasing your aims try to think about how you would answer, in one sentence, the question 'what is the purpose of your research?'

In the carpet retailer example in Section 4.2, the aim of the research could be phrased as 'to investigate the real-time use of end-user-operated screen painters in a workshop environment, in order to accelerate the development of user interfaces'.

In the more conventional (and less research-oriented) language translation services example in Box 2.3, the research aim might be 'to investigate development approaches for the design and implementation of small-scale extranets'.

Define your objectives

The next step is to establish precisely the things that you will need to achieve or deliver in order to meet your aims. This will have the effect of clarifying exactly what you are planning to do in your research. It will also help to verify that your aims are feasible, given your research constraints.

For each of your aims (and it is more than likely that you will have only one), you should produce a list of objectives, each starting with the word 'to'. You are essentially attempting to answer the question 'what are you planning to do in order to meet your aims?'

It is important that your objectives are action-oriented, as you will then be able to use them to determine the tasks and products that will be needed to meet them. So try to use verbs such as 'identify', 'establish', 'describe', 'determine', 'develop' and 'evaluate', rather than 'explore' or 'investigate', as these are too open ended and vague (and more suited to aims). Well-constructed objectives are frequently referred to as being SMART (Specific, Measurable, Achievable, Relevant and Timely).

Using the carpet retailer example, objectives will include: 'to identify suitable screen painters', 'to define workshop facilitation procedures and roles', 'to establish effectiveness measures for interface development', 'to develop mechanisms and formats for documenting interface designs'.

We have already seen the much less ambitious research objectives in the Project Brief for the language translation services example, namely: 'to identify best practice, as used in industry, for designing an extranet', 'to identify appropriate implementation technologies for small-scale extranets' and 'to evaluate the suitability of structured methods for designing extranets'.

Test the objectives

Once you have defined a set of objectives you will need to test them, by asking:

- Are your objectives specific and unambiguous, or could they be misinterpreted?
- Are the objectives too big? Can you meet them in time? Can they be broken down or replaced by smaller, less ambitious objectives?
- Are your objectives too trivial?
- Are there too many objectives?
- Are the objectives too broad or vague? Can you refine them, so that they are focused on the issue or question that you are really trying to address?
- Do you have the skills to meet them?
- Do you have access to the necessary people and resources?
- Can your success/failure in meeting the objectives be measured? If not, you will not know if you have met them, and neither will your assessors.

Refine aims and objectives

In many cases you will find that your objectives do not pass the above tests. The most common failings are that the objectives are too vague, in which case you will need to rethink or rephrase them, or that they are too ambitious for a development project.

Looking at the example of the carpet retailer, it is obvious from just those objectives listed above that this would be a significant research project, and would be extremely difficult to meet within the constraints of a typical student project, even if the system development component were relatively trivial. To meet the stated research aim as part of a predominantly system development project would be near impossible. In this case the best course of action would probably be to make the research aim less ambitious, for example to focus purely on the conventional use of screen painters to accelerate interface design.

still be conducted in a rigorous fashion and be based upon authoritative sources. In undergraduate projects the literature review will tend to focus on well-established theory and more readily available data, while in postgraduate projects the literature review will more often be based on theory that is only just emerging and thus less widely reported in the literature.

A well-conducted literature review is critical to the success of your project for a number of reasons:

- It will establish the technical, academic and business context of your project.
- It will increase your knowledge in areas directly relevant to your project, thereby leading to a better product.
- It will help you to identify potential project topics and to decide whether a topic is feasible and capable of meeting your requirements.

- It will help you to identify and decide upon a development methodology and technical environment.
- It will assist in the definition of research questions and identification of necessary research methods.
- It will feed directly into the planning of your project, by highlighting potential project issues and providing insights into the conduct of similar projects.
- It will help you to justify your project and confirm its originality.
- It will demonstrate to your assessors that you have the relevant knowledge of the area and that you have applied an appropriate degree of academic rigour to your project.

Broadly speaking, there are three types of literature review:

- **Preliminary searches.** These would be carried out while exploring potential project ideas, and usually consist of short high-level exercises designed to give you sufficient insight into topics to allow you to assess their suitability.
- **A formal literature review.** This is a single more rigorous review, usually started during the definition and set-up of your project, and often completed as part of your project proper. This is the most important type of literature review for most development projects, as it is the one that delivers most of the benefits listed above, and is a mandatory requirement for many courses.
- **Mid-project targeted reviews.** These are carried out when specific issues arise during your project that require targeted research. For example, during requirements analysis you may identify technical requirements that you had not anticipated during the definition of your project. This in turn may lead to a literature review in order to identify appropriate solution and design approaches.

The basic process for a conducting a literature review is illustrated in Figure 4.1. The literature search activities of the first four boxes are discussed in sections 4.4 to 4.7. The writing of the literature review is covered in section 10.3, as most students will write their formal review towards the end of their project. However, it is important to begin the process of drafting your review as early as possible, and you may also be required to write an outline review as part of your project proposal. You may therefore want to read the relevant sections in Chapter 10 before starting your search.

In many development projects the main literature search will take place during project set-up, followed by the production of a high-level review as part of the project proposal. The completed literature review will be produced towards the end of the project and presented in the final report. In many projects it will be necessary to conduct follow-up searches during the project, either to keep up to date with emerging theory, or to address issues that have arisen from the initial search or from development activities.

In projects that involve theory development not only will the literature review be used to develop new theory at the beginning of the project, it will also continue as a key activity throughout the life of the project, as the new theory is put into practice, then reviewed and refined in the light of the literature.

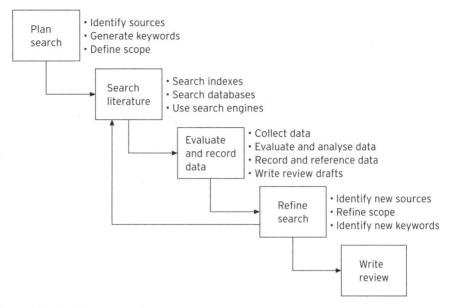

Figure 4.1 The literature review process

4.4 Planning your literature search

The key message when it comes to planning and conducting your literature search is: start early! Carrying out a proper search of the literature is a time-consuming exercise, and nearly always takes longer than students expect. This is a particular problem with students who have not received formal tuition in research methods, as is usually the case with those on computing courses.

In order to ensure that you do not waste time and effort on irrelevant or fruitless searches it is important to spend a little time planning your search. Without a framework and schedule for your search you will not maximise the use of your time, and will spend a lot of energy searching inappropriate sources of data and constantly rethinking your search strategy. You will also tend to run out of time, and have to settle for less than optimal data.

The following are the four main things that need to be planned:

1. **Your time.** Unless you set quality time aside for your literature search, you will fail to conduct an effective search. The literature search is an essential part of most projects, and cannot be fitted into odd spare moments. You need to plan blocks of time so that you can immerse yourself in the search process. If you are constantly dipping in and out of the search, you will spend most of your time picking up on your previous train of thought, logging on to catalogues and databases, and requesting printed bibliographies. Conversely, you should not expect to carry out your search in one or two large blocks of time, as many of your data sources will come to light as a result of examining previously acquired data.

2. **Where you intend to search.** You need to be fairly disciplined about which sources of data you are planning to search. There will not be time within a typical development project to trawl every index or bibliography within your subject area, so you need to plan which sources you are intending to focus on. You should avoid looking at just one data source, as this will colour your research by missing the aspects that are better addressed by other sources. For example, if you search textbooks alone, you will miss the latest developments in your research area, as books are by their very nature historical references. As part of deciding on your data sources you should address the following questions (Bell, 1999):

- What types of publication will you search (books, journals, newspapers, reports, etc.)?
- Do you want to constrain your search to a specific publication period (e.g. the last five years)?
- Are you planning to search UK publications only?
- What facilities do you have access to (e.g. libraries, company archives, Internet)?

3. **What you are looking for.** You will need to decide precisely what you are searching for, which means defining your subject areas (for browsing) and keywords (or search terms) for searching. Keywords can be generated by looking for relevant terms, words or phrases in your lecture notes and textbooks. They can also be explored in discussions with your tutors, project supervisor or fellow students. A thesaurus and glossaries are useful aids in expanding your keywords, so that you are not limited to the particular terms that you have been presented with in your lectures. You should expect to refine and add to your keywords as your search progresses, but if you start out with a poorly defined set of keywords the entire process will be built on shaky foundations. Many students claim that they are unable to find any information on their subject. It is *extremely* unlikely to be the case that nothing of relevance has been published. It is almost always the case that the set of keywords used for their search has been too narrowly defined. If in doubt, start with a wide search, and if that yields too much data, narrow your search to more manageable proportions.

4. **How you are going to record your data.** There are a number of ways of recording the results of your literature search, such as specialist software packages and card index files. Some of these are discussed below (see Section 4.8). The essential thing, regardless of the mechanism you are using, is to set up your filing system early and to update it religiously. Far too many students neglect to document their search in a rigorous and structured fashion, with the result that they lose essential references and find themselves repeating or missing work. You do not have the time to waste on needless searches.

Probably the single most important thing for you to do as part of your search planning is to investigate the library resources at your university. As well as consulting your project handbook and library guides, you should talk to the librarians about facilities and data sources. You should also enquire as to when the library is least busy, as you will get very frustrated if you spend a lot of your valuable time queuing or waiting for resources to be free.

4.5 Sources of data

There are three categories of literature sources, as described by Saunders *et al.* (2003):

1. **Tertiary literature sources.** Tertiary sources contain information about where to find other, more in-depth sources of information. They consist of indexes, abstracts (summaries of articles, together with references or links to the full article) and bibliographies. Tertiary sources may be published as paper documents or accessed electronically using databases, CD ROMs or the Internet.

2. **Secondary literature sources.** Secondary sources consist of widely published works such as books, journals (magazines and periodicals) and newspapers. Increasingly, secondary sources can be found on the Internet (a fee is often payable for the full article) as well as on paper. This is especially useful in the case of journals, as some specialist titles many not be available from your university. Secondary sources sometimes contain tertiary sources, such as bibliographies, or primary sources, such as conference papers or company reports.

3. **Primary literature sources.** Primary sources refer to the original or first publication of information, in research reports, theses, conference papers and company reports.

Each of the primary and secondary literature sources mentioned above has relative pros and cons, which are summarised briefly in Table 4.1. Note that you must take special care to ensure that the publications you obtain are authoritative or recognised, as opposed to unsubstantiated opinion, speculation or marketing hype, which are all potential problems with the Internet and with some newspapers.

4.6 Searching for data

The key to conducting an effective search is to be systematic and rigorous. If you have planned your search properly you should have a clear idea about where you are going to search, what you are looking for and how you are going to record your efforts. In this section we discuss how various search approaches and tertiary sources can be used to obtain relevant literature.

Table 4.1 Summary of literature sources

Source	Pros	Cons
Books	Widely available, and easy to access in libraries and increasingly over the Internet. Authoritative and recognised academically. Information is well presented and aimed at variety of knowledge levels. Provide good introduction to broad topic areas. Good source of further references.	Broad scope can lead to lack of specialisation and depth. Material may be out of date. Competition for popular titles in libraries.
Journals	Tend to be highly specialised, and targeted at either academics or professionals. Up to date, owing to frequency of publication. Academic journals are highly authoritative and recognised. Professional journals are practical in nature. Wide availability in libraries and increasingly via Internet (although often in summary form or as a contents list).	Some professional and trade journals can be difficult to obtain. Can require high level of existing knowledge.
Newspapers	Widely available. Accessible style. Up to date. Good source of topical business developments and statistics.	Reporting can be biased. Generalist and therefore rarely in depth. Rarely authoritative or recognised (there are exceptions, such as some financial titles).
Conference papers	Can be highly specialised. Up to date, often groundbreaking.	Hard to find (indexing is poor), and sometimes hard to obtain (other than in summary form). Typically require high level of existing knowledge. May not have been subject to peer review.
Research reports and theses	Highly specialised, and frequently in depth. Up to date.	Hard to find (indexing is poor) and obtain (often expensive, e.g. Mintel). Some commercial and government reports may be biased.
Company reports	Some companies make reports easily available, and you may be able to gain privileged access (depending on company and project circumstances). Narrowly focused.	Highly biased. Many are available in summary form only. May contain confidential material, which cannot be quoted.
Video and radio broadcasts	Widely available (live, on tape, and increasingly in Internet archives). Accessible style. Sometimes cover conference sessions. Up to date.	Reporting can be biased. Mainly generalist and therefore rarely in depth. Rarely authoritative.
The Internet	Widely available. Easy to search and use. Source of original articles, and of electronic versions of other secondary and primary sources. Invaluable tertiary source (indexes, company contacts, abstracts, etc.). Up to date.	Internet articles are often of dubious quality and of unknown authorship. Full articles and papers often not available. Can be very time consuming (easy to be distracted from search plan).

Table 4.2   Computing-related publishers' websites

Publisher	Internet address (URL)
Pearson Education (covering Prentice Hall, Addison-Wesley, Longman, Benjamin Cummings)	www.pearsoneduc.com
Butterworth-Heinemann	www.bh.com
Wiley	www.wiley.com
McGraw Hill	www.mcgraw-hill.com
O'Reilly	www.oreilly.com
Macmillan (including Palgrave)	www.macmillan.com
Blackwell Publishing	www.blackwellpublishing.com
Thomson Learning	www.thomsonlearning.com
Sybex	www.sybex.com
Peachpit Press	www.peachpit.com

Browsing

As well as carrying out focused searches using precisely defined search terms, it is useful to browse potential sources of data. This will usually involve a visit to your library and university bookshop, where you should look through any relevant books mentioned by your tutors, course notes and in the bibliographies within your course textbooks. You should also browse through other books in the same subject area or library classification. It may also be worth browsing publishers' catalogues. Most catalogues are now available on the Internet (Table 4.2), with search facilities of variable quality and sophistication (some will only allow searches on authors and titles, rather than subject matter). Most catalogues will include tables of contents, and some may include sample chapters.

You should also browse the journals and newspapers held by your library (see Table 4.3 for a selection of journals and newspapers). Although most academic journals are well indexed in tertiary sources, many professional and trade journals are poorly indexed. The latest journals will also be poorly indexed, as there is always a delay between publication and indexing. Once you have located journals that appear to be of use to you, you may need to scan archived copies manually for specific articles of relevance. Alternatively, you might be able to search an electronic index for the journal using the Internet or a CD ROM database.

You might also try browsing Internet news services, on-line publications and textbook and journal websites in order to assess their relevance, and to look for search engines and links that might be of use to you. It is very important to timebox this activity, as it is much harder to scan articles on-line than on paper, and it is all too easy to get sidetracked by clicking on links that appear promising but that lead to dead ends.

Browsing is an activity that you should repeat throughout your search. As you find books and journals that you were previously unaware of, it is useful to browse other publications in the same library classification or subject area.

Table 4.3 Selected journals, journal publishers and newspapers

Publication	Internet address (URL)
Byte	www.byte.com
Communications of the ACM	www.acm.org/cacm/
Computer Weekly	www.cw360.com
Conspectus	www.conspectus.com
The Economist	www.economist.com
European Journal of Information Systems	www.palgrave-journals.com/ejis/
Financial Times	news.ft.com/home/uk
Guardian	www.guardian.co.uk
Harvard Business Review	www.hbsp.harvard.edu
IEEE (American Institute of Electrical and Electronic Engineers)	www.computer.org
Academy of Information and Management Sciences	www.alliedacademies.org/ims/
Information Systems Journal	www.blackwellpublishing.com/journals/isj/
Information Systems Research	isr.katz.pitt.edu
Journal of Information Technology	www.tandf.co.uk/journals/routledge/02683962.html
Journal of Strategic Information Systems	www.elsevier.nl/inca/publications/store/5/2/5/4/4/7/
Journal of the Association of Information Systems	jais.aisnet.org
Journal on Computing	joc.pubs.informs.org
MIS Quarterly	www.misq.org
Telegraph	www.telegraph.co.uk
The Times	www.timesonline.co.uk
Wall Street Journal	www.wsj.com

Using tertiary sources

Searching a tertiary source, such as an index, is a much more precise and structured activity than browsing. It is also more effective and efficient at finding data of relevance. Most indexes, catalogues and abstracts are now published as electronic databases, sometimes with a printed version as well. A few highly specialised indexes and abstracts are available on paper only (as are bibliographies in textbooks), but their numbers are reducing rapidly. Databases are increasingly available over the Internet, with few being accessible only from CD ROMs.

The main advantage of electronic databases is that they can be searched more rapidly and flexibly than printed sources. However, the advantage of printed indexes is that because you are physically scanning the index as you search for your keyword you may spot other articles and terms that you would not otherwise have found.

Indexes provide information such as the authors, titles and contents of articles and reports, together with their publishers, journal or book titles, reference numbers (such as ISBN numbers) and dates of publication. In addition, abstracts provide summaries and/or extracts of the articles that can be reviewed before requesting the full article (usually for a fee). Internet-based indexes and abstracts may also include hypertext links to the full articles, if they are available on the Internet.

In order to search indexes and abstracts stored in databases you will need to specify a number of keywords, which the database search engine will then use to locate articles of interest to you. The best strategy is to combine all the keywords that you are interested in as a set of search terms that the database will then use together to locate articles that are of maximum significance to your research. For example, if you wish to find articles on the use of prototyping tools within a workshop environment, for the purposes of requirements analysis, you might combine the keywords 'workshop', 'prototyping' and 'requirements analysis' in order to narrow down the data that is found to be of most direct relevance. To combine keywords, you will use the Boolean logic term 'AND', or enter the individual keywords into some sort of list box, depending on which database you are using. Note that you may also need to exclude certain articles by specifying that you want specified topics or keywords excluded, usually by using the Boolean logic term 'NOT'.

You should also try to specify as many synonyms for your keywords as possible, as different articles will use different terminology to refer to the same concepts. For example, as well as searching for 'requirements analysis', you should also search for 'requirements definition', 'systems analysis' and so on. You need to be careful in offering alternative keywords to a database that you do not inadvertently ask the search engine to combine the keywords, and look for articles that contain all of the keywords. To specify alternatives you will either use the Boolean logic term 'OR', or a list box.

Indexes and abstracts are frequently subscription-only services, so you will need to visit your university library in order to find out which databases and printed indexes your university subscribes to. You should also try to attend any training sessions offered by your library in using the principal databases. Some databases may be accessed only from terminals within the library, as they are stored on or accessible only from servers within the university. Others may be accessed from home, given the correct user account and password. Paper indexes will have to be used within the library, as they are never available for loan.

Two of the most important databases are BIDS (Bath Information Data Services), which covers a wide range of journals and conference papers, and your university's OPAC (Online Public Access Catalogue), which covers publications held by your university. You will also be able to access the OPACs of other universities, by following links from www.niss.ac.uk.

Table 4.4 lists some of the key databases for research related to computing or business systems. To maximise the effectiveness of your search you should use as many tertiary sources as possible, as each index will provide access to a unique range of articles, which will differ from the articles listed by other indexes.

You should document each search that you make, by noting the database or index searched, together with the keywords used, in order to avoid repeating searches unnecessarily. It is also a good idea to make a note of which searches were particularly effective, as you may wish to repeat them, possibly with minor variations, at a later date.

Table 4.4 Selected tertiary sources

Source	Internet address (URL)
BIDS	www.bids.ac.uk
NUA	www.nua.com/surveys/
ISWorld Net	www.isworld.org
Information Technology Management Web	www.itmweb.com
Elselvier Science	www.socscinet.com/lis/journals.html

Internet search tools

As well as providing access to index and abstract databases, the Internet provides search tools of its own that can be effective in finding and accessing literature. Most search engines are designed to find websites and web pages that are of interest to you, rather than individual articles and documents (although some articles will be published as web pages). Most of the best known search tools are general-purpose search engines that have the potential to provide links to virtually any web page that matches your search terms, whether relevant or not. They may also have directory structures (in fact some search tools, such as Yahoo, are built directly on top of directories) that enable you to browse around a subject area in the same way that you might browse a library catalogue.

In addition to general search tools, such as Google (www.google.com), there are a number of specialist directories and search engines that are designed to access websites within a particular subject area. For example, the NISS website (www.niss.ac.uk) provides a searchable directory of OPACs, the UK government site (www.ukonline.gov.uk) searches government websites only, while the search tools at IsWorld (www.isworld.org) provide 'an entry point to resources related to information systems technology for information systems academics and practitioners'.

Once you have used a search tool to locate potentially relevant websites, you should scan the list of websites returned, in order to assess whether you have defined your search terms tightly enough. General-purpose search engines in particular will tend to return enormous lists of largely irrelevant websites that you cannot hope to evaluate in any depth at all. It is essential that you be disciplined in picking out the few of real relevance from the short descriptions in a search tool's results list. You should expect to repeat your searches multiple times, until you have narrowed down the list of sites to a focused and highly relevant group.

It is tempting for students to use only general-purpose Internet tools that they are familiar with to search for websites and articles, as they can access them easily and already know how to use them. You should avoid doing this at all costs, as it will severely limit the data you will have access to. Many of the more specialist articles and journals will not be found using general Internet search tools. You will also find that most Internet articles and reviews are of dubious quality and authorship, and many will appear on a website or page that is here today and gone tomorrow.

If you find an article or website that is of genuine relevance and interest to you, it is important that you establish its source and obtain a full reference for it (see Section 4.8). The 'bookmark' or 'favorites' facility within your Internet browser is a useful way of noting the addresses of websites that you wish to return to, or to use in your research. However, the Internet address of an article alone will not be sufficient as a full reference.

| 4.7 | ### Evaluating the literature |

Once you have located an article or book that is of interest to you, you will need to acquire or access a copy of it. Most of the relevant material will hopefully be available within your university library, but you may also need to download articles from the Internet or order copies from publishers, companies or conference organisers. You should be aware that a fee is usually payable if your library does not hold or subscribe to a particular journal. You may also need to borrow a publication from another university library on an inter-library loan (a fee may also be payable for this).

Most development projects will be well within the boundaries of established theory, and so it should therefore be possible to find highly relevant material by searching the most easily accessible databases and your library OPAC. You should then be able to discard a lot of the material you obtain following a relatively brief scan of each article or book.

The questions you need to ask yourself when evaluating an article are not associated with whether you agree with its conclusions (this may come later in your literature review), but rather to do with its relevance and quality. Dawson (2000: 75) documents a comprehensive list of such questions (some of which are summarised in Table 4.5), which he suggests are not used as a checklist, but are borne in mind implicitly while scanning or reading an article. Note that an elegantly written article is not necessarily authoritative. Some of most persuasive and stimulating of newspaper stories are based on pure conjecture or speculation.

As you carry out your literature search, you should be continually adding to and refining your searches. Most of the articles and books that you obtain will contain numerous references to other works, and introduce you to new concepts and keywords that you can use to refine and extend your search.

As discussed earlier, a literature search can be extremely time consuming, so it is important to know when to stop. A general rule of thumb for literature searches within a research project is to call a halt when you stop discovering new references and find yourself repeatedly looking at the same articles. In a system development project, where the literature search is a much smaller part of the total effort, you may need to stop earlier than this in order to meet your project schedule. In this case you should stop searching when the articles themselves cease to contribute anything of any substance to your project.

Table 4.5 Evaluation questions

- What ideas, techniques and quotations can you gain from the article?
- Is the author clearly identified, and is he/she well recognised within his/her field?
- Can the article make a direct and meaningful contribution to your project?
- How important is the article within its field?
- Is the article up to date, and is it still relevant within its field?
- How respected and authoritative is the publication?
- Does the article add anything new to your research?
- Is the article well researched, referenced and logically presented?
- Is the article based on fact, logical reasoning, speculation or opinion?
- Are the conclusions consistent with the facts and arguments?
- Is the article biased or unbalanced?
- Are the article and/or its author quoted in other material?

Sources: Author's experience, Dawson (2000).

4.8 Recording references and data

There is little point in undertaking a time-consuming search of the literature unless you record the information that you have gathered and where you obtained it. Many students will adopt an approach of photocopying, downloading or printing articles. There are many advantages to this, but on its own it is not sufficient, and for some literature sources (such as video) it will not be possible. It is vital that you make notes or annotate the article copies with details of how the article will contribute to your project, where the data came from, and how you found it. It is also useful to make notes on articles that you have not found useful, as you do not want to waste time during your project rereading articles that you have already reviewed and discarded.

The key to managing the data that you obtain during your literature search is to record it rigorously as you go along. It is all too common for students to record data in a haphazard way, or to concentrate on the search process in the mistaken belief that they will remember where an article came from and so can record its reference later. This invariably leads to repeated searches, and a great deal of frustration.

There are various ways of recording data and references, ranging from software packages, such as Reference Manager for Windows, to card index filing systems. While some students find a software package approach helps them enormously, others find a card index system less cumbersome and more efficient, particularly if the amount of research they are undertaking is small, or much of the data has been obtained on paper.

Referencing systems

Recording and providing full references for all the material you refer to or use in your project is essential for a number of reasons:

- It enables you to find the material when you need it.
- It demonstrates that your project is grounded on published and authoritative theory.
- It enables others to identify and access the material you have used or referred to.
- It will be a requirement of your final project report and possibly of your project proposal.

What you must avoid at all costs is presenting work or an idea as your own, even inadvertently, when it is actually the work of others. If you include in your final report or project proposal passages of text that you have lifted directly from a publication of any sort, you must provide a full reference for it. Likewise if you have drawn directly on ideas from the literature, even if you have not quoted it verbatim, you must acknowledge the source(s) of those ideas. If you fail to do so, you will be guilty of plagiarism or even breach of copyright.

There are several systems of referencing in common use within universities, such as the Harvard system, the Vancouver system and the American Psychological Association (APA) system. These systems set out formal conventions for referring to literature sources within a passage of text and within a bibliography. Most universities will have a standard that they expect you to adopt, and will usually provide guidance in how to apply that system. If you have a free choice in adopting a system, then you should find out which system your supervisor prefers or which one is most commonly used within your course. Regardless of which system you adopt, you use it consistently throughout your work.

In order to use any of the reference systems you will need to record the same basic information for each item of literature that you obtain (Table 4.6). In

Table 4.6 Referencing data for journals and books

Book	Journal
Full names (including initials) of the authors or editors	Full names (including initials) of the authors
Year of publication	Year of publication
Full title of book	Full title of article
Edition number	Full title of journal
Publisher	Volume and issue number of journal
Place of publication	Page numbers within journal
Title and author of chapter (if more than one contributor)	
Page numbers (for specific references or quotes)	

addition, if you have obtained an article from the Internet, you should record its Internet address (URL) and the date that you accessed it.

Harvard system

When you refer to an article or book within the text of your report you should include just the surname(s) of the author(s) and the year of publication, for example:

'Bell (1999) has suggested that' or 'it has been suggested (Bell, 1999) that'.

If a work has more than one author, you should either list all the authors' surnames or, if there are more than two, use *'et al.'*, for example:

'Cadle and Yeates (2001)' and 'Saunders *et al.* (2003)'.

If you are referencing more than one work from the same author in the same year, you should distinguish between the two using a single letter suffix, and if you wish to refer to a specific page you should add the page number after the date:

'Dawson (2000a: 75)'.

For each article or book referred to in your report, you must then include a full entry in the list of references in your bibliography, which will usually be included as an addendum to your report. The Harvard system format for a full book reference is:

Surname, forenames or initials of each author (year of publication) *Full Title* (edition), place of publication, publisher.

For example:

Bell, J. (1999) *Doing Your Research Project* (3rd edition), Buckingham, Open University Press.

Saunders, M., Lewis, P. and Thornhill, A. (2003) *Research Methods for Business Students* (3rd edition), Harlow, FT Prentice Hall.

The Harvard system format for a full journal article reference is:

Surname, forenames or initials of each author (year of publication) 'Article title', *Journal Title*, **Volume** (issue), page numbers.

For example:

Netril, J. (2002) 'Art of graph drawing', *Journal of Graph Algorithms and Applications*, **6**(2), 131–147.

Internet referencing

If you have obtained a journal article or an electronic version of a book from an Internet site, you should add the Internet address (URL) and access date to the end of the reference, for example:

Yin, J., Alvisi, G., Dahlin, M. and Iyengar, A. (2002) 'Engineering web cache consistency' *ACM Transactions on Internet Technology*, **2**(3), 224–259. Available from http://www.research.ibm.com/people/i/iyengar/toit02.pdf (10 January 2003).

If the article you are referring to has been published solely on the Internet, you should attempt to record as much information as you would collect for a printed article. In many cases journal volume and issue numbers will not exist, but you should attempt to record at least the following:

- Full names of the authors (this may be an organisation).
- Year of publication.
- Full title of article.
- Full name of on-line journal or website.
- Publisher or organisation responsible for maintaining the website, if different from author.
- Place of publication, if known.
- Internet address (URL) of article.
- Date of access.

For example:

DSDM Consortium (2002) 'The Underlying Principles' *DSDM Website*. Available from http://www.dsdm.org/en/about/principle.asp (accessed 7 January 2003).

4.9 Research strategies

A detailed discussion of research strategies and approaches is beyond the scope of this book, and beyond the needs of most development projects. A brief overview of research approaches, and some of the most common strategies for computing related research, is given in Table 4.7. If your project has a large research component you will need to learn more about relevant research strategies, and associated data collection and analysis techniques, in which case you should consult one of the many excellent research methods texts, such as Saunders *et al.* (2003).

The key research-related activities for a development project are likely to be the literature search and the literature review, together with the critical analysis

Table 4.7 Common research methods and approaches

Research approaches

Inductive	An inductive approach is one in which you develop a theory as a result of analysing the findings of your research.
Deductive	A deductive approach is one in which you use your research to test a predefined theory. This is the most common approach in development projects, as the relevant theory is generally well developed and presented in the literature, and time constraints may make a more time-consuming inductive approach impractical.
Combined	Inductive and deductive approaches are not mutually exclusive, and in some projects it may be wise to combine them. For example, by defining a theory, which is then tested and reviewed in the light of research findings, leading to subsequent refinement or redefinition.

Research strategies

Action research	Action research is a strategy whereby the researcher aims to add to the body of knowledge in an area by applying theory to a practical problem, and evaluating the results. This is by far the most common research strategy in a system development project, and in some ways can be used to define what a system development project is all about.
Case study	A case study involves the in-depth investigation of a specific situation, such as a particular problem, company, event, strategy or technology. For example, a case study might investigate the results of implementing an intranet within a major company, and attempt to confirm or challenge existing theory using the results. Case studies should ideally be more than descriptions of a situation, but should also attempt to draw conclusions. The advantages of case studies include the ability to explore in detail *why* something has happened. The disadvantages include the danger of generalising from a specific case.
Survey	The survey approach involves gathering and analysing large amounts of data from a wide audience, often using questionnaires, but sometimes also using techniques such as structured interviewing.
Experimental	An experimental approach involves repeating a set of activities with different sets of variables, in order to collect data that allow us to test a hypothesis or develop a theory. Some development projects, such as those with an element of theory development, will adopt a pseudo-experimental strategy, where the variables being manipulated include such things as system modelling techniques, interface designs and hardware configurations.

and evaluation of your findings (see Chapter 10). However, a significant number of projects will also involve techniques such as interviewing and the design of questionnaires, either for research purposes, or more often as part of establishing system requirements. For this reason, interviews and questionnaires are covered in Chapter 7.

In any given project, it is possible to combine strategies, and to use a range of data collection techniques, such as interviews, document analysis, questionnaires and observation.

4.10 Summary

1. Research at its most basic consists of a systematic investigation, leading to a novel insight or conclusion that can be backed up by the results of the investigation.

2. Research objectives within a system development project are of two main types: critical evaluation and theory development.

3. A literature review is an essential part of any project, with the exception of HND projects. A literature review is often a required part of the initiation of a project, where its primary purpose is to demonstrate that the problem domain has been properly explored and understood.

4. A literature review consists of two main parts: a search of the literature for relevant data, followed by a critical review of the data. There are three types of literature review: preliminary searches, a formal literature review and targeted mid-project reviews.

5. There are three categories of literature sources, as described by Saunders *et al.* (2003): tertiary literature sources, secondary literature sources and primary literature sources.

6. Many Internet articles and reviews are of dubious quality and authorship, and many will appear on a website or page that is here today and gone tomorrow.

7. The key to managing the data that you obtain during your literature search is to record it rigorously as you go along.

8. Recording and providing full references for all of the material you refer to or use in your project is essential. Failure to do so will leave you open to accusations of plagiarism.

9. There are several systems of referencing in common use within universities, such as the Harvard system, the Vancouver system and the American Psychological Association (APA) system. These systems set out formal conventions for referring to literature sources within a passage of text and within a bibliography.

5 Setting up your project

5.1 Introduction

The aim of this chapter is to provide guidance in the setting up of your project. Many university courses do not cover project management, and if they do so they present it in the context of a full-blown commercial project. So this and the next chapter cover in some detail the activities and issues related to project management *in the specific context of a student project*. This chapter also completes the proposal process started in Chapter 2.

Project set-up should not be overlooked or skimped, as it lays the foundation for the whole project. A great many students pay lip service to project start-up, and then find themselves floundering in the middle of their project, when things start to get complicated or they are faced with issues and decisions that they have not anticipated in advance.

It is possible to execute a project without proper planning, but you will find it much harder and more stressful. In general, time spent in setting up your project will be time well spent, and will save you time and effort overall.

Learning Outcomes

After reading this chapter, you will be able to:

- Set up a simple but effective filing structure for your project

- Create a project plan

- Understand the need for well-defined project team roles and structures

- Complete the documentation of your project set-up

5.2 Getting organised

Before getting into the details of setting up your student project, you should collect together all the work that you have done to date. This means, if you have not already done so, setting up a project filing system and project diary or

Table 5.1 Suggested filing system sections

Background documents	Never throw anything away! Background documents will include such things as the initial research that you carried out when selecting your topic, any checklists you used, plus correspondence from potential clients and supervisors.
Project start-up documents	This will consist of your formal proposal documents, i.e. Project Brief, Project Initiation Document.
Project plans	Always keep close at hand a copy of your latest project plan, together with any previously issued plans. When you come to write up your final report it is important to have evidence of how your project progressed against the plans you produced.
Literature search results	As discussed in Chapter 4, you should be rigorous about recording data, references and search results.
System development documents and models	This is likely to be the largest and most important section in your filing system, as it includes all of your key deliverables, with the exception of your implemented system.
Fact-finding results	This is the input to your analysis of system requirements, and will include interview notes, workshop minutes, memos, completed questionnaires, etc.
Project control documents	This section will build up as your project progresses. It will include risk logs, progress reports, issue logs.
Correspondence	There may be very little correspondence, but what there is should be carefully filed as it often has a significant impact on your project.
Draft reports	This will include draft sections from your final report, literature review, project presentations and any other required interim reports. Ultimately it will also include your completed final report.
Project handbook	It is always useful to have easy access to a copy of your project handbook.
Meeting agendas and minutes	For a group project it is important to keep and circulate records of your discussions and decisions.

notebook. This is not a complicated exercise, but it is well worth doing, as otherwise it will become increasingly difficult to manage your project as you accumulate increasing amounts of information and paperwork. It will also demonstrate to your supervisor and assessors that you have adopted an organised and efficient approach to your project.

A suggested filing system is given in Table 5.1. At the start of your project some of these sections will be empty, but it is still worth setting them up from the beginning.

The exact mechanisms that you use for holding the documents and information are up to you, and will depend largely on your personal preferences, skills and the requirements of your course, if there are any. One thing to avoid is an over-dependence on your PC or laptop. There is an increasing tendency for students to try to store everything in electronic format, just because they can.

While the PC is a useful tool for such things as managing your project plan, creating reports and producing system models, there is little to be gained by scanning in your handwritten notes and printed documents. When thinking about how to file a document you should always ask yourself what would be the most efficient mechanism, rather than what would be the most technically impressive. For most students the best answer will be a mix of computer files, notebooks and paper folders.

Whatever mechanisms you choose, you should take care to keep duplicate or back-up copies of all important notes and documents. It is your responsibility to ensure the security of your own work, and few assessors will accept your loss of some vital piece of information as an excuse for late or substandard work.

In addition to organising your documentation, you should set up a project notebook and diary, which should always be close to hand when carrying out any project-related activities, so that you can jot things down as they occur to you. This should be relatively informal, and should include things such as:

- A diary with brief notes on what you have done each day. You will find this useful in meetings with your supervisor, and when writing your final report.
- A regularly updated 'to do' list.
- Questions for your supervisor, other project team members, together with follow-up actions for yourself.
- Ideas on how to solve project issues, or address system requirements.
- Notes on newly identified issues or risks.
- Useful titbits of information, such as websites or software tools that you come across in informal discussions with your peers.

The other thing that you need to organise as soon as possible is access to or acquisition of essential resources, such as computer equipment, lab time or library service passwords. While many of these things will only be needed later in your project, some will be subject to long lead times, or may be needed from day one.

5.3   Project planning

The main things that we need to add to the Project Brief discussed in Section 2.7 are details of how and when we are going to deliver the project. The Project Brief gives us a solid idea of what the project is aiming to achieve. It will also have established some constraints, assumptions and milestones for input to the planning process. However, in the form presented in Section 2.7, it does not document how you are planning to approach the development and research. Nor does it define what you plan to do on a day-to-day, or even week-to-week, basis.

Many students fail to appreciate the need to plan their projects, and dive straight into the first 'doing' activity without a clear idea of what they will be doing next, let alone two months down the line. This is rather like setting out on a long journey without a clear idea of where you are going, what form of transport you will use, or the route you should take. If your journey is a familiar or short one, you will not need to give these matters much thought, and will make your plans as you go through your front door. However, in undertaking your first project you are setting out on a totally unfamiliar journey of a type you have no experience of. Your project plan will act as a route map to help guide you, and without it you will almost certainly get lost.

Specifically, your project plan should attempt to meet the following objectives:

- To ensure that you can complete all of the necessary project activities in time.
- To establish what you need to do on each day (it will feed directly into your daily 'to do' list).
- To help in booking and scheduling necessary resources.
- To identify when you need to acquire certain skills.
- To identify project dependencies and conflicts.
- To demonstrate to your assessors that you have thought your project through.
- To enable you to track progress. After all, how else will you know if you are behind or ahead of schedule?
- In a group project, to establish who will complete each task, and to let everyone know what they and other group members are doing.

It is important to recognise that project planning is not an exact science. The reality of project execution will never exactly match your plans, no matter how experienced you are. As your project progresses you will find that tasks take longer or shorter than expected, and you will inevitably encounter unexpected events. However, this is not an excuse for sloppy planning, as the more intelligently constructed your plans are, the better able they are to adapt to change. What it does mean is that you will need to monitor your plans carefully, and adjust them from time to time.

You may also be undertaking a project with a significant degree of uncertainty attached to it. For example, you may have little firm idea of what your prototyping environment will be until you have completed your requirements specification. This means that you will need to make some working assumptions in creating your initial plans, which you will then replace with the findings of your project as you reach the appropriate stage. This could have a serious impact on your plans, but if you have made sensible assumptions and built in some contingency, you should be able to minimise the effect on your overall timescales.

5.4   Creating a project plan

This may be your first exposure to planning a project. It can appear quite a daunting task if you study a project management textbook, such as Yeates and Cadle (2001), or have attended a project management module. However, these will have dealt with the needs of industrial projects, which have very different needs from the typical student project. Often there are contractual or financial implications captured within industrial project plans, which need to be very tightly defined and which involve a significant amount of effort and time to produce. This is rarely (if ever) the case in a student project. Industrial projects may also involve complexity, size and organisational issues of a far greater magnitude than you will encounter in a student project. To understand the scale of the planning process for a student project, it can be helpful to look at past projects, although few project reports will cover planning activities in much detail.

The guidance given below may also help to reassure you that planning for a student project is not an overwhelming bureaucratic exercise. It should also demonstrate that you really will need to address all of the associated points at some point in your project, and by far the best time to do this is at the start.

Although the planning process set out below appears to be linear, it will in fact be an iterative process. As you undertake each of the planning tasks, you will throw light on earlier issues and questions, as well as introducing new issues, such as timing conflicts. You may also find that your first draft plan does not fit with your overall timescales, or that on closer inspection you have missed some interdependencies that need to be added. Finally, once you start your project proper, you will need to monitor and make adjustments to your plan in the light of experience.

Producing a task list

In order for your project plan to be effective, you need to identify small units of work that you can schedule on a day-to-day basis. These are usually referred to as tasks.

A task is a piece of work that cannot meaningfully be broken down any further, but that is small enough to be estimated accurately. In the context of a student project a task will normally involve between 2 and 15 hours of work, with most falling between 4 and 10 hours. Any smaller than this and you will not be able to handle the detail that results, and it will not serve any real purpose in helping you to manage your time (quite the reverse in fact, as even the tiniest of issues will have an impact on a task that is very small). Any larger than 15 hours or so, and you will not be able to estimate the task accurately. Furthermore, large tasks will almost certainly be hiding lower-level tasks that you should be scheduling, investigating and monitoring in their own right.

Far too many student plans list a dozen or so key milestones or phases, such as 'set up project', 'analyse requirements', 'design interfaces' and so on. This level of planning is no use whatsoever in helping you to understand what is involved in carrying out your project, or what you need to be doing on a daily basis.

Work breakdown

The classic way to arrive at a list of project tasks is to create a work breakdown structure. To do this, you start with a list of the high-level phases of your project,

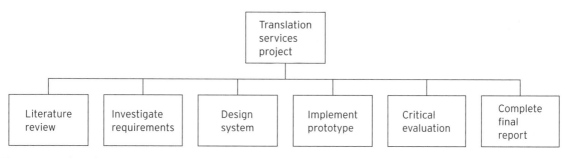

Figure 5.1 Phase-level work breakdown structure

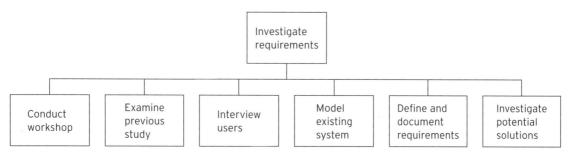

Figure 5.2 Second-level work breakdown structure

as shown in Figure 5.1 for the language translation services example introduced in Section 2.7. Not all of the phases will be equal in size. It is not important to balance them, but it is important to ensure that you have covered all of the main phases of your project (you may also want to include your set-up phase if you are producing an early plan).

The next step is to break down each of your phases into the activities involved in each stage, as shown in Figure 5.2 for the 'Investigate requirements' phase from Figure 5.1. Some of these will resemble the objectives listed in your Project Brief.

At the second level your work breakdown structure is likely to contain a number of activities that are still at too high a level to estimate accurately. Some of the activities listed will span several weeks, and really be collections of lower-level tasks. Others will indeed be tasks, especially if their parent phase was short. Figure 5.3 shows the breakdown to task level of the 'Model existing systems' activity from Figure 5.2.

You may need to go further than three levels of breakdown, but for most student projects three levels will be sufficient. This corresponds to the three-level structure suggested by some of the more popular planning tools, such as Microsoft Project.

The bottom level (end-leaves) of your work breakdown structure will represent a minimum list of tasks that you will need to plan for and carry out in your project. There are some activities that the work breakdown approach tends to overlook, however. These cover the tasks associated with the management and control of your project, including interim reports and presentations, and progress meetings. You will need to add these to your task list.

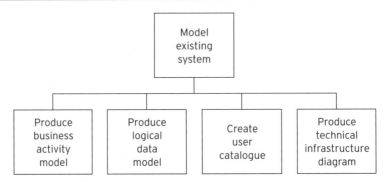

Figure 5.3   Task-level work breakdown structure

It may sound like you will generate vast quantities of tasks that will be difficult to manage. However, if you follow the rule of thumb that tasks should generally take between 2 and 15 hours to complete, and perhaps come up with a task list with an average of 6 hours, then even for a 300-hour project you will only be looking at around 50 tasks (little more than one sheet of A4 paper with one task per line).

Product breakdown

An alternative, or complement, to the work breakdown approach is to examine and break down the products that you plan to deliver during your project. The basic strategy is the same as for the work breakdown structure, but instead of looking at the project from the perspective of what you are planning to do, you look at it from the perspective of what you are planning to produce, and then relate those products to the tasks needed to deliver them.

This is a particularly useful approach if you are using a methodology that provides a ready-made product breakdown structure.

Adding timings to tasks

Once you have a list of tasks you need to estimate how many hours of work you think each one will take to complete. It is important to differentiate at this point between the duration of a task and the number of hours of work involved. For example, it may take only four hours of work to produce a technical infrastructure diagram for your proposed system, but you may need to spread this work over two days. So in this example the number of work hours required is four, but the duration is two days.

As a student you will have little real experience of estimating how long project tasks will take, unless you are undertaking a workplace project. Nevertheless, you should be able to produce an initial estimate for most of your project tasks based on your experience of coursework. For other tasks you may need to consult with your supervisor, discuss timings with your fellow students or examine past projects. You may even be able to find some project-specific guidance from your literature search. You should be wary, however, of lifting estimates blindly from previous projects or from articles, as the work involved in completing tasks varies greatly from project to project.

Some tasks, such as those associated with prototyping, fact-finding and the writing of your final report, can be very open ended. For these tasks it may be appropriate to adopt a timeboxing approach, where you estimate the minimum time needed to complete them to an acceptable standard, and stick rigidly to that within your project. Without this approach you may find that tasks over-run badly, and you never seem to reach the end of them, causing knock-on effects to the rest of your project.

Identifying task dependencies

The next stage in constructing your project plan is to identify which tasks are dependent on each other, and therefore what sequence they should be carried out in. For example, if you had the tasks 'create user interface prototypes' and 'demonstrate interface prototypes', it is self-evident that one is dependent on the other, in that you cannot demonstrate anything until you have at least started the production of your prototypes. A great many of your tasks will have interdependencies of this nature. Others will not be directly dependent on each other in quite such an obvious way, but may still have an optimum sequence.

While most tasks will be dependent on at least one other task, they generally belong to interdependent sequences that are conducted in parallel with other sequences. For example, the tasks associated with investigating and defining requirements will be highly interdependent on each other, but will be totally independent of the tasks associated with acquiring and training in Java programming tools.

Task dependencies can be documented using an *activity network*, using the simple notation of Figure 5.4 (known as *activity-on-the-node* notation). An activity network can be further enhanced to form the basis of your project plan, by adding start and end dates to each task. However, most students (and professionals) will choose to adopt a Gantt chart approach to both dependency documentation and scheduling, as discussed below.

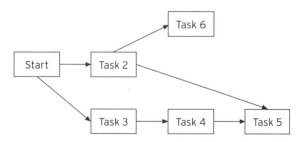

Figure 5.4 Activity network notation

Identifying planning constraints

Before attempting to schedule your tasks you will need to identify any constraints that you will need to take into account in deciding when tasks can or should be carried out. The most obvious constraints are the milestones that you need to achieve in order to meet the requirements of your course. Such milestones will of course include the submission date for your final report, but may also include interim report and presentation deadlines.

The other main type of planning constraint concerns the availability of resources, including your time and, for group projects, the time of other team members. This is a critical area, and one that is frequently overlooked by students. During the course of your project there will inevitably be times when you are unable to work on your project, perhaps because you are sitting exams, and other times when you have substantial amounts of time to devote to it. It is essential that you draw up a week-by-week picture of the time you will feasibly be able to spend on your project. Other resource constraints might include access to development tools, and these need to be noted down as milestones on which some of your project tasks will depend.

Contingency planning

Most new project managers (and many experienced ones) are hopelessly optimistic in assessing what they can get done in a set period of time. The reality of a project is that you will suffer delays and setbacks, as few will take place in a laboratory where you can exercise compete control over your environment.

In order to allow for tasks overrunning, and for events that delay you or introduce new work, you must build some contingency into your plans. There are four basic types of contingency, all of which you should consider using, depending on the nature of the tasks you are undertaking:

■ **Task-level contingency.** This is where you identify high-risk tasks and allow some additional time in your estimate to cater for possible overruns. You should use this sparingly, as many tasks and activities can be timeboxed to some degree without affecting the overall quality of your project.

■ **Phase-level contingency.** This is applied to a phase or to the whole project, and consists of building some slack time into your plans when scheduling your plan. In commercial projects it is a common practice to allocate tasks to people on a plan so that they are never utilised for more than 75–80% of their available time. This then gives the project manager some extra capacity to cope with unexpected events, such as additional tasks arising from sickness.

■ **Alternative plans.** Some tasks may have more time-efficient but less desirable alternatives that could be used if your project falls behind. For example, you may have planned on using an interviewing approach to fact-finding, but may be able to replace some interviews with questionnaires or e-mailed questions if you run out of time.

Scheduling

The final step in producing your initial project plan is the scheduling of project tasks, so that you have a target start and end date for each task, and a complete picture of how and when the project is planned to be executed. Note that for group projects you will also need to allocate tasks to individuals, but this is dealt with in Section 5.5.

In student projects scheduling is usually relatively straightforward, as there are small numbers of tasks with fairly simple dependencies. For a plan with 50 tasks, you should be able to produce a reasonably accurate schedule in less than an hour.

The most effective way to schedule your project is to create a Gantt chart, by following the steps listed below. If you are using a project-planning tool, such as Microsoft Project, your job will be easier as some of this will be automated or prompted. All of the figures below were created using Microsoft Project, but you could use pen and paper if you prefer.

1. Create an unscheduled chart by listing your project tasks and milestones on the *y* (side) axis, and a date line on the *x* (bottom) axis. Figure 5.5 shows an unscheduled Gantt chart extract covering the tasks of the 'Investigate requirements' phase of Figure 5.1.

2. Identify task and milestone dependencies using arrows (Figure 5.6) or by making a note of the names of any predecessors next to each task.

3. Take each task in turn and establish the earliest date that it can start, according its task dependencies and preferred sequencing. Draw a bar to reflect how long its duration will be given the resource constraints (mainly your availability) of the relevant period of the project (Figure 5.7).

4. Double check that you are not over-committed, and that the plan has some slack time in it to allow for slippage.

Task Name	Work	Oct '02				Nov '02				Dec '02				Ja
		30	07	14	21	28	04	11	18	25	02	09	16	23	30
Investigate Requirements	**55 hrs**													
Conduct interviews (head office)	6 hrs													
Conduct interview (self-employed translators)	6 hrs													
Plan workshop	2 hrs													
Conduct workshop	4 hrs													
Examine previous study and system docs	5 hrs													
Produce Business Activity Model	3 hrs													
Produce Logical Data Model	6 hrs													
Create User Catalogue	2 hrs													
Produce technical infrastructure diagram	3 hrs													
Define and document requirements	10 hrs													
Investigate potential solutions	8 hrs													
Complete requirements analysis (milestone)	0 hrs												11/12	

Figure 5.5 Unscheduled Gantt chart extract

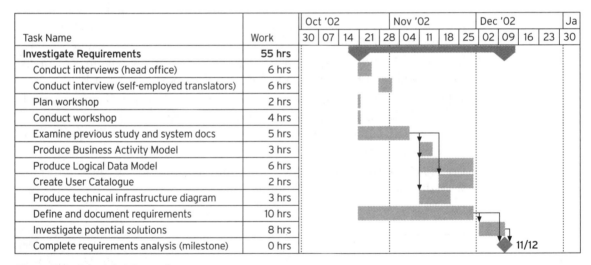

Task Name	Work	Oct '02				Nov '02				Dec '02				Ja
		30	07	14	21	28	04	11	18	25	02	09	16	23	30
Investigate Requirements	**55 hrs**													
Conduct interviews (head office)	6 hrs													
Conduct interview (self-employed translators)	6 hrs													
Plan workshop	2 hrs													
Conduct workshop	4 hrs													
Examine previous study and system docs	5 hrs													
Produce Business Activity Model	3 hrs													
Produce Logical Data Model	6 hrs													
Create User Catalogue	2 hrs													
Produce technical infrastructure diagram	3 hrs													
Define and document requirements	10 hrs													
Investigate potential solutions	8 hrs													
Complete requirements analysis (milestone)	0 hrs												11/12	

Figure 5.6 Unscheduled Gantt chart extract with dependencies

Task Name	Work	Oct '02				Nov '02				Dec '02				Ja
		30	07	14	21	28	04	11	18	25	02	09	16	23	30
Investigate Requirements	**55 hrs**													
Conduct interviews (head office)	6 hrs													
Conduct interview (self-employed translators)	6 hrs													
Plan workshop	2 hrs													
Conduct workshop	4 hrs													
Examine previous study and system docs	5 hrs													
Produce Business Activity Model	3 hrs													
Produce Logical Data Model	6 hrs													
Create User Catalogue	2 hrs													
Produce technical infrastructure diagram	3 hrs													
Define and document requirements	10 hrs													
Investigate potential solutions	8 hrs													
Complete requirements analysis (milestone)	0 hrs												11/12	

Figure 5.7 Scheduled Gantt chart extract

5. Double check that the task sequence makes sense and that you are not planning to carry out too many tasks in parallel.

6. Verify that you can complete the project within the required timescales, and that you can achieve all of the external milestones. If the project appears to be overrunning, then review each task to ensure that you have allocated your time effectively, and that there are no periods when you are seriously under-utilised. Also review your dependencies, in particular to check that you have not specified that tasks must run after one another, when in reality they can overlap to some extent.

In a typical planning exercise you will cycle through the above steps a number of times, and so a tool of some sort will be useful to you as it will make adjustments much easier to apply. However, you should beware of using the 'auto-scheduling' facilities that claim to generate an optimum plan for you. In reality they will apply strict parameters to the plan, and you will find that you spend more time adjusting these parameters to your liking than you would have spent in manually scheduling your plan.

If you have adjusted your plan to give you the optimum utilisation of your time and it still fails to fit within your project timescales, you will need to make some hard decisions, ideally in consultation with your supervisor. The only real answer, if you have estimated accurately and are unable to free up any more of your time, is to reduce the scope of your project in some way, for example by dropping a non-essential deliverable or by limiting the functionality of your implementation.

What you must not do is to artificially reduce your task estimates so that the plan fits with the end date. All that will happen if you do this is that you will create the illusion that you will finish in time, but will then fall behind and have to negotiate a reduced scope late in your project or face the prospect of finishing late. Neither of these consequences is likely to find favour with your assessors.

5.5 Team organisation

Group projects have a lot to recommend them, as they are more representative of the real world than an individual project. In a commercial setting few projects are carried out by a single person, and the experience of working as part of a team in a student project can be invaluable as you move into a commercial setting.

Just as in a commercial project, student project teams need to be organised and managed carefully to ensure that all members are used effectively and that their needs, as well as the needs of the project, are satisfied. There are two parts to this. Firstly, the team must be set up correctly, as discussed below. Secondly, the team must be managed properly: this covered in Section 6.4.

In some projects students may be allowed to create teams of their own choosing, while in most projects team members are selected by tutors. If you are given a free choice try to resist the temptation to create teams made up of close friends. This is invariably a bad idea as friendships can be severely tested during a project, and can seriously undermine the effectiveness of the team. It is far better to select teams based on their skills and strengths than on their social interests. The ideal scenario is one in which the strengths of the team members complement each other, so that each part of the project has someone who is ideally suited to take responsibility for it.

Assigning responsibilities

Once you have introduced yourselves to each other, your first task in organising your team is to establish what skills and personal objectives you have. You should then attempt to assign roles and responsibilities to each member of your team, the most important role being that of team leader.

The most frequently cited reason for breakdown in a group project is the lack of a clear leader. In selecting a leader you should not engage in a popularity contest, or turn the choice into a battle of egos. The important thing is to select the person who has the most appropriate skill set. The ideal leader would possess a high degree of organisational ability, be decisive but diplomatic, be technically and academically gifted, and have good people skills. Assuming that you do not have such a paragon within your team, you should probably look to the person with the best organisational and people skills.

The team leader's main responsibilities will include the maintenance of the project plan, the organisation and possibly the chairing of team meetings, and on occasions arbitrating in disputes. The team leader should not see themselves as the only decision maker in the team, and they should not bully other team members. This is inappropriate behaviour for a project manager (which is what the team leader will be acting as), and will be picked up by your project supervisor and assessors.

Depending on the size and nature of your project, you might consider assigning other key team roles such as secretary (responsible for minute-taking and filing, etc.), main client contact, alongside more technical roles such as lead analyst, technical architect, etc. In most group projects, there will be an opportunity for a number of team members to take part in most activities, but it can be helpful if one individual takes responsibility for coordinating a particular area. For example, while everyone might take part in the interviewing process, the lead analyst may have overall responsibility for organising appointments and collating the results.

If there are roles that no team member is willing to fill, or roles that more than one person would like to take on, you may need to consider sharing or rotating them between team members.

While not everyone in the team has to be assigned a specific team role, care should be taken to ensure that no one individual takes on too much responsibility. If you have agreed to take on a major team role, such as leader, you may need to take a slightly smaller technical role within the project as much of your time will be taken up with team management duties. On the other hand, do not worry if you have not picked up a specific team role, as there will be plenty of opportunities within the execution of the project to make a full contribution through more technical roles.

Assigning tasks

Once key responsibilities have been decided, you will need to allocate project tasks to individuals. Some tasks may be carried out by the whole group (e.g. workshops) or in pairs (e.g. interviews), but most will be single person tasks. In a group project there are two basic approaches to task allocation:

- Assign whole areas or 'chunks' of the project to individuals. This can be done by identifying self-contained areas of activity, such as the literature search or the database design, or by identifying functional 'chunks' of the final system that can be assigned to individuals to design and build.

■ Spread tasks around, so that everyone takes part in each type of activity.

Both approaches have something to recommend them, and so in reality the best strategy is to adopt a combined approach. Assigning whole subsets of the plan to individuals can make the planning process more straightforward, and also makes it easy to identify the contribution of each individual within the project, which is an important assessment criterion. Spreading tasks around should mean that each team member can experience as many types of work as possible, and also helps to ensure that everyone can contribute throughout the life of the project, rather than dipping in and out for short periods of intensive activity.

Once tasks have been assigned to individuals, you will schedule them in much the same way as discussed in Section 5.4, although issues of matching the timings of tasks with availability will be more complicated owing to the variance in people's timetables and other commitments.

Team meetings

The organisation and purpose of team meetings will be discussed in more depth in Chapter 6. However, it is important, regardless of how you run meetings or what you use them for, to set up your schedule of meetings at the earliest opportunity.

You are likely to hold meetings on a weekly or fortnightly basis, and/or before important milestones on your plan. If you delay the setting up of meetings, you will find it difficult to organise meetings that will fit into everyone's diaries, and if you need to book a meeting room this may prove impossible at short notice.

5.6   The Project Initiation Document

The Project Initiation Document (PID) is one of the most important deliverables of any project. Even if your university does not require that you produce one, you are well advised to do so, as it will greatly improve your chances of completing your project successfully. In many universities a PID will form part of the project proposal process, although it may be called something different, such as Project Definition Document, or Project Proposal. In other universities the PID may be a required early deliverable of the project, with the proposal process relying on a Project Brief. The importance of the PID is reflected in the fact that it will often attract around 10 per cent of the overall marks for the your project. Similarly you will typically be expected to spend around 10 per cent of your project time on its production, most of which will go into the investigations and groundwork discussed in previous chapters.

The main aims of a PID are to define the scope and objectives of your project, and your plan of work for its completion. In short, a PID should describe:

Table 5.2 Project Initiation Document contents

Item	Description
Title	Your title should convey the flavour of your project in one short sentence.
Background	A few paragraphs should be sufficient to cover the background to your project. Try to explain the overall aims of your project, its type and the work you have done to date. You should also describe your external client, if you have one.
Objectives	The list of objectives should collectively describe what the final deliverables and achievements of your project will be, covering three areas:
	■ Academic objectives, covering such things as your research objectives, particular theory or techniques that you will explore and apply, and any required objectives of your course.
	■ Personal objectives, including skills that you plan to acquire.
	■ System and business objectives, including system components that you will deliver, functionality/main requirements that you will satisfy and key business benefits.
	You should ensure that all of your objectives begin with the word 'to', and are phrased so that your success or failure in meeting them can be tested or measured. Test each objective to check that it conforms to the checks in Box 4.1, and the SMART acronym (Specific, Measurable, Achievable, Relevant and Timely).
	The best approach to setting objectives is to define a series of smaller objectives, rather than building your project around a single large objective. This has the benefits of giving a feeling of making progress, as you achieve each objective, and of ensuring that your project is not dependent on one single 'do or die' objective.
Justification	You should justify your choice of project by explaining how the project will meet the requirements of your course, why the topic interests you and what you will gain from the project.
Scope	The scope of a project is a description of what activities you plan to carry out, and of the functional or academic boundaries of your project.
	In order to clarify the scope it can be helpful to list what you are *not* going to be covering. Functional boundaries will help to define which parts of a problem or business you will be addressing.
Approach and deliverables	A description of your development and research approaches, methods and tools.
	You should also include a brief justification for your choice of methods and tools.
	Deliverables should include all of your key development products and research outputs.
Major milestones	Timings for your main deliverables and activities. You must ensure that they are aligned with your university's project submission timetable.
Constraints and assumptions	Any project-specific constraints and assumptions should be noted for review by your supervisor. Avoid bland statements that apply to all projects, such as the constraint that 'the project must be completed on time'.
Resources	Any special resources or tools that you will need to complete your project. It will reassure supervisors that that you have not overlooked the need for specific hardware or software. Your supervisor may also be able to assist in identifying where you can access or acquire them.
Major risks	Risks are the things that you aware of that might happen, and if they do will have an effect on your project. For each risk you should have a fall-back position in case they do occur.
Project organisation	For a group project this will include all of the team members, together with their primary roles and responsibilities.
	You should also include any external clients, technical advisers, and your project supervisor (if known).
Project plan	Your initial project plan, as described in Section 5.4.
Preliminary literature review	Some universities may require you to include the results of your preliminary literature search.

■ *what* you are planning to do;

■ *why* you have chosen to do it;

■ *how* you are planning to achieve it;

■ *who* will be doing it;

■ *when* you are planning to do it.

Without this information you would be undertaking your project 'blind'. The PID provides a firm foundation for executing your project, and acts as a baseline for monitoring and managing your progress. You should also regard the PID as a 'contract' between yourself, the university (represented by your project supervisor) and any external clients.

Project Initiation Document contents

Table 5.2 lists the contents of a typical PID. As you can see, much of it is lifted directly from the Project Brief described in Table 2.7, with the additional information defining how and when the project is to be executed.

Before merely duplicating the details of the Project Brief, you should verify that its contents are still true and accurate, as you may have carried out a significant amount of planning and further investigation since its initial creation. It is important that your PID is clear and unambiguous, so you should ensure that any concerns that you had when producing your Project Brief have been addressed.

If some areas of your PID are based on assumptions that cannot be confirmed until you reach a particular milestone, then you should say so clearly. Many of your later activities and deliverables will be dependent on the results of earlier activities, and so cannot be predicted or planned with total conviction until you are part way through your project. For example, your choice of a user interface tool might well depend on a detailed analysis of user interface requirements.

No supervisor or client will expect you to stick rigidly to the terms of your PID in the face of evidence that you should be doing something different. However, you must ensure that there are as few surprises as possible, by stating which deliverables and estimates are based on assumptions concerning earlier activities, and by indicating that you will need to confirm their details at a later date. Do not attempt to do this for all of your deliverables as an excuse for sloppy planning. Most of your deliverables and activities should be relatively predictable, or capable of being timeboxed.

Box 5.1 shows how the Project Brief from Box 2.3 has been updated to create a PID (note that in the interests of space the Project Plan has been limited to the extract from Figure 5.7).

Reviewing and baselining your project

If the PID is part of your project proposal process, you should double check it against the 'killer questions' in Table 2.4.

Box 5.1

Example Project Initiation Document

Title
Development of a system to support the work of a language translation business.

Background
Borders is a firm offering a wide range of language translation services to private and commercial customers. Most of their clients are small to medium enterprises (SMEs), requiring the translation of documents between different, mainly European, languages. They also provide translators for business trips, conferences and meetings. They have a permanent staff of eight translators, but supplement these with a network of self-employed translators to cover as many languages as possible. The self-employed translators carry out over 50% of Borders' assignments.

This main aim of this project is to develop a system to support the management of translation assignments for Borders. A secondary aim is to investigate best practice for implementing an extranet in businesses of similar size to Borders.

Investigations carried out so far suggest that the solution is likely to be an extranet, consisting of a central database of clients, translators and assignments, with an Internet-based interface to enable the self-employed translators to access the system.

Objectives
- To produce requirements specification for translation services management system.
- To design the entire system for management of translation services.
- To identify best practice, as used in industry, for applying structured methods to the design of an extranet.
- To identify appropriate implementation technologies for small-scale extranets.
- To design target technical architecture for Borders.
- To implement a prototype covering the core functions of the system.
- To evaluate the suitability of structured methods (specifically SSADM) for specifying extranet applications.
- To acquire and demonstrate Java programming skills.

Justification
This project will enable me to explore analysis and design techniques in depth, and in a real-world environment. It will also enable me to develop an understanding of how the skills acquired during my studies fit together over the full system development life cycle (excluding maintenance). The topic also offers an opportunity to investigate how extranets are designed and implemented in SMEs, which is an under-researched area at present. The external clients are happy for me to take a prototyping approach to the implementation of the user interfaces, which should allow me the flexibility to meet project deadlines, by selecting an appropriately sized first implementation.

The topic also offers me an opportunity to acquire some further technical skills in web development, and on a project that has sufficient depth to provide some real challenges.

Scope
The functional scope of the project and of the resulting system design is limited to Borders' core business activities, namely:

- the assigning and distribution of written translation assignments to translators;
- the booking of verbal translation assignments;

- the tracking of assignments;
- customer management (excluding those activities related to payment processing);
- the maintenance of a translator skills database.

The prototype application will cover a subset of the above functionality, to be decided during functional specification. The technical architecture design will cover the needs of head office and of the remotely located translators.

Approach and deliverables
The project will cover the entire Systems Development Life Cycle (with the exception of the maintenance phase) using a spiral GUI model, and SSADM notation. SSADM has been chosen as it is the most widely recognised structured methodology, and so will provide an ideal vehicle for meeting my primary research objective of evaluating the suitability of structured methods (specifically SSADM) for specifying extranet applications.

The project will include a literature review, in order to identify best practice in applying structured methods to the specification of an extranet in an SME, and to identify appropriate implementation technologies for small-scale extranets. Primary data collection will include structured interviews as part of my evaluation of the effectiveness of SSADM.

- Requirements Catalogue.
- Business system options (alternative outline solutions).
- Functional specification.
- Data model, database design and implementation.
- Prototype application, covering subset of total functionality.
- Test infrastructure.
- Test plans, implementation plans and user guide.
- Literature review.
- Evaluation of SSADM's effectiveness in specifying this type of application.

Major milestones
Detailed plans will be produced as part of the Project Initiation Document, but the following milestones appear achievable from initial planning:

- Project Initiation Document   20 October
- Requirements analysis complete   12 December
- Interim project report   11 January
- Functional specification complete 20 February
- Technical design   17 March
- Test infrastructure set up   2 April
- Prototypes and database delivered 22 May
- Final report   10 June

Constraints and assumptions
The requirements analysis phase must be completed by mid-December, as the staff at Borders will be unavailable to me in the run-up to the end of their financial year.

The project assumes that my only missing skills are the area of Java programming.

As stated in the course handbook, the project must be completed by 10 June.

Resources

The project is expected to make use of hardware and software that is freely available to me at home, at Borders or at the university. In any event, Borders is prepared to pay for any additional developer licences if they can be justified.

Risks

The main risk to the project is the availability of the self-employed translators. They do not work exclusively for Borders and therefore their time cannot be allocated to the project in the same way as for internal staff. The fall-back position, should their availability cause issues, will be to concentrate on the requirements of internal staff.

The other significant risk is that the project assumes that the only skills that I will need to acquire are in Java programming. If the system design requires additional new skills, then the scope of the implementation will need to be restricted.

Project organisation

The project will be conducted entirely by myself.
The project supervisor will be Dr Lambrou.
The client sponsor is Mr Border, of Border Translation Services.
The main user contact and representative will be Ms Gould.

Project Plan

Task Name	Work	Oct '02				Nov '02				Dec '02				Ja
		30	07	14	21	28	04	11	18	25	02	09	16	23	30
Investigate Requirements	**55 hrs**													
Conduct interviews (head office)	6 hrs													
Conduct interview (self-employed translators)	6 hrs													
Plan workshop	2 hrs													
Conduct workshop	4 hrs													
Examine previous study and system docs	5 hrs													
Produce Business Activity Model	3 hrs													
Produce Logical Data Model	6 hrs													
Create User Catalogue	2 hrs													
Produce technical infrastructure diagram	3 hrs													
Define and document requirements	10 hrs													
Investigate potential solutions	8 hrs													
Complete requirements analysis (milestone)	0 hrs												11/12	

If you have already been allocated a supervisor, you should have been consulting them during the production of your PID. Even so, you should review the PID carefully with your supervisor, before agreeing it formally both with them and your client (if applicable).

If you have not been allocated a supervisor, you may be able to review your PID with a project coordinator or your tutors, before submitting it as a formal project proposal. Once you have been allocated a project supervisor, you should discuss the details of your PID with them. Even though you are probably quite committed to the contents of your PID, having put a significant amount of work into it, you should be prepared to accept constructive criticism and make adjustments if necessary. Your supervisor will have a great deal of experience in judging projccts, and will also ultimately be one of the people who assess your work, so you should listen carefully to their advice.

If your project involves an external client, you will need to discuss your PID with them as well. There can be quite a drawn-out process of making revisions to your PID, before producing a version that both your client and supervisor are happy to baseline as your project 'contract'.

5.7 Summary

1. A project filing structure will help you to manage your project as you accumulate increasing amounts of information and paperwork. It will also demonstrate to your supervisor and assessors that you have adopted an organised and efficient approach to your project.

2. You should keep duplicate or back-up copies of all important notes and documents. Few assessors will accept your loss of some vital piece of information as an excuse for late or substandard work.

3. You should set up a project notebook and diary, which should always be close to hand when carrying out any project-related activities, so that you can jot things down as they occur to you.

4. Planning for a student project is not an overwhelming bureaucratic exercise. Although the planning process may appear to be linear, it will in fact be an iterative process. The basic steps in the process are: produce a task list, add timings to tasks, identify planning and resource constraints, add project contingency measures and schedule tasks.

5. Most new project managers are over-optimistic in assessing what they can get done in a set period of time. Contingency planning is therefore essential.

6. In order to allow for tasks overrunning, and for events that delay you or introduce new work, you must build some contingency into your plans.

7. Just as in a commercial project, student project teams need to be organised and managed carefully to ensure that all members are used effectively and that their needs, as well as the needs of the project, are satisfied.

8. You should then attempt to assign roles and responsibilities to each member of your team, the most important role being that of team leadcr, as the most frequently cited reason for breakdown in a group project is the lack of a clear leader.

9. The Project Initiation Document (PID) is one of the most important deliverables of any project. The main aims of the PID are to define the scope and objectives of your project, and your plan of work for its completion.

Project execution

6 Managing your project

Introduction

The aim of this chapter is to provide guidance on managing your project once it is up and running. As with the previous chapter there is no attempt to discuss project management as it applies to commercial projects. The focus once again is on the management of student projects, which have very different needs from those of industry.

Each university will have its own requirements in areas such as interim progress reporting and meetings with supervisors. While these requirements represent the minimum that is needed to satisfy your university that your project is on track, they are insufficient on their own to enable you to manage your project effectively, nor is that their intention.

Project management processes are independent of the type of activities you are undertaking. So the principles discussed here can be applied to any stage of your project, regardless of your topic or the nature of your system development. Indeed, the same principles could be applied to projects in entirely different fields of study.

Learning Outcomes

After reading this chapter, you will be able to:

- Understand how to make the most of the relationship with your project supervisor

- Understand how to manage your client

- Set up effective procedures for working in a team

- Apply techniques for managing your time and overcoming common project issues

- Set up effective project control and project tracking mechanisms

6.2   Working with your project supervisor

Your project supervisor is one of the most important support resources available to you. Supervisors have three main roles: firstly they will act as project management consultants, secondly they will ideally be advisers in your field of study, and finally they will be one of your assessors.

In an ideal world you would get to choose your supervisor so that they were experts in your specific project topic and had unlimited amounts of time to devote to your needs. However, the real world is not like this, and in many universities you will be allocated a supervisor, rather than being given a free choice. Even if you are given a degree of influence, you will be competing with other students who are undertaking projects in the same field. The result is that your supervisor may have some knowledge of your topic, but may not be your university's ultimate authority in the field. Nevertheless they will almost certainly know more than you do, and in any case will be able to point you towards sources of information and support that you would otherwise not have access to (such as other academics). In any event, the topic-specific expertise of your supervisor is secondary to their experience and knowledge of how to conduct an academically based project.

The second area in which the real world conflicts with the ideal is in the amount of time your supervisor has available to support your project. Most supervisors are busy teaching, researching and engaging in numerous other activities. They are also likely to be supervising a number of projects in addition to yours, so while your project might be the most important task in your life, it is just one among many for your supervisor.

Most universities provide limits or guidelines on the amount of time your supervisor is expected to spend on any single project, and even if they do not, there will be strict practical limits. This means that you must be efficient and effective in the use of your supervisor.

Being efficient means ensuring that you turn up promptly for meetings, that you keep your supervisor up to date on your project, and that you document things properly. Being effective means ensuring that the issues you raise and discuss with your supervisor are the important ones, that you give advance notice of issues you want to discuss, and that you prepare in advance for your meetings. Finally, remember that the relationship you create with your supervisor will be critical to the success of your project. If you are enthusiastic, show initiative, and work in an organised and professional manner, time will be made for you and your supervisor will share your enthusiasm. If you appear to lack interest, then so will they.

The role of your supervisor

First and foremost you should view your supervisor as an adviser and critical reviewer of your work. You must not expect them to do your project for you. The kinds of things that a supervisor may be able to do for you include:

- reviewing and agreeing your project proposal;
- reviewing project progress and future plans;
- reviewing project deliverables;
- providing guidance on potential solutions;
- advising on your project approach and the application of techniques and tools;
- discussing issues and potential changes to your project;
- suggesting ideas and new avenues of investigation;
- pointing out risks and issues;
- identifying and securing resources;
- advising on the handling of personal problems;
- reviewing draft documents;
- writing letters of introduction;
- providing references for employers.

While there are many areas in which your supervisor can provide advice and guidance, you should not fall into the trap of consulting them on every minor decision and issue. Even if your supervisor had the time to support you in this way, you would endanger the objective of demonstrating your ability to work on your own.

Students often find it difficult to judge when to ask for help and advice. While your project is a self-managed piece of work, just as in industry you are not expected to undertake your project in a vacuum. One of the key learning outcomes from your project should be an understanding of when and how to consult managers and expert advisers.

The essential thing when faced with an issue is to think it through properly before discussing it with your supervisor. Ideally you should have a range of possible solutions to hand, and use your supervisor to confirm your preferred solution, or to guide your decision-making process. Do not expect them to solve your problems for you. For more minor issues (ones that are not critical to the overall success or failure of your project), you should make your own decision, and document the issue together with your solution for inclusion in your next progress report or meeting.

Some project supervisors will prompt you with reminders as you near significant milestones in your project, while others will not. However, you should not rely on your supervisor to chase you for action, as you are responsible for your final deliverables and for managing your own time, not your supervisor.

One of the key activities of a project supervisor is to critically review your work. In doing so, they will highlight things that you are doing well and encourage you to continue doing them, but they will also point out weaknesses, and make suggestions about how you could approach things differently. You should make every effort to explore these suggestions, and consider them in full before rejecting them. It is quite acceptable to reflect on a point of criticism and to then make an informed decision to challenge it. It is all too easy to slip into a defensive frame of mind when you have invested a lot of time and effort in a project. However, you should try hard not to reject advice and criticism for purely emotional reasons. Critical reviews of your work, both positive and negative, are intended to guide you towards a better outcome. They are not intended as comments on you as an individual.

In an academic project (one without an external client), your supervisor may also be your project sponsor. In effect they will be the ultimate customer or recipient of your project's main deliverables. In such projects, the student will usually be investigating or exploring a topic as input to the research of their supervisor. This has undoubted benefits for you, as your supervisor will have a direct personal interest in ensuring that your project proceeds smoothly. However, it also has its drawbacks, as your supervisor may begin to focus on the detail of your deliverable, rather than your needs and objectives as a student. If this starts to happen in your project (and thankfully it rarely does), you will need to highlight the issue and discuss how it can be resolved. This is not an easy thing to do, and you may need to take some advice from other academics, such as the project coordinator or your personal tutor. Again, this may prove a valuable learning experience, as the same issues occur in industry.

Meeting with your supervisor

During the initial meetings with your supervisor you will tend to spend much of your time reviewing and debating the details of your proposed project. A supervisor's general experience of what makes for a successful project at your university, coupled with their specific knowledge of your academic background and achievements, makes their advice in this area invaluable.

The kinds of questions that your supervisor might explore include the following:

- Is the topic challenging enough? Does it have sufficient depth or breadth?
- Is the project achievable? Do you have the time, resources or knowledge to undertake the tasks you are proposing?
- Is the project original, or does it merely repeat the work of others?
- Is your proposed approach suitable for the problem concerned? Have you thought through all of the key risks and issues?
- Does the topic really interest you? If not, your motivation may well suffer later in the project.
- Are the academic objectives of your project clear?
- Have you carried out sufficient background research to ensure that the project is viable?

The other key thing that you need to discuss and agree during your initial meetings is how you will interact with your supervisor during the course of your project. This will normally consist of a mix of regular progress meetings and reports, formal submission deadlines and less formal correspondence, such as e-mail or 'open door' time when you can drop in to discuss one-off issues.

You should not expect your supervisor to be available to you 24 hours a day, seven days a week. Few supervisors will be willing to provide you with their home or mobile phone numbers, but most do check e-mails regularly. Using e-mail you are likely to get far more timely responses to urgent issues than if you wait until your supervisor is free during office hours.

Depending on the duration of your project and the time available in your supervisor's timetable, you will probably agree to meet with your supervisor every week or fortnight at the start and towards the end of your project, with less frequent meetings during the middle execution phase. The actual format and style of the meetings will depend largely on the personal preferences of yourself and your supervisor. There may also be university standards for how often and how formal your meetings should be.

Regardless of how frequently you meet, you should try to schedule your meetings as far in advance as possible. It will be difficult for you to meet regularly if you leave it until the last minute to arrange a mutually convenient time.

While it is common practice to meet less often during the middle stages of your project, many supervisors get uneasy if you do not contact them for a long time. Without regular progress updates they will not be sure that you are working effectively (or even that you are working at all), and will be less able to help when issues do arise, as they will be out of date and uninvolved in your project.

There is nothing that supervisors dislike more than an initial meeting with a project student, followed by weeks of silence and a late panic just a week or two before the final report deadline. As you near the final report deadline, your supervisor will be increasingly tied up with the projects of a whole range of students, and so will have little time to address complex issues in your particular project. In addition, if you have shown little visible interest and commitment towards your project over the preceding weeks or months, you will already have undermined your working relationship with your supervisor.

Agendas and minutes

In order to make the most of the limited time you will have with your supervisor, you should prepare in advance by drawing up an agenda that covers the issues you need to address in your next meeting. Every project is different, and every supervisor meeting will be unique, but there are some core points that you should always aim to discuss, as listed in Table 6.1.

If possible, you should send a copy of the agenda to your supervisor prior to your meeting. It can also be helpful, if you want to discuss a deliverable in detail, to attach a copy of the relevant documents to your agenda, although your supervisor may not have time to read them in advance of your meeting.

If you have arranged a meeting and subsequently find that you cannot make it, you should rearrange it as soon as possible. If you have regular problems with attendance at meetings it will give your supervisor the impression that you are failing to manage your project effectively. If these problems are due to a clash with other commitments, try to reschedule your remaining meetings to better, more predictable times.

Table 6.1 Standard agenda items for supervisor meetings

Item	Comment
Last meeting's action points	There is little point in reading through the minutes or notes of your last meeting (unless a long time has elapsed and your supervisor needs reminding about the details of your project). In order to maximise the use of your time, you should simply review the action points that were agreed at your last meeting.
Progress since last meeting	It is not sufficient just to say that things are 'going OK'. You need to talk about the tasks that you have worked on and the deliverables that you have completed. You also need to discuss the things that you had planned to do but have not done, and any consequent slippage against your plans. You should have thought about the consequences of this slippage in advance of your meeting, and be ready to discuss the actions you have taken or plan to take to get you back on track.
Issues and questions	This will include problems that have arisen since your last meeting. You may have solved them already, in which case you may wish to confirm that you have done so correctly. If you have not solved them, you should have thought the problems through, and be prepared to discuss your ideas for their solution. Do not expect your supervisor to solve your problems for you, as their job is merely to provide guidance. It is also useful to review solved problems in order to demonstrate that you are managing your project effectively. You may also have a number of questions about how to approach activities and tasks within your project. The range of such questions is almost limitless. They could, for example, include questions about to booking resources, where to obtain information, how to access training materials, and how to apply modelling techniques. If you have a long list of issues and questions, you should prioritise them and make sure that you deal with the most important ones first. If you are running short of time, you may well be able to postpone some of the minor issues until your next meeting.
Review of deliverables	Includes any draft reports or development products that need to be reviewed with your supervisor. You should bring copies (for yourself and for your supervisor) of any relevant documents to the meeting.
Risks	You should discuss any worries you have about events or issues that may affect your project over the coming weeks. Your supervisor may be able to reassure you that your worries are unfounded, or suggest some preventative action to ensure that they do not materialise.
Plan for next period	You should review your latest plan, and discuss the activities you are planning to undertake during the period before your next meeting. It is possible that your plan will need some revision following your earlier discussion of issues.
Agreed actions	You should close your meetings by reviewing all of the follow-up actions agreed with your supervisor during your meeting.

It is important during your meetings to listen carefully and make notes. If you are given advice that you do not understand, then you should clarify it at the time. It can very frustrating, and waste a lot of time, if your supervisor is continually repeating advice or answering the same questions.

After each meeting you should either photocopy or type up your notes, and send a copy to your supervisor. Many supervisors prefer notes to be limited to your agreed action points, while some may ask for a full set of minutes (particularly for group projects). The main purpose of supplying your supervisor with a copy of your notes is to provide them with an aide-mémoire, as they are likely to be supervising many projects, some of which will be superficially similar to your own. It may also prove helpful if for some reason you have to change your supervisor, or are involved in a rare dispute over your final project grade.

Your supervisor as assessor

The things that your supervisor will ultimately assess you on are likely to include your ability to manage your own project, to work independently, and to show initiative and commitment. Your day-to-day contact with your supervisor will therefore be taken into account in your final project mark. Too much reliance on your supervisor, and they will view your contribution as being less than it should have been. Too little, and they will not have a full appreciation of the problems and complexities that you have encountered. They will also be highly critical of deficiencies in your project that you could have sought assistance with (demonstrates a lack of initiative).

6.3   Working with a client

Working for an external client on a real-world problem can be interesting and rewarding, and may provide useful experience to take into the workplace. If that client is also your employer it enables you to demonstrate newly acquired skills, and possibly to explore new career opportunities.

However, there are also inherent dangers in taking on a project for an external client, many of which are related to conflicting priorities and objectives. Your main priority in undertaking a project should be to satisfy the academic requirements and objectives of your course. Your client's main priority will be the success of their business. If your client sees your project as contributing directly to the success of their business then you may well receive a reasonable level of support. However, if some of your academic objectives are not obviously required to meet the needs of their business, for example by requiring you to undertake tasks that appear unnecessary to your client, that support will quickly evaporate. If your client has taken on your project merely out of a sense of public duty (or because you are known to them personally), then the direct contribution to their business is non-existent, and their ongoing support will often be minimal.

Table 6.2 Tips for managing your client

Tips	Comment
Act early	Many of the benefits of working with a client are associated with investigating real-world requirements. As these should take place early in your project, you have an ideal opportunity to start work on the client-based aspects of your project as soon as possible. This will enable you to take advantage of the initial backing of your client and to demonstrate your commitment and professionalism. If there is a significant delay to your starting work on your project it will give the appearance of lack of interest, which will quickly be mirrored by your client.
Emphasise business benefits	In your communications with your client you should stress the business benefits of your project.
Make efficient use of time	Ensure that you plan in advance for all activities involving your client or their representatives. This may involve developing a highly structured approach to interviewing, analysing company documents thoroughly before following up with targeted questions, and making sure that every client site visit has a real and clear purpose. Chapter 7 deals with many of these issues in some detail.
Clarify and document well	You should document all contact with your client thoroughly, and make every effort to clarify issues on the spot, rather than relying on follow-up visits. Client time is a valuable commodity, and you should not waste it by revisiting issues that you should have resolved previously.
Agree formal PID	Your PID needs to be understood and agreed formally by your client. If they fail to appreciate the details of your project or, worse, cannot spare the time to assess it properly, you should be uneasy about their real levels of commitment.
Report progress	The progress reports that you provide for your client should be brief (two or three paragraphs, possibly by e-mail) and above all should be regular. You should focus on what you have done since the last report, and what you plan to do before the next one. Do not leave it too long between reports, as this will give the impression of lack of commitment on your part.
Use your supervisor to manage issues	If you have a major issue that jeopardises the success of your project you should review it with your supervisor before raising it with your client. You should attempt to resolve lower-level issues with your supervisor wherever possible.
Diarise early	Try to book your client visits and your access to resources as early as you can.
Have fallback position	In any client-based project you must have a contingency plan that includes a fall-back position in the event that you do not receive the support you anticipated. No assessor is likely to accept the excuse that your project failed because your client was unavailable.
Establish business contacts	The main client sponsor of your project is likely to be a relatively senior figure within the business. This is important to ensure that your project has real backing. However, you should also try to establish lower-level contacts within the business, as you are will find it easier to get access to them (you should have identified key contacts already in your PID).
Shield your client from academic deliverables	In all dealings with your client you should focus on the business deliverables, even to the extent of producing a tailored 'client' version of your final report.

When you initially approach a prospective client about your project, they can appear very enthusiastic, and may well promise to give you the access, resources and time that you need. Once you are up and running, and you have started to make demands on the time and resources of your client or their business, things rarely go as smoothly as you had hoped. This is mainly due to the pressures of time that exist within a business. Your project will usually be viewed as an 'optional extra', and so if people are under pressure it will be your project activities that they drop or postpone in order to concentrate on their real business priorities. While this is unlikely to be quite as big an issue if your client is also your employer, it will still happen from time to time, particularly if what you are working on appears to be a largely academic activity.

Table 6.2 provides some tips on managing these issues, mainly by minimising the demands you make on the time of your client, and by capitalising on their early enthusiasm for your project.

If your client is also your employer there are some additional issues that may arise within your project:

- You may feel less able to assert or defend your academic objectives, and you are likely to share the view that business interests come first.
- You may be more easily coerced into changing the scope and direction of your project.
- Other more pressing business tasks may start to eat into the time you had set aside for your project work.

The only way to overcome these issues in the workplace is to enlist the firm support of your managers up front. Ideally, you should try to negotiate some relief from your normal day-to-day duties, but in a busy business environment this can prove extremely difficult.

It is inevitable in a client-based project that issues of varying significance will arise. If they endanger your academic objectives, it is important to deal with them as soon as possible. This may mean negotiating a change of project scope with your supervisor and/or client. In many situations you will be able to reshape your academic project to meet your university deadlines (they will rarely be shifted to meet the needs of an external client), while still delivering the original scope to your client, albeit to later timescales.

Above all, if your project does start to go astray you should contact your supervisor first. They will have experience of managing the types of issue that you as a student will face, and will advise you on how to approach your client.

6.4 Working in project teams

Good teamwork is essential to the delivery of any group project, as without it the contributions of individuals will not be optimised or coordinated. For most group projects teamwork will also be used as a key assessment criterion. The main elements of teamwork are as follows:

- **Team organisation and structure.** This includes the careful planning and tracking of project activities, and the clear assignment of tasks and roles to individuals. Team organisation was discussed in Chapter 5.

- **Effective communication.** Without good communication any team would find it impossible to operate effectively. Teams that adopt a mix of regular formal meetings (see next section) and efficient informal communication (either face to face, via telephone or using e-mail) are able to coordinate their efforts, avoid wasting time on duplicated or unnecessary work, and to identify and resolve issues efficiently that affect everyone on the project.

- **Individual working practices.** Some people find it difficult to work in teams, either because they fear that their own contribution will be hidden or undermined by the rest of the team, or because of a lack of confidence in their own abilities. It is the shared responsibility of the individuals concerned and of other team members to find ways of integrating everybody into the team. This can be helped by making individual contributions very clear, by fostering an open atmosphere in which problems can be aired and discussed without prejudice, and by identifying tasks that play to individuals' strengths. The same issues are encountered in industrial projects, so experience gained in working as a member of a team, however reluctantly, can prove invaluable as you move into employment.

- **Team spirit.** A strong sense of shared purpose and of mutual trust is important in ensuring that everyone performs to their full potential, and the needs of the team as a whole are recognised and worked towards. To help establish team spirit some groups find it helpful to adopt a team name or logo. Others hold regular social events, most notably at the start of the project, or following the achievement of major milestones.

Team meetings

In addition to meeting with your project supervisor (as discussed in Section 6.2) it is essential that you set up a series of regular team meetings. The frequency of team meetings will vary with the overall length of a project, but will typically be weekly for a single semester project, or fortnightly for a year-long project. As a general rule, shorter more frequent meetings are more effective than longer infrequent meetings.

Team meetings are essential to the success of a group project, as they are the only truly effective way of ensuring that progress is monitored, that issues are resolved and decisions are made with the full involvement and understanding of all team members. You should adopt a fairly formal approach to team meetings, as without it your meetings will either descend into a social occasion or repeatedly fail to address key project issues. Some of the features of a well-organised team meeting are listed in Table 6.3.

As well as holding team meetings you will need to maintain less formal contact between team members. The best way of doing this is often using e-mail as there is permanent record of such contact, but you can also use face-to-face

Table 6.3 Features of a well-organised team meeting

Feature	Comment
Chairperson	The chairperson should prepare the agenda, ensure that suitable accommodation has been booked, and check that everyone is able to attend, or has had the opportunity to send in any contributions on paper or by e-mail. In many teams the role of chairperson is rotated to give everyone the opportunity to experience the role, and to share the workload.
Agenda	Each meeting should have a clear agenda, with items such as:

- Last meeting's action points
- Progress report from each individual
- Project issues and concerns from each individual
- Reviews of deliverables
- Discussion of approaches to, and problems with, project tasks
- Review of the plan, and **agreed** actions for each individual for the coming week/fortnight
- Issues for discussion with your supervisor

In addition, you may dedicate further meetings to the production of key deliverables or to workshop-style activities, but these should not displace your regular progress meetings.

Minutes	The actions arising from each meeting along with all team decisions must be carefully documented in a set of minutes that is typed up quickly and distributed to all team members (often using e-mail). This will prevent time being wasted on repetition of discussions, ensure that all decisions are understood by all team members, and provide an audit trail for use in the case of future dispute. Producing minutes should not be too arduous if a standard layout is reused for each meeting (most points can also be documented in a bulleted list). The role of meeting secretary should be rotated. However, most teams will identify an overall team secretary who should ensure that a copy of each set of minutes is deposited in the team's filing structure (see Table 5.1).
Accommodation	Try to find suitable accommodation that will allow you some privacy and preferably facilities such as a flipchart. Avoid holding your meetings in a social setting, such as a bar or canteen, as you will find it hard to adopt a professional approach in such surroundings.
Decision process	Occasionally, you will come across issues where there is no obvious answer, or where you are unable to achieve consensus within the team. In order to handle these cases you will need to set up a decision-making process, such as voting. Whatever system you adopt, you should make sure that all team members are happy with it before you need to use it.

meetings for work carried out in pairs, or set up a team website (useful for publishing minutes and agendas). To help with this it can be useful to circulate telephone numbers and e-mail addresses of all team members right at the start of your project.

The team's filing structure as detailed in Table 5.1 will act as the central repository for all project documents, with copies made easily available to team members using a website, a shared file space or e-mail. All team members should supplement this with their own informal notes, project notebooks and diaries, as discussed in Section 5.2.

Team breakdown

While group projects are open to exactly the same issues as an individual project, they also have some additional risks associated with working in a team environment. The most serious of these is a breakdown of team relations, usually arising from one or more of the following:

- **Non-contribution of one or more individuals.** If an individual is failing to work as a member of the team the issue should be discussed openly in a team meeting, and not in corridors or the bar. The aim should be to provide every opportunity for the individual to contribute fully (for example by identifying more suitable tasks, identifying any personal issues that might be affecting the individual or ensuring that their role and responsibilities are understood fully), not to find ways of excluding them. If, despite the best efforts of the team, you are unable to bring the individual back into the team, you should raise the issue with your project supervisor.

- **Lack of commitment to the goals of the team.** In some teams there may be an absence of team spirit or clear goals for the team. Again, this should be discussed openly in team meetings, before raising it with your supervisor.

- **Internal disagreements.** Occasionally disputes can arise within a team, either between two individuals who have fallen out for personal reasons, or because a specific project decision is being challenged. If the issue is a disputed decision, then it should be clarified at the next team meeting, and resolved using the team's agreed decision-making process. If the issue is an interpersonal problem it may not be resolvable within the team and will need to be passed to your project supervisor as soon as possible.

- **Poor organisation.** Teams more often fall apart through a general lack of organisation than any other specific cause. The most frequent issues are poor planning, unclear roles and responsibilities, and lack of communication. All of these points should be addressed at the beginning of the project, but if problems arise during the course of the project they should be raised at an early stage with your supervisor (you are unlikely to be operating effective team meetings in this case).

6.5   Managing your time

Your project is likely to be the largest academic task you undertake while at university. Added to this, it is largely self-managed, and is spread over a long period of time. These factors bring with them a number of new and important challenges, which many students find hard to manage. You may have met previous coursework deadlines by leaving it quite late, and then putting in a few days of concentrated effort right at the end. While this is far from being the most effective approach to completing coursework, you may well have got away with it in the past. However, please note: **this will not work for your project.**

The sheer size and complexity of your project, combined with the length of time needed to set up and complete some of the individual tasks (especially those dependent on other people, such as interviewing, or resources, such as searching the literature), make it vital that you make optimum use of your time, over the entire duration of your project. In Table 6.4, we discuss a number of tactics for managing your time effectively, and for resolving the issues that will inevitably confront you in the course of your project.

6.6   Project tracking and control

Many of the concepts covered in this section have been mentioned earlier in this chapter. However, they are worth discussing in a little more depth, as they are all essential to the smooth running of your project. They will also demonstrate to your supervisor that you are managing your project in a professional manner.

Using your plan

The project plan that you produced at the start of your project should be viewed as a working document that evolves and adapts as your project progresses. You should constantly review and consult your plan in order to determine what you need to be working on, and what the consequences might be of any issues that arise. You should not view your project plan either as a one-off exercise in order to satisfy your assessment criteria, or as a script that you should follow regardless of the events that unfold.

Ideally, you should aim to set aside around 5 minutes each day to check that your plan is still a reasonable reflection of what you need to do. If you find that it is getting out of date, then you may need to spend a little time adjusting your plan, perhaps by making some notes on a paper copy. Once your plan has got to the stage where the majority of tasks need annotating you should probably carry out a more detailed replanning exercise. If you are using a planning tool such as Microsoft Project it is relatively easy to revise an existing plan, and experiment with various options for rescheduling tasks. However, if you can get away with some minor pen and paper adjustments this will almost certainly be the best use of your time.

Table 6.4 Tactics for managing your time

Tactic	Comment
Start early	As your deadline approaches things will appear to take longer while time gets ever shorter. Some of this is psychological, as the slightest delay has an impact on your project, which is now out of contingency. Some is real, as resources are under pressure and supervisors are busier. So start early, and enjoy watching the late starters panic.
Work consistently	Try to balance the workload across the duration of your project. This will help maintain your interest and momentum, and allows for rescheduling of tasks if delays occur. If you work in bursts, there is less flexibility within your plan.
Resist peer pressure	There always seems to be someone on hand to tell you that you have plenty of time, and should work on your project some other time. They will be the ones panicking later.
Do not let things drift	If you are falling behind schedule or getting bogged down, stand back and review your project. Examine whether you are using techniques or tools in the optimum way. Discuss the issue with fellow students or your supervisor. Do not let it continue to drift.
Balance your commitments	Examine your other commitments. If you are running short of time you should try to identify non-project activities that can be postponed, carried out in a different way, delegated to someone else, or cancelled.
Schedule your use of resources	Try to find times when the competition for resources is lowest. This applies particularly to such things as library resources, IT facilities and meeting rooms. Early mornings and weekends are usually the times of lowest demand.
Identify when you work best	You probably know this already. Some people work best in the mornings, others in the evening. So maximise the use of your time by postponing mundane tasks to times when you are less effective, so that your most productive time is spent on important or complex activities.
Make notes	There will be times when you cannot work on your project, owing to other commitments. Plan for these, and make some rough notes on where you are and what to do next. This way, when you pick your project up again you do not waste time reminding yourself of where you had got to.
Block out time	Most students work best if they block out periods of time that they dedicate to their project, and nothing else. Try to remove yourself from contact with social circles during this time, in order to minimise interruptions.
To do lists	Create a weekly list of tasks plan, based on your project plan. Prioritise this, and use it to create an achievable 'to do' list for each day that you work on your project. Try to make sure that this list is reasonable, as it can be very discouraging if you do not appear to meet your goals for the day.

Table 6.4 *(Cont'd)*

Tactic	Comment
Identify background tasks	Some tasks can be fitted into small gaps in the course of a day. These include reading, organising and filing your notes, tying up loose ends, and even annotating draft reports. Prepare for these small gaps by having materials such as articles, your project notebook and draft reports ready to hand.
Use your project notebook	If an idea or issue occurs to you in the middle of carrying out a planned task, then note it down and move on. Do not get sidetracked. Students frequently do get sidetracked owing to a fear that if they do not work immediately on an idea they will lose it. Write it down and this will not happen.
Avoid unnecessary perfectionism	It is all too easy as you become engrossed in your project to aim for a perfect result, when all you need is a product that is fit for purpose. This is a particular problem when it comes to presentation. While the format and appearance of your final deliverables are undoubtedly important, the same standards should not be applied to working documents, interim products or informal communications.
Schedule breaks and refreshments	One of the benefits of starting work early in your project is that you can afford to schedule breaks in your working sessions. Working for long stretches without a break usually leads to falling productivity. Ideally you should try to relax and take time out. If not, you will become too involved and get into state of anxiety and perfectionism. Conversely, try to avoid the trap of stopping every 15 minutes, or breaking up important trains of thought.
Tie up your loose ends	Ensure that you do not leave too many tasks in a 90% complete state. While this may be unavoidable for some tasks, if you make a habit of it, you are leaving yourself with a large tidying-up job, which will be far more time consuming to complete than if you had finished your tasks properly while they were fresh in your mind.
Get an alarm and use it!	No comment needed.

A good approach is to produce a new 'clean' copy of your plan that incorporates all of your pen-and-paper adjustments, before each progress meeting with your supervisor. You should keep copies of each version of your plan, as it will form an important input to your final report.

Managing issues and risks

If your project is properly planned and managed then the number of issues that you encounter should be kept to a minimum. However, you can never eradicate them entirely, so you should be prepared to keep on top of the issues that will inevitably arise as your project progresses. Issues can be defined as any event or

Issue	Description	Date raised	Target date for action	Action required/outcome	Responsibility (Group project)	Date issue resolved
1	JE unavailable for interview until late December. Requirements definition threatened due to lack of accountancy input.	6/11	12/11	Action: Identify alternative interviewee. Interview needed during November. Outcome: TY booked for 20/11.	PW	10/11
2	JV software not delivered on time.	16/11	7/12	Action: Chase order. Find alternative supplier or software if no progress. Outcome: Software delivered 2 weeks late.	AG	29/11
3	Requirements for user interface more complex than anticipated. If scope of prototype maintained, project would miss deadline. Major/urgent issue.	16/12	20/12	Action: Agree reduction in scope of prototype, or negotiate reduced interface complexity. Outcome: Prototype to exclude all management reporting.	PW	19/12
4	Access to computer lab severely restricted until early February due to inter-semester recabling. Development work due to start on 12/1.	18/12	11/1	Action: Identify alternative lab facilities, or reschedule development timings. Outcome: Lab time in W1 campus booked.	PW	19/12

Figure 6.1 Extract of example Project Issue Log

problem that threatens the outcome of your project, either in terms of what it will deliver, or in terms of its timings and costs. In a commercial project issue management can be a large and challenging exercise, reflecting the size, complexity and business implications concerned. In a student project, a straightforward spreadsheet or table (see Figure 6.1), which logs all project issues and the actions taken to resolve them, should be sufficient. Your spreadsheet should include:

- description of the issue and its consequences;
- date the issue was identified;
- description of the action required to resolve the issue;
- description of how the issue was resolved;
- target date for resolution;
- the person responsible for resolving the issue (in a group project);
- date the issue was resolved.

Your issue log should be kept up to date, with issues added as they arise. In this way it will help you to manage project issues, as well as providing evidence for your assessors that you were rigorous in your handling of issues.

You need to be careful to avoid using your issue log as a means of noting every minor question or follow-up action that occurs to you. If you do this, your log will quickly become unwieldy and will have the effect of obscuring genuine issues. Remember that issues are events that in some way threaten the success of your project. For general questions, you should use your project notebook.

While an issue refers to something that has happened, a risk refers to something that may happen, and that would then threaten the outcome of your project. Again, in a commercial project the management of risks can be a complex operation, while in a student project it should be relatively straightforward.

Most risks will be obvious at the outset of your project, while others will become apparent only once your project is under way. In a student project the most commonly identified risks include:

- non-availability of resources, such as journals, library facilities, and in particular IT facilities;

- lack of access to clients, business documents and premises;

- tasks that overrun, owing to lack of experience either in estimating their duration, or in applying them to a real-world situation;

- other commitments, such as coursework or employers, making unexpected demands on your time;

- lack of team cohesion or poor contributions from individuals (group project);

- unexpected or higher than anticipated costs.

In order to identify risks, you should consult the literature (including past projects of a similar nature) and discuss them with your supervisor. You should them set up a simple risk log (there will often be less than ten readily identifiable risks), which should summarise the following:

- Description of the risk and its likely consequences.

- Warning signs that would indicate that the risk is about to become an issue.

- Description of what actions you might be able to take, either to avoid the risk, or to resolve the issue that would arise should the risk become reality.

Box 6.1

Example of risk log entry

Risk:
Learning how to use Java SDK might prove more difficult than anticipated, leading to unacceptable delays in the programming of software. Plan allows for 4 weeks' duration.

Warning signs: If lesson 4 not completed by end of week 2, then it is unlikely that the task will be completed on time.

Possible actions:
Use Microsoft FrontPage (already skilled in tool).

Reduce scope of prototype to allow for continued use of Java SDK.

At the end of each week you should spend a few minutes checking the warning signs that you have documented in your risk log. If you are concerned that a risk is about to become an issue, you can then take appropriate action, which might include contacting your supervisor if you feel that your project is under serious threat.

In a group project all team members must be able to raise issues and risks. The team leader will be responsible for maintaining the log and ensuring that actions are followed up. It can be useful to set up the issue and risk logs so that they are visible to all team members, possibly by using a web page. Failing that, both logs should be reviewed briefly at each team meeting. The team secretary should also make sure that up-to-date copies are kept in the team's filing structure.

Controlling change

If issues arise that cannot be resolved without a change to the project as defined in the PID or project proposal then you must ensure that you have agreement from your supervisor for the change. If you do not have a meeting scheduled in the near future, you should try to gain agreement for the change by e-mail or an informal face-to-face meeting.

If you fail to do this you may waste valuable time working on a change to your project that your supervisor later refuses to endorse, either because it undermines the basis for your project and its acceptability to the university, or because they are able to identify a more appropriate course of action. In the worst case, your unapproved change may even fail to meet the assessment criteria of your university.

If your project involves a client, and the proposed change affects elements of your project that will directly affect them, you must also get their agreement before proceeding with the change.

Reporting progress

While the principal mechanism for reporting your progress will be your supervisor meetings, it is also a good idea to make some notes each week, summarising your progress and any issues you have encountered. This does not need to be a formal report as such, but if you have arranged to produce a regular progress report for an external client you may want to adopt a standard format. The entries in your notes should be kept simple and brief:

- Progress during the past week, covering both the tasks you have completed, and the tasks you have failed to complete.
- Planned tasks for the coming week.
- Issues encountered, and actions taken or planned to resolve them.
- Points of interest for input to your final report.

A brief set of notes should take no longer than 10 minutes to complete, and will prove invaluable when you carry out the critical evaluation of your project for your final report.

In a group project you may want to adopt a standard layout for your progress notes. The notes can be used as an aide-mémoire for the verbal progress reports at team meetings, and then filed as a permanent record of how the project progressed.

6.7 Common problems

In addition to the teamwork, client-related and time management issues discussed above, there are a number of other common problems that can affect student projects. Table 6.5 describes some of these problems, together with possible actions to overcome them.

6.8 Record-keeping and good housekeeping

We have repeatedly referred to the importance of good record-keeping throughout this chapter. However, it is worth emphasising once more that it is all too easy during a lengthy project to forget why you made certain decisions and to forget significant details of the work you have undertaken, and which may prove important when writing your final report. It is a sad fact that poor record-keeping is a feature of most of the substandard projects that were reviewed in the preparation of this book. Poorly documented projects were all too often characterised by wasted time, poor decisions and ineffectual management.

In the previous chapter we discussed the setting up of a filing system. There is little point in doing so unless you use it. When you are in the middle of a project you may well begin to regard documentation as a chore, even if it takes little time (which it should do), and start to neglect its upkeep. Try to avoid this by setting aside a few minutes at the end of each week to tidy up your files, and ensure that you have copies of all important notes, data and documents. This investment in time will be paid back many times over during your project.

It is also important to ensure that you have back-up copies of all important documents and computer files. It is your responsibility to ensure that your files are safe and secure. Your project assessors are unlikely to accept poor housekeeping as an excuse for late or partial delivery of your project.

Table 6.5 Common project problems

Problem	Actions
Lack of motivation	The best way to maintain your motivation is to choose a topic that interests you in the first place. However, if your motivation still begins to wain, try to identify your most enjoyable tasks. You will inevitably enjoy some project tasks more than others. Try to intersperse your work schedule with these, or use them as a reward for completing less enjoyable tasks. Break down your tasks into small steps. As you achieve each step you will get a feeling of progress. It is often easier to find small slots of time, in which a small step can be achieved, than longer stretches.
Getting sidetracked	As well as causing issues with time management, getting sidetracked can sometimes lead you to explore areas that are outside the scope of your project. Not only does this waste time, it may also lead you to miss the objectives you originally set for your project. If you check your plan regularly, you should pick up on the fact that you are getting sidetracked. If the reason for getting sidetracked is that you have identified an important new area that your project would benefit from exploring, then you should discuss it with your supervisor before changing the scope of your project.
Panicking	If you find yourself starting to panic, and make rash decisions or cut activities short, then you should raise the issue with your supervisor. Alternatively, it may be that you are getting too emotionally involved in your project, and need to take a short break in order to be able to look at your project rationally.
Hardware or software failures	If your project is heavily dependent on the use of specialist hardware or software, you must ensure that you have examined the possibility of technical problems as part of assessing your project risks. If possible you should identify alternative software and hardware products. You should also ensure that you secure access to them as early as possible in your project.
Loss of materials	In order to safeguard yourself against the loss of paper or electronic materials you should take regular back-ups of all important documents and data, including programs.
Personal problems	The best way to handle the impact of personal problems on your project is to discuss them with your supervisor as early as possible. Do not attempt to just absorb the impact of the problem within your project, as if issues surface later you will be less well placed to appeal to your university's extenuating circumstances procedures.

6.9   Summary

1. Project supervisors are one of the most important support mechanisms and resources available to you. They have three main roles: firstly, they will act as project management consultants; secondly, they will ideally be advisers in your field of study; and finally, they will be one of your assessors.

2. You should try to schedule your meetings with your supervisor as early as possible. Supervisors will get uneasy if you do not contact them for a long time. Without regular progress updates they will not be sure that you are working effectively and will be less able to help when issues arise.

3. In undertaking a project for an external client, your main priority should be to satisfy the academic requirements and objectives of your course.

4. Good teamwork is essential to the delivery of a group project, as without it the contributions of individuals will not be optimised or coordinated. For most group projects teamwork will also be used as a key assessment criterion. The main elements of teamwork are: team organisation and structure, effective communication, individual working practices and team spirit.

5. Team meetings are essential to the success of a group project, as they are the only truly effective way of ensuring that progress is monitored, that issues are resolved and decisions are made with the full involvement and understanding of all team members.

6. While group projects are open to exactly the same issues as an individual project, they also have some additional risks associated with working in a team environment, such as: non-contribution of one or more individuals, lack of commitment to the goals of the team, internal disagreements and poor organisation.

7. While you may have been able to meet previous coursework deadlines by leaving it quite late, and then putting in a few days of concentrated effort right at the end, this will not work for your project.

8. The project plan that you produced at the start of your project should be viewed as a working document that evolves and adapts as your project progresses. You should not see it either as a one-off exercise in order to satisfy your assessment criteria, or as a script that you should follow regardless of the events that unfold.

9. Project issues can be well managed using a straightforward spreadsheet or table that logs all issues and the actions taken to resolve them. If issues arise that cannot be resolved without a change to the project as defined in your Project Initiation Document or project proposal then you must ensure that you have agreement from your supervisor for the change.

10. While the principal mechanism for reporting your progress will be your supervisor meetings, it is also a good idea to make some notes each week, summarising your progress and any issues you have encountered.

7 Systems analysis

7.1 Introduction

The aim of this chapter is to provide guidance on issues and activities that are common to the analysis stage of any student development project, regardless of the method or approach being used. Many of the techniques discussed in this chapter are either missing from methodology-specific systems analysis courses and textbooks, or presented in the context of a commercial project, rather than a student project. It is therefore these techniques that students frequently struggle to apply effectively during their project, as they have not had the opportunity to explore them in a practical fashion while completing coursework.

Learning Outcomes

After reading this chapter, you will be able to:

- Identify the key sources for system requirements

- Understand how to apply requirements investigation techniques within a student project

- Define and record requirements in a manner appropriate for student projects

- Appreciate how system models can be adapted for use in a student project

- Understand how to investigate potential system solutions

7.2 Investigation and information sources

Fact-finding or investigation lies at the heart of all system development projects, regardless of their size, complexity or type. Before you can embark on the specification, design and construction of your application, you need to be clear about what your system needs to do, and this will require you to obtain information about a potentially wide range of subjects.

Table 7.1 lists some of the key areas that you will need to investigate, and while the emphasis of many systems analysis courses is rightly on the first item in the table (system requirements), you may also need to consider many of the other items, particularly if your project involves an external client.

Where to find information

The sources of information available to you will depend on the nature of your project. For academic projects, such as those involving the development of innovative software, or of applications to test a theory, the main sources of information will include the following:

- **Literature search.** As discussed in Chapter 4 your literature search should include journal articles, books, company reports and case studies, all of which will be good sources of system objectives, application features and potential solutions.
- **Lecturers.** Many university-based projects are carried out on behalf of lecturers or researchers, in which case the academic staff will take on the role of the project's 'client'. Other projects might be self-initiated pieces of work, but carried out under the close supervision of one or more members of the academic staff.
- **Businesses and their customers.** Information can be gathered directly from the websites of businesses, either by analysing and modelling transactional sites, or by reviewing published materials, including case studies and software/business process overviews. Information about businesses and their customers can also be gathered using interviews and questionnaires; however, you should be cautious about spending too much time 'cold-calling' or e-mailing businesses, as the success rate of such an approach for purposes other than pure research is low.
- **Fellow students and personal contacts.** You may be able to use fellow students or personal contacts as pseudo-users (or real users in some cases) in establishing the requirements for a system, or as subjects for testing theories, techniques and software.

If you are developing a system for an external client, then one of the main reasons you will have chosen this type of project is the rich set of information sources that should be available to you, such as the following:

- **Company representatives and system users.** Interviews with representatives of your client business will be a key source of requirements, but for a compete picture and to maximise the use of your time they should not be used in isolation (see Section 7.4 for guidance on interviewing).
- **Company documents.** Even very small businesses will have a significant amount of documentation on existing systems (both paper-based and computerised), and on new requirements.

Table 7.1 Areas requiring investigation

Area	Explanation
System requirements	Information about what your system or application is required to do should be the main focus of your investigation. System requirements will cover processes, data, interfaces and non-functional issues such as volumes and performance targets. If you are replacing an existing system, remember that the majority of what your new system will need to do will already be done by the existing one.
Current problems	In reality this is a subheading under system requirements. In many projects most of the requirements will be stated in terms of current operational or system problems that the new system will need to resolve.
System objectives and success factors	As well as having a number of things that it needs to do, your system will have a number of objectives that it needs to meet. For a client-based project, objectives may include financial benefits, improved employee morale, removal of capacity constraints, etc. For a more academic project, objectives may include testing the application of a theory, or evaluating the effectiveness of a tool. Success factors will include acceptance criteria (e.g. who will need to agree that the final system is 'up to standard' and fits the requirements), and post-implementation measures (such as system take-up, performance and problems).
Existing systems and infrastructure	As well as investigating any systems that you are proposing to replace (most new systems are replacements), you need to investigate existing systems that you will need to interface with. They may place tight restrictions on your potential solutions, and make significant demands in terms of the data or processing you will need to provide for them. In addition, you should investigate the technical infrastructure that currently exists. Your system will almost certainly need to make use of it. Student projects are rarely given a blank cheque to entirely replace existing installations.
Potential solutions	As soon as you have established outline requirements you should start to look into potential solutions, albeit at a superficial level at first. Many students either make the mistake of opting for the first solution that presents itself to them, or start investigating potential solutions so late that they do not have time to consider a full range of options.
Organisational or cultural factors	Most students have not experienced the constraints that organisational or workplace culture places on systems. The levels of education, dynamism and openness that exist in an organisation will greatly affect both the nature of your application (particularly the user interface) and the implementation or training strategies that you can adopt.
Internal policies and procedures	You will need to establish whether the organisation has any strict policies with regard to the types of software and hardware you should use, the way in which you should work, and the way that they conduct their business. For example, organisations (including universities) may demand that you develop code using a particular language (so that others can maintain or modify it), or that you use hardware from a specified supplier. They may also have standards for what user interfaces should look like, or how documents should be formatted. Many businesses will also have well-established principles and policies governing areas such as data access, accountancy practices and relationships with suppliers and customers. You may also need to investigate internal procedures for agreeing and controlling system developments and expenditure.
Internal politics	Internal politics may affect how certain departments and individuals work with each other, and what they are prepared to accept in terms of changes to their working practices. Some individuals will be more influential and/or open to new ideas than others. Do not underestimate the effects of internal politics. If you are developing an application in an environment where people are operating to different agendas it can sometimes be impossible to achieve a solution that is acceptable to everyone, or occasionally to anyone.

■ **The workplace.** The workplace itself is a valuable source of requirements for a system. By observing physical working practices and by analysing existing computer systems (either by observing their use, or by using them yourself) you will gain an important insight into what works well currently and what needs to be changed in your new system. You will also be able to observe informal procedures that are not necessarily documented anywhere, but that are important in ensuring that tasks are completed efficiently.

7.3 Analysing documents

Try to obtain company documents as early as you can/as they provide an excellent and efficient way of gaining an understanding of how existing systems work, and of establishing a framework for the rest of your investigation. If you have a good basic understanding of the existing systems, and of the business procedures and terminology in operation, it will make your interviews far more productive. You will not need to waste valuable contact time exploring what should be background information, and will instead be able to focus your information-gathering on real issues and the requirements of the new system.

If you are able to communicate in a common business language it will establish some credibility with your clients, and demonstrate that you are well prepared and able to work unaided. It is against the background of existing systems that the requirements of your system will be discussed: requirements are most often expressed in terms of which features should be retained and which should be replaced or improved. On the negative side, clients will not be impressed if you ask too many naive and basic questions.

When analysing documents you must check carefully that their contents are still relevant, as some may well be out of date. You will also need to prioritise your analysis, as it is unlikely that you will have time to analyse everything.

Company documents to be analysed include the following:

■ **Previous project outputs.** You may not be the first person to have carried out a project in the area you are investigating. The outputs from previous projects may have highlighted problems or requirements that your project could address.

■ **Existing system and procedure manuals.** Some businesses will have sophisticated step-by-step manuals describing how tasks should be undertaken. Others may have simple printed checklists that are pinned up on workplace notice boards.

■ **Change request and problem logs for existing systems.** Most systems will have a mechanism for reporting problems or noting requests for new features.

■ **Training materials.** In addition to system user guides, you may have access to training materials that will present the operations of the existing systems in a logical and accessible fashion.

■ **Forms and reports.** On-screen or printed reports and forms can provide invaluable information on current business processes and data. You should ensure that you obtain copies of all the forms that are in use, especially those that have been created manually, as they usually represent informal additions to the existing system, and will probably need to be included in the new system. You should also look at several completed copies of each type of form to identify fields that are consistently unused, and to identify additional information that is repeatedly being added to the forms. Any reports and forms that have fallen into disuse are candidates to be eliminated from the new system, but you should check first that they are not just being ignored because users are unaware of them. If you find that a number of reports or forms are always used in conjunction with each other, you should consider whether they should be merged.

■ **Memos and other correspondence.** It is possible that the system you are working on has been the subject of correspondence regarding requirements or the shortcomings of the existing systems. However, correspondence of this nature can be difficult to obtain.

7.4 Interviewing

Interviewing forms the backbone of most requirements-gathering exercises in student projects, and it is not difficult to understand why, as it has a number of clear benefits:

■ Interviews are relatively simple to arrange. There will typically be just one interviewee, and so only one person whose diary needs to be coordinated with the interviewer(s). By comparison, workshops can be extremely difficult to organise, owing to diary clashes among the participants.

■ The personal nature of interviews encourages people to express their views and needs fully, and enables issues to be probed in detail.

■ Interviews can be conducted effectively by just one interviewer (although in a group project, two would be the optimum number).

■ Interviews are not constrained in the way that questionnaires are. This often leads to useful asides and insights that might have been missed using other techniques.

■ Interviews help to build relationships between the interviewer or project team and the interviewee.

The danger is that in many student projects interviews are used to the exclusion of all other methods of information-gathering. This inevitably leads to problems, as there are several drawbacks to interviewing:

■ Interviews are deceptively time consuming. While on the surface a 30–40 minute interview may not appear to take up much of your time, you need to add on preparation time, travel time and write-up time. Added to this, you may find that interviews are rearranged at short notice, which will usually lead to more preparation time and scheduling problems.

- Interviews are almost always heavily time-constrained. It is unusual to be granted interviews of over an hour, and most will be around 30 minutes. This is not sufficient to uncover all of the information that you need to carry out your development, regardless of how many interviews you manage to fit into your schedule.

- The number of interviews you can arrange in the limited time available to you is often quite small. You may also have some difficulty gaining access to the right people, particularly in the workplace where time is short and student projects can be regarded as an unwelcome interruption.

- Interviewees may have political or personal agendas that colour their views. They may for example feel threatened by your system, and so provide misleading information or attempt to promote a particular way of working. They may also describe what they think they should be asking for, rather than what they believe is really needed.

- Over-reliance on interviews will usually mean that the resulting system has been influenced by the views of a small number of individuals.

- It can be difficult for some interviewees to express their thoughts clearly, and conversely for the interviewer to understand what is being described.

Most students have little or no experience of interviewing, and so often find it more difficult to obtain detailed information using interviews than using other techniques, such as observation and analysis of documents. The main problems arising from this lack of experience are an absence of control, leading to issues with time management and getting sidetracked, and an inability to drill down into underlying detail. To an extent these problems can be offset by thorough planning, although this can in turn lead to problems arising from the desire to stick to a preprepared 'script' or structure, thereby missing the opportunity to probe and explore unexpected insights.

Preparing for interviews

Once you allow for late starts and interruptions you will find that the number of areas that you can discuss in any given interview is limited. You therefore need to plan carefully and set clear objectives for each interview. Table 7.2 describes the purpose of the main types of objective.

For each interview you need to think about what your objectives are, and how best to word and sequence your questions to meet them. In most interviews you will have a number of distinct objectives, possibly of different types. A good tactic is to open with general questions (usually associated with scoping or descriptive objectives), and to follow them with more probing questions. This has the effect of putting your interviewee at ease, rather than making them feel that they are being examined in some way.

Table 7.2 Types of interview objectives

Type of objective	Purpose
Scoping	To obtain high-level descriptions of requirements and current systems. Can also be used to confirm the overall objectives and priorities of the project, and to set the scene for the rest of the project. Scoping objectives are usually addressed in early interviews with senior individuals.
Descriptive	To describe in detail the processes, data and benefits associated with particular requirements or the operation of current system functions.
Specific	To address specific issues, or drill down into specific areas that require clarification.
Exploratory	To explore potential solutions to requirements, and to encourage creative or innovative thinking.
Prioritising	To establish the relative priorities of system requirements and problems.

A point of real confusion for many students is the level of detail that interviews need to go into. All too often the transcripts included in final reports reveal that the interviews failed to get much beyond scoping objectives. This is perhaps due to an impression gathered from coursework and examination scenarios that this is all that is required. However, coursework scenarios are deliberately and artificially simplified to enable them to be analysed, modelled or programmed within strict time limits. In your project you need to investigate requirements to a far greater level of detail and precision. In a coursework setting you may be presented with scenarios taking up no more than a page. No business or department is simple enough to be comprehensively described in anything approaching a single page of text.

Types of question

In order to get the most from the interviewing process you will need to make use of three types of question:

1. **Open questions.** These are questions that encourage the interviewee to expand on an issue or topic. They are often used to gather opinions, rich descriptions and suggestions, for example by asking, 'how do you think this problem could be solved?'

2. **Closed questions.** These are questions that have a specific and often quantifiable answer, such as 'how many customer enquiries do you receive per day?'

3. **Probing questions.** These questions are designed to follow up or drill down into an issue or answer, for example by asking, 'can you describe that process in a little more detail?' or 'can you give me an example/sample of that?'

Table 7.3 Examples of different types of question

Type of objective	Purpose
Open	How do you think the process of checking deliveries could be improved?
	Can you describe how the customer enquiry system works?
	Why do you think so many orders get cancelled?
	What are the highest priorities for the new system?
	Describe the biggest issues with the current system.
	What do you like about the current system?
	Do you have any suggestion for how we could solve that problem?
	What do you do if a customer is late?
	Do you have any views on how this report should be laid out and accessed?
Closed	How many times do you print this report each day?
	Which files do you check?
	How many orders do you take each day?
	Which report do you check first in the morning?
	Do you use the supplier look-up function?
	How long does it take to fill in the current form?
	Who authorises this type of order?
Probing	Can you give some examples?
	Why do you use this form and not that one?
	What did you mean by regularly; can you give me a figure?
	What will be the financial benefits of doing it that way?
	Can you clarify what happens if there is not enough stock?
	Why do you think it would be better to do it like this?
	Do you have a copy of the form that I could have?
	Why do you find it a problem to use this function?
	Have you found ways round that?

Students often feel uncomfortable asking probing questions, as they are afraid of appearing intrusive or ignorant. You should try to overcome these fears, as your interviewees will be far happier to clarify points on the spot than be asked to cover the same issues again at a later date. They will also tend to be far more experienced in their role as interviewee that you are in yours as the interviewer, and will fully expect to be asked probing questions.

You should try to use a combination of all of the types of question. In the early stages of your information-gathering you will tend to ask more open questions, whereas later on you will find yourself asking more closed or probing questions as you attempt to clarify specific points of detail. If you rely too heavily on one particular type of question, which sometimes happens if you lack experience, you will get only a partial view of requirements. For example, if you ask too many closed questions you will deny your interviewees the opportunity to give you information on areas that you had not considered fully, or perhaps were not aware of. If you ask too few closed or probing questions you will struggle to obtain the precise information that you need to design an effective system. Table 7.3 gives examples of the different types of question.

Before each interview you should think carefully about how best to meet your interview objectives. Try making a list of all the questions and issues that you need to explore or clarify, and then check them by asking the following questions:

- **Is this something that the interviewee is well placed to answer?** There is little point in asking questions that the interviewee does not have the knowledge or experience to answer; it will merely take up time and undermine your credibility as an interviewer.

- **Can I obtain this information more easily elsewhere?** Some questions, such as those relating to detailed descriptions of existing processes, are best explored by examining documents or by observation. Interviews are a valuable and scarce source, so you use them to investigate areas that you cannot easily investigate using other more accessible means. It is particularly irritating for interviewees to be asked questions that you could and should have answered for yourself with a little preliminary reading.

- **How should I phrase the question?** Decide whether the question should be open or closed. If you are looking to confirm a fact, then you will ask a closed or probing question. If you are looking to elicit an opinion or rich description, you should ask an open question. Some areas are best investigated by asking an open question, then following that up with a number of preprepared closed questions, if the original answer is not precise enough, or by using probing questions that you think up on the spot.

- **What is the relative priority of this question?** You may well run out of time during the interview. In this case you should have thought in advance about which questions you could drop most easily.

- **How should I sequence the questions?** In most cases there will be a logical sequence to some of your questions. For example, if you are investigating a set of processes, then you should sequence the questions to follow the natural flow of the processes. Alternately, you may find that your questions group themselves around a number of distinct concepts or topics. If, after grouping and sequencing your questions, you are left with a number of unrelated questions, you should leave those until the end of your interview, and ask them as a group.

Interview approaches

As well as considering the individual questions that you wish to ask in an interview, you need to decide on how you are going to conduct the interview. There are three main types of interview:

1. **Structured interview.** In a structured interview the interviewer follows, with little or no deviation, a script consisting of a list of questions prepared in advance. The questions are typically closed, but some open questions are usually included as a way of opening the interview. An extreme version of structured interview consists of a face-to-face questionnaire. Structured

interviews are often used towards the end of the requirements-gathering stage, when high-level requirements are well understood, and the remaining issue are narrowly focused. They are also useful in establishing the views of a range of people on a limited number of specific topics, where open responses would render analysis and comparison difficult.

2. **Unstructured or open interview.** Open interviews involve posing a small number of broad open questions, such as 'what are the main features you would like the new system to have?', in order to give the interviewee an opportunity to talk widely about a subject. They tend to be used near the beginning of a project, where the interviewer is attempting to gain a general impression of the requirements, priorities and scope of the project. In the hands of experienced and skilled interviewers they can be very effective, with probing questions being used to drill down into points of detail as they arise. The benefit of an unstructured interview is that it does not constrain the interviewee, and so they are more likely to express their real views and expose underlying issues. However, many students find them difficult to handle, as they are inexperienced in detecting when to drill down and in encouraging the interviewee to expand on important topics. In many cases the transcripts of open interviews show that they close too early, and fail to get beyond high-level generalities.

3. **Guided interview.** A guided interview is something of a halfway house between structured and open interviews. Instead of using an interview script, as in a structured interview, you will use a list of topics and ask open questions that encourage the interviewee to cover the required topics. As with open interview, you should use probing questions to clarify issues and to ensure that your list of topics is covered in sufficient detail. In addition you may supplement your topic list with some more closed questions in areas where you need specific answers. The guided interview can be used at all stages of your requirement investigation, as it strikes a balance between the precision of the structured interview and the unconstrained nature of the open interview. This balance can also be adjusted to suit the circumstances of an interview, with more open questions at the beginning of the project, and a more scripted structure towards the end. Students are likely to find the guided interview the easiest approach to operate.

Whichever approach you adopt, you should always aim to open with non-controversial questions in order to put your interviewee at their ease. You should also plan to end each interview with a general and open question such as 'is there anything else that you think I should be aware of/need to know?'

Selecting interviewees

It is advisable to set up your interviews at the earliest possible stage in your project. This is because it can be difficult to get appointments with key individuals at short notice, and because you are more likely to get a positive response at the start of your project when enthusiasm is at its greatest.

You should aim to draw up list of the people that you think will be able to meet the objectives of your interviewing process. This will involve identifying people at various levels of responsibility, representing all of the functional areas affected by your project. The best way of identifying potential interviewees is by asking your project sponsor or supervisor. Once your interviews are under way, you will find that the interviewees (particularly those in a management position) will also suggest other people that you should interview.

Do not rely on interviews with just one or two individuals. In client-based projects many students make the mistake of limiting their interviews to their sponsor and perhaps one other key manager. Although this is an effective way of investigating the scope, priorities and objectives of your development, it will not provide you with detail on how the system should be designed to meet the day-to-day requirements of the workplace, or on how the existing system works in reality.

Try to encourage your sponsor to pick out people who together will provide a representative sample of experts, users and policy makers. There is a tendency among students to target managers or senior personnel, in preference to lower-level staff members, who are often the people who are expected to use the system. A good strategy is to start your interviews with managers in order to establish overall objectives, scope and priorities, then to move on to lower-level staff to add detail on actual processes and problems, before moving back to people in management to confirm your findings.

Box 7.1

Example of interviewee selection

Anna is developing a system to support the membership system of a local sports centre. Her sponsor is the manager of the sports centre, so her first interview was with her. One of her questions concerned other useful interviewees, which resulted in three suggestions: the admin manager, the accountant and the head receptionist.

It transpired during her interviews that other key personnel included the admin clerk who actually processed membership applications and reminders, all three of the sports coaches, who regularly consulted the membership system, and one of the experienced but junior receptionists who had devised some hand-drawn forms to capture informal membership queries.

Once Anna had conducted her initial interviews (nine in total), and analysed their results, she re-interviewed several people, ending with the centre manager, to clarify details and to discuss potential solutions.

When scheduling your interviews it is a good idea to spread them out, so that you have time to analyse the results of each interview, or follow up with observations or document analysis, before embarking on the next. A common error in student projects is to carry out a concentrated set of interviews at the beginning of the project, and then be left with few opportunities to query the results or discuss solutions later on. Most interviewees will have strict limits on their availability, and will often grant you just one interview, so you must ensure that you use their time to maximum effect by scheduling your interviews carefully.

Conducting interviews

As soon as you have made an appointment with an interviewee it is important to confirm in writing the timings and location of your interview, together with a brief outline of the purpose of your interview. This will enable them to think in advance about what you will be asking them. This is particularly important for people who are not used to being interviewed, and who may be quite nervous about the whole process. At the start of each interview you should introduce yourself, restate your objectives, and confirm the format and timings for the interview. You should aim from the very first to appear professional and to put your interviewee at their ease. This will often involve a little small talk at the beginning of the interview, but try to make sure that this does not eat into your time too much.

While experience is undoubtedly an important factor in conducting successful interviews, Table 7.4 lists a number of things that you can do to ensure that your first interviews proceed as smoothly as possible.

As you gain experience in interviews, you will become more relaxed, and your interviews will flow more easily. In the early stages it can be helpful to review your questions and plans with your supervisor, and to practise your interview technique on fellow students. In a group project, you will probably attempt to share the interviews, so you should consider running an informal training session where you take turns as interviewer and interviewee.

During the interview you should attempt to make brief but comprehensive notes on everything that is discussed, as you will not be able to recall much detail if you rely on your memory alone. The best way to do this is to adopt an informal style of shorthand, which you can annotate immediately after the interview to ensure that you will understand the notes subsequently. In a group project you should consider conducting interviews in pairs, with one person taking on the role of lead interviewer, and the other the role of note-taker.

If you are following a script or list of topics, then you can create a recording form using your questions as section headings to give your notes some structure. Figure 7.1 shows an example of some interview notes that use a form to record questions and responses, and to note any follow-up questions that occur to the interviewer during the interview (a template for this form can be downloaded from the companion website).

Many students feel it necessary to reformat or write-up their interview notes for inclusion in their final report. There is little or no point in doing this, unless your interviewee has requested a copy, as most supervisors are happy to see copies of your original handwritten notes in your final report. It is far more useful to spend the time assessing the information they contain and to use it to record requirements formally (see Section 7.5).

Table 7.4 Tips for successful interviewing

Tip	Comment
Be on time	Nothing irritates busy interviewees more than students turning up late for appointments. Being late undermines your credibility before you have even started, and displays a lack of respect for your interviewee.
Clothing	Dress appropriately. If your interviewee represents an organisation with a formal dress code, try to emulate it. This is what a professional consultant would do.
Know your topic	Ensure that you have done your background reading and research. It will reassure your interviewee that you are serious and well informed about your project.
Know your interviewee	Check your interviewee's position and role within the organisation.
Pay attention	Try to pay attention and to maintain some eye contact with your interviewee. It can be quite easy to let your attention drift during an interview, especially if your interviewee is talking about a peripheral issue.
Be open and avoid bias	Do not try to impose your views on your interviewee. By all means make suggestions, but listen carefully to the response and do not try to argue against a genuinely held opinion.
Do not criticise others	Never criticise other interviewees, even if you appear to be invited to do so.
Watch your body language	Sit upright, smile and do not fold your arms!
Have a close-down plan	You should think in advance about what to do if you start to fall behind schedule. It is far better to drop less important questions than to try to rush your interviewee's answers.
Expect some distractions	In a perfect world you would choose a location for an interview that minimised distractions. The reality is that as a student you will have little influence over the location, so should expect some disruptions, such as telephone calls.
Keep checking your plan	In a structured or guided interview you should have a plan or list of what you need to cover. Keep checking that you are sticking to it, but do not do this at the expense of exploring an unexpected but significant side issue.
Do not over-promise	Interviews are to some extent a two-way process, and your interviewee may use your interview to probe your project. If this happens do not raise expectations by over-promising what you will deliver. Explain the scope of your project, and how the interview will feed into it, but do not make false claims.
Clarify points on the spot	If you do not understand something, then say so. If you do not do so, then you risk being given answers later in the interview that falsely assume you understood the earlier point.
Ask probing questions	If your interviewee gives you a reply that is too superficial, or hints at an issue that you need to explore further, then follow up immediately with a probing question. Always ask for examples and quantitative measures (in cases where interviewees use phrases such as 'too many', request samples of documents and clarify where you might be able to find more information on a topic).
Listen, don't talk	Do not dominate the interview by talking too much. Your purpose is to gather, not impart, information.
Summarise	Every so often you should summarise or recap briefly on what you have learnt. This gives your interviewee the opportunity to correct any misunderstandings and gives them the impression that you have been listening. This is especially important in more open or unstructured interviews.
End on time	Never overrun unless your interviewee makes it clear that they are happy to do so (check with them before you reach the last few seconds of your appointment). If you have had to drop some important questions, you may be able to arrange a follow-up interview.

Interviewee:	Sally Jeffries, Tennis coach
Date/Time:	2 November
Location:	Club meeting room

Question	Response	Additional Questions/Information
Can you tell me which functions of the membership system you use?	Only reports and queries Prints subs list before each coaching course Checks fees paid by members for 1-1 sessions Uses member list to send out mail shot	Format of queries? – always asks admin clerk to look up or print the info out. No easy access to PC to view on screen. Would prefer to do things herself – delays are a problem and mail shot lists sometimes wrong
How often do you use the system?	Requests prints at start of every day for 1-1 sessions. Others once or twice a week.	If admin clerk not in, then can't get info e.g. in evenings – many courses are in evenings
Are there any features or data missing from the current system?	No facilities for recording team details More info needed on ability levels and courses attended – relies on own notes Plus access to update member details	What team details? Team names, members of team, fees for joining (if any), type of team, who can join

Figure 7.1 Extract of interview notes using formal recording sheet

On the surface it might appear that the best approach to documenting an interview is to make a tape recording. However, the effort required to listen repeatedly to a recorded interview, and to transcribe its salient points, is significant, and is rarely worth it. In addition, many interviewees are uncomfortable with tape recordings, and are more likely to withhold controversial views in favour of saying what they think they should say. Some organisations even ban the use of tape recorders. In some cases a tape recording can be useful as a back-up to your notes, where they can be used to clarify points that you have not captured fully, but only if you are sure that they will not get in the way of a free exchange during the interview.

At the end of each interview you should thank your interviewee for their time, and confirm details of what will happen next, both in terms of the results of the interview and of the overall project.

Following up on interviews

As soon as possible after completing each interview you should review your notes, while things are still fresh in your mind. You should make sure that

Table 7.5 Checklist for planning and conducting an interview

- ☑ Set objectives, ensuring that interviews are the most appropriate information-gathering technique
- ☑ Identify potential interviewees from all functions and at all levels affected by the system
- ☑ Make appointments with interviewees, ensuring that interviews are sequenced and spaced out appropriately
- ☑ Send interviewee summary of interview objectives
- ☑ Design questions using open, closed and probing styles
- ☑ Decide on approach and structure of interview
- ☑ Prioritise and sequence your questions
- ☑ Review and rehearse timings for the interview
- ☑ Read background information on subject area
- ☑ Adopt a professional approach to the interview (by following the tips in Table 7.4)
- ☑ Use a mix of open and closed questions, followed up with probing questions
- ☑ Review notes as soon as possible after interview
- ☑ Clarify and confirm outstanding queries using e-mail if possible

you can understand your own writing, particularly if you have used any form of shorthand, and add some further notes if not.

It is often a good idea to create a short summary of key points and follow-up actions (such as additional interviews, observations or documents that you need to analyse), as your notes may contain a lot of information that you already have or that is not of direct relevance to you. Any new system requirements should be noted immediately in your Requirements Catalogue (see Section 7.5), together with suggested solutions.

If on reflection you need to confirm or clarify some of the points arising from an interview, the best approach is often to send a short e-mail to your interviewee, rather than trying to contact them in person.

Table 7.5 provides a checklist for planning and conducting interviews.

7.5 Observation

For some inexplicable reason, students frequently overlook observation as an information-gathering technique. This is a great pity as it can be one of the most effective techniques available for gaining a rapid insight into current practice and problems in a workplace, in a way that reveals what people are really doing, rather than what people or documents say should be happening. It may be that students are wary of the workplace, or perhaps believe that observation is in some way 'unscientific'.

Observation can be used at a number of points in the investigation phase of a project. It is an excellent way to gain an overall impression of the dynamic operation of current systems and the working environment at the start of a project. It is much more difficult to visualise how current systems, whether computerised or manual, operate from verbal or written descriptions.

Observations can also be used to investigate particular processes that are central to the system, or that involve a significant amount of personal interaction or manual intervention. In practice, few formal procedures are followed to the letter or carried out in a fully predictable manner. For example, procedures may take longer than you had imagined, or may be sequenced in a way that you had not anticipated. In addition, it is also sometimes useful to witness problems at first hand, as it may be the case that what appears on paper to be a trivial problem is actually a major inconvenience in the workplace.

Finally, in many projects it is important to make the end users feel that they have had the opportunity to air issues and ideas they have regarding the new system, and to see that you are prepared to get your hands dirty and come to the workplace.

As with any technique, observation has a number of drawbacks, which are significant enough to mean that it can rarely be used in isolation:

- **Focus on the current systems.** By definition, observation of the workplace is most effective at analysing current processes and problems. In most observation sessions you will be able to combine passive observation with questioning of the people you are observing. This provides you with an opportunity to explore suggestions for improvements and additions to current systems. However, you are unlikely to get a coherent view of the overall requirements for the new system, or of radical suggestions for changes to current practice.

- **Unnatural behaviour.** When people are observed they tend either to put on their best behaviour or to act in a more outspoken and exaggerated fashion than usual, although it becomes less of an issue as people get used to the observer. This may give you a false impression of what happens under normal circumstances. One advantage that you may have as a student in a client-based project is that people are less likely to feel threatened by your presence than they would if you were an internal employee or consultant, so this problem, while it still exists, is lessened.

- **Time.** Observation is a time-consuming activity. In order to gain a complete picture of what is happening within an organisation you would need to observe the workplace for a considerable amount of time, in order to allow for a full range of processes and events to take place. For this reason, observation is best used to gain an overall picture, and to examine a few specific processes and problems.

- **Disruption.** Even if you attempt to be as unobtrusive as possible, your presence as an observer will to some extent disrupt the workplace. Many managers will be reluctant to allow extended or repeated observations in the same area.

The following are the main approaches to observation as a requirements investigation technique:

- **Passive observation.** Passive observation involves recording what is being done and what systems are being used with the minimum of interference on your part. The purpose of this type of observation is to examine what happens in the normal course of events. You may use passive observation to assess how long certain activities take to complete and how processes interact with each other. It may also reveal how certain problems with current systems are resolved, and highlight informal mechanisms (such as unofficial forms and reports) that have been developed to overcome shortcomings.

- **Participation.** Participation involves you taking on the role of one of the people you are observing. You may be able to spend a few days during a vacation being trained in how to carry out current tasks, and then undertake those tasks for real. This is only really feasible if the tasks are relatively straightforward, as you will not have time to learn complex tasks. Participation is a good way of experiencing the problems and reality of current activities, but can only be used to examine a limited number of areas owing to time constraints and the adverse impact you are likely to have on workplace productivity.

- **Active observation.** This involves supplementing passive observation with questions, in order to clarify what is being done and why. It is perhaps the most time-efficient type of observation, but will necessarily reveal less natural behaviour than passive observation. With active observation you need to be careful to strike a balance between observing and questioning. Otherwise your observation will become more like an interview.

- **Scenario testing.** In scenario testing you will ask individuals to demonstrate how they would handle specific events using whatever systems and tools they would normally use. This requires a degree of trust on the part of the people being observed that their actions will be treated sensitively or in confidence. Without this trust some people may feel obliged to show you how things should be done, rather than how they actually do them.

One of the biggest benefits of observation is that it often reveals manual systems, workarounds and forms that would not be revealed by analysing documents or necessarily by interviewing selected personnel, as in the following examples taken from two different projects.

Box 7.2

Examples of observation scenarios

1. Christina was investigating the use of a number of reports that were printed each morning for use in checking stock levels in a clothing warehouse. Each report dealt with a different type of garment, and listed items where stock levels were believed to be low and needed to be verified so that

new stock could be ordered if necessary. Interviews and procedure manuals had suggested that each report was printed off in turn, and checked by a warehouse clerk, before moving on to the next type of garment.

However, observation revealed that the clerks actually printed off all the reports, then split them up and re-sequenced the pages, so that the items were in the same order as they were stored on the shelves in the warehouse. This greatly reduced the amount of time the clerks spent walking around the warehouse, more than making up for the time they spent re-sequencing the reports.

2. Angelos was undertaking a project with a major food retailer to make some minor changes to a new vehicle booking system that had been under trial in one of their larger stores. On his first visit to the store the manager had shown Angelos round and explained how the system was used to maintain a diary of the vehicles that were due to make deliveries each day. The booking clerk had listened to the manager's explanation and had demonstrated how the system worked.

On Angelos's second visit he started to observe the delivery booking process without the manager being present. After a few minutes it became obvious to Angelos that the clerk was not using the system very much, and kept referring to a paper diary that he kept next to his PC. It turned out that the clerk was not using the new system to make bookings at all, because he found it difficult to operate and it took too long to update. Instead he was using a paper diary, and only adding the bookings to the PC system during quiet spells to keep his manager happy.

The best way to record a observation is to make notes, either in textual format or using drawings and diagrams such as flowcharts. As with interviews it is helpful to use an informal type of shorthand as things often happen quickly, and in bursts of activity. A useful tip is to record your observations on sheets with two columns; one for noting what is happening, and the other for jotting down questions or follow-up actions. If you are using a participation or scenario-testing model then you may be able to use a more formal system of note-taking, by annotating a procedure manual or a preprepared script or process model for the scenario being observed. In some circumstances you may be able to use recording devices such as videos or tape reorders. However, in most cases this will severely disrupt normal operations and will inevitably lead to people acting a part.

You should also use your observation sessions to gather documents relating to the existing system. If you are carrying out passive observation, then you should make a note of the samples that you would like to collect, and ask for them after the session. Otherwise you will disrupt the natural flow of what you are observing.

Regardless of how you record your observation it is essential that you analyse your notes as soon as possible after the session. You will quickly forget small details that you have observed, or what you meant by a particular comment. So check through your notes and either rewrite them in a more easily understood form or annotate them to ensure that they make sense when you refer to them later.

Table 7.6 gives a checklist for planning and conducting observations.

Table 7.6 Checklist for planning and conducting observations

- ☑ Establish objectives and identify who/where to observe
- ☑ Ask permission and book timings
- ☑ Decide on the type of observation you will be using
- ☑ Design your note-taking scheme
- ☑ Introduce yourself and your project to those being observed
- ☑ Take notes on everything that you see, and questions that the process raises
- ☑ Ask for samples and clarification (after observation has been completed if you are using a passive model)
- ☑ Thank the people that you have been observing, and ask if they have any questions or comments they would like to make
- ☑ Write up or annotate your notes immediately following your observation, while things are still fresh in your mind

7.6   Questionnaires

Questionnaires, while being an extremely useful tool for research, are of limited use in investigating requirements. In certain circumstances they can be of some use as a supplement to other techniques, but on their own they are unable to provide sufficient depth or a full enough picture to provide anything like a comprehensive picture of requirements.

The main function of questionnaires in a development project is to clarify issues or points that have been raised during your requirements analysis, where the views or experiences of a wide range of users are needed to establish facts rather than opinions. This is usually achieved by distributing a questionnaire consisting of closed questions to either a large sample or an entire population of users, depending on the numbers involved. As a general rule you should avoid asking open questions in a questionnaire as they are difficult to analyse in large numbers, and people are often reluctant or unable to provide unambiguous or complete responses, even if the wording of the questions is itself unambiguous, which is notoriously difficult to achieve.

The types of closed question that are most commonly used include the following:

- **Numeric.** In a numeric question the respondent is asked to answer with a number. For example, 'On average, how many times a day do you refer to the stock listing report?'

- **Range.** Respondents are asked to state which range or category they fit into. For example, the question in the previous paragraph might be easier to answer if respondents are asked to place themselves in one of several bands, such as 0, 1–2, 3–5, 5–10, over 10. In using a range question you need to be careful that all possibilities are covered, that the bands are not too broad or too narrow, and that there are not too many options.

- **Ranking.** A number of options are presented to users, who are asked to put them in order of preference. For example, you might be considering several methods for distributing a report (paper, e-mail, website, etc.), and wish to establish the preferences of users.

- **Selection.** In a selection respondents are presented with a list of items, and asked to indicate which items (if any) apply to them. For example, in trying to establish the familiarity of users with various types of technology, you could ask respondents to indicate if they are regular users of websites, e-mail, text messaging, etc.

- **Scale.** In a scale question respondents are asked to indicate, usually by circling a point on a line, where they lie along a scale, such as from 1 to 5, low to high, 0–100%.

In addition to tightly defined closed questions of the types listed above, you can add comment boxes for respondents to add further information that they feel is relevant to the question being asked. This is usually done by adding an 'other, please specify' option to a list or range question.

If you do choose to ask open questions in a questionnaire it is essential that they are tightly focused and clear, as you do not have the opportunity that exists within an interview to clarify your questions or the respondents' answers. You should avoid any use of broad questions, such as 'what would you like the new system to do?' While this is a reasonable opening question in an unstructured interview, you will find that the responses in a questionnaire will be far too brief to be at all useful.

Table 7.7 provides a checklist for the production and administration of questionnaires for use in investigating system requirements. For a full discussion of research questionnaires you should refer to a business research text such as Saunders *et al.* (2003).

Questionnaires are most useful when there is a large and distributed population whose behaviour and views are difficult to assess using other techniques. They can also be effective in circumstances where there is no existing system, and you wish to collect data on the priorities and likely take-up rate for your proposed system. However, the creation and analysis of an effective questionnaire is both difficult and time consuming, and response rates are often disappointing. You can improve response rates by delivering and collecting questionnaires in person, or by asking the questions face-to-face or by telephone. Nevertheless, in a student project your time is invariably better spent using other techniques that encourage open dialogue, and enable you to probe for details.

7.7 Workshops

If handled correctly, workshops can be an extremely effective and rapid way of identifying and investigating system requirements. For this reason, they are regarded as fundamental to the success of many RAD projects. In a well-run workshop a number of interested and informed parties are brought together and

Table 7.7 Checklist for producing and administering a questionnaire

☑ Assess the information you wish to gather, and confirm that questionnaires are the only viable approach (they rarely are).

☑ Draw up a set of closed questions, and double check for clarity and precision. Note that the number of questions that you can ask within a single questionnaire is relatively small, as response rates will drop quickly if your questionnaire takes much longer than 15–20 minutes to complete.

☑ Design an answering mechanism (e.g. range, scale) that allows for a full set of responses.

☑ Ensure that any open questions are tightly focused and unambiguous.

☑ Design your questionnaire layout, ensuring that:

- Questions are well spaced out, and the response boxes are clearly identifiable
- A plain and formal 10 or 12 point font (such as Times Roman or Arial) has been used
- The opening questions are easy to answer and non-controversial
- Questions are numbered to aid analysis
- A brief introduction and clear instructions for returning your questionnaire have been given
- Anonymity is assured.

☑ Test your questionnaire on fellow students or a small sample of respondents.

☑ Select your sample, bearing in mind that response rates may be as low as 20%, even if issued with management backing within an organisation.

☑ Design your distribution method. Face-to-face and telephone questionnaires have the best response rate but are labour intensive. E-mail and postal questionnaires have better response rates than web-based questionnaires, but take time to address and collate. Web-based questionnaires are useful when respondents are external to the organisation(s) concerned, and where addressing is difficult.

☑ Ensure that you have permission to distribute your questionnaire.

☑ Distribute your questionnaires, and chase up a few days before your collection or return date. If using e-mail or postal distribution, include a brief letter of introduction.

☑ Analyse your returns as soon as possible, even if you are expecting more responses. Analysis always takes longer than you think.

encouraged to discuss, exchange and debate their views and ideas. Because this is happening in an open manner, the people involved are inclined to share their ideas and to feed off the ideas of others. The result is a rich and creative set of requirements that have been thoroughly explored by experts in their field, and that have a degree of consensus that would have been time consuming to achieve had they been identified in one-to-one situations.

The major drawback of workshops is that they require a great deal of planning and, more significantly, a higher level of skill than other investigative techniques in order to work well. If handled badly, workshops can descend into acrimonious disputes, can become sidetracked or may even be hijacked by one participant. Students rarely have the skills and experience to run workshops that have the potential to be contentious or involve large numbers of participants. However, as many student projects are relatively uncontroversial and small in scale, workshops will often be a useful supplement to other investigative techniques, given the right preparation and the right mix of attendees.

Workshops can be used for a number of purposes during the life of a project (we have already looked briefly at their use in brainstorming ideas for project topics in Chapter 2). While their most common use is to provide a rapid initial view of system requirements from a range of viewpoints at the beginning of your investigation, they can also be used to explore potential solutions, to confirm that you have fully understood all of the requirements, to assign priorities to the set of requirements, and to walk through your proposed or prototype solution. Regardless of when you use them, workshops invariably help to create a sense of ownership of the final system among users, which can be invaluable in managing its acceptance.

In many projects workshops can form the basis of a key academic or personal objective, as few students will have had the opportunity to experience running a real workshop during their studies.

Preparing for a workshop

It is often claimed that the best way to prepare yourself for taking an active part in running a workshop is to observe an experienced facilitator in action. If you have the opportunity to do this, then you should grab it. However, the reality is that few students will be able to sit in on a real-life workshop in this way. Instead you will need to rely on role-playing exercises. If you are part of a group project then this will be much easier, as you can set up some small-scale workshops using members of your team as the main participants, supplemented with fellow students if your group is small. If you are undertaking an individual project, then you should try to enlist the help of fellow students, at least one of whom will need to assist you in the running of the real workshop as described below.

The best role-playing workshops will involve a similar number of participants to your real workshop, and you should attempt to set up the room in a similar fashion. It is not necessary to base your role-playing exercises around the same sort of topic. Indeed, it is better to choose a topic that all participants have some real-life experience of, for example planning a perfect holiday, choosing a university course, finding your ideal accommodation.

Setting an agenda

As with interviews you need to set clear objectives for your workshops (see Section 7.4). You should then create a highly structured agenda around these objectives, consisting of a series of activities or discussions designed to meet your objectives. These activities may include discussions, brainstorming exercises or walkthroughs, and should be set up in such a way that they encourage participation from all your attendees. Unless you are very experienced, you should not attempt to construct your agenda 'on the fly'. While most workshops will throw up a few unexpected topics that you will need to explore as and when they arise, it is difficult to control an entire workshop on this basis.

In putting your agenda together, try to avoid posing too many questions that can be answered quickly, without debate. Instead, you should identify a small number of open-ended questions that will take between 15 minutes and an hour to discuss. If questions take less than 15 minutes to debate, then they will tend to be dominated by one or two more vocal attendees, or result in closed answers. Conversely, if they take longer than an hour then they are too large in scope, and will be difficult to bring to a conclusion. Even one hour may be too long if attendees are unused to this type of exercise, so you may wish to consider breaking them up into smaller topics that are closer to a 30-minute maximum. As a general rule you should not use closed questions in a workshop, unless you can work them into a more general discussion as an aside.

While the objectives of requirements investigation workshops vary enormously, Table 7.8 represents a commonly used overall framework that can be adapted to suit a range of situations.

Workshop roles and invitees

Workshops are extremely difficult to manage on your own. The level of interaction and the speed of information disclosure make it almost impossible to facilitate the process and capture information at the same time. Even if you are able to interview the workshop, you will not be able to note issues that come up during the proceedings for further exploration later on; a process that is critical to the success of a workshop.

As a minimum, you will need one person to act as a scribe or note-taker, and one as the facilitator of the workshop. Ideally, you will have two or more note-takers who will then also be able to prompt the facilitator with issues and follow-up questions that they may not have picked up during the cut and thrust of the debate. In a group project, this should be easy to organise, and if you are carrying out more than one workshop you should try to rotate the roles (do not, however, rotate roles within a single workshop, as this will severely interrupt the flow of the discussions).

The most important role is that of facilitator, who is responsible for ensuring that the workshop is as productive as possible. Guidelines for carrying out the facilitation role are given in the next section.

In considering which people you are going to invite to a workshop you should apply a similar set of criteria as you would for selecting interviewees. However, there are some other practical considerations that are specific to workshops:

- **Mix of experience and responsibilities.** It is important to invite a proper cross-section of users; otherwise you will not get a full range of views. In particular, you should try to ensure that all parts of the organisation that will be directly affected by your project are represented.
- **Seniority.** In some organisations, you may experience problems if attendees have different levels of seniority. In hierarchical organisations junior members may feel unable to express their true opinions if they contradict those of their

Table 7.8 Framework for structuring a requirements investigation workshop

Introductions	As well as introducing yourselves and your attendees, you will also need to outline your agenda and the rules of the workshop. You may want to include an ice-breaker if the attendees are not well known to each other. For example, you could pair up the attendees (including yourself), and ask them to talk with their partner for 5 minutes, and then introduce each other to the rest of the group, including one interesting fact about them that no one else will know.
High-level opening	It is a good idea to adopt a top-down approach, with broader topics being covered first, followed by more focused topics as the workshop progresses. A common approach is to open with a general question or discussion that will draw out a contribution from everyone, such as: ■ What are the ten things that you most like/dislike about the current system? ■ What are your top ten requirements or expectations for the new system? ■ Describe a typical day/morning ■ Describe the steps/tasks in walking through a key process ■ Describe the life cycle of a specific document/piece of information/supplier/customer/product, etc. ■ What is the first thing you do with the current system on a Monday morning?
Focused topics and questions	This is where you move through the topics and questions that you have designed to meet your objectives for the workshop.
Review and conclusions	Depending on the length of your workshop, you may need to review your findings and agree your conclusions at several points during the workshop. One idea is to break the workshop into 2-hour chunks, and conduct a 10–15-minute review after each one.
Follow-up	At the end of the workshop you should inform attendees about what will happen to your findings and what the next steps in your project are.

managers or other more senior attendees. To overcome this you may need to organise more than one workshop, in order to draw out the ideas and views of people from different levels across the organisation.

■ **Geographical spread.** If you are undertaking a project for a client that covers a large geographical area, you may need to hold workshops at different locations in order to cover the organisation fully.

■ **Potential alienation of non-invitees.** In order to keep the number of attendees down to manageable levels you may need to exclude some people who might otherwise have had a role to play in the workshop, and who may feel resentful at being left out. If you fear that this is the case, you should interview the individual concerned *prior to the workshop*, and make it clear that they were excluded for purely practical reasons.

It can prove difficult to find a date that is convenient for all of your invitees to attend a workshop, especially as the time involved is usually much longer than for an interview. To minimise these problems you should try to organise the workshop in plenty of time, otherwise you will face a last-minute struggle to schedule the workshop, and may be forced to shorten it or make changes to your attendees.

Once you have settled on a firm agenda, you should send an outline of it to all attendees, together with information on the date, the location, practical arrangements such as the dress code and refreshments. By informing attendees about what is expected of them, you will help to put them at their ease, and give them the opportunity to think in advance about the topic and to collect together any relevant documents that they feel may be relevant.

Conducting a workshop

The location for your workshop should be as free from interruptions as possible (including mobile phones), and should ideally be away from your attendees' normal place of work, although this may prove impractical. The room should have a whiteboard and/or flipchart board, plus space on the walls for completed flipchart sheets. A common arrangement is to place seating in a semi-circle, possibly around a U-shaped table, as in Figure 7.2.

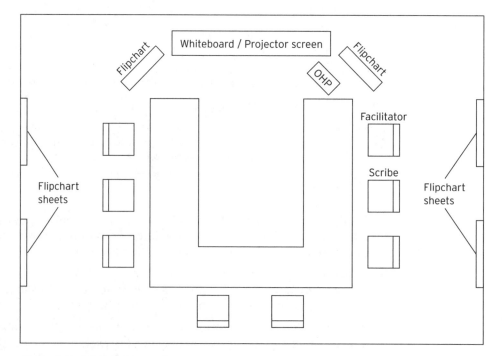

Figure 7.2 Workshop room layout

In addition to the workshop agenda, you will need to create a set of rules to ensure that the workshop runs as smoothly as possible. There are a number of 'golden rules' that are commonly adopted by workshops:

- Everyone's views are valid.
- No criticism of people or ideas.
- Every idea counts.
- One person speaks at a time.
- The agenda must be followed.
- Disagreement should be accepted.

If you are acting as the facilitator (and in most cases you will be), it is your job to ensure that the workshop runs smoothly and sticks to the agenda. It is also your responsibility to draw out the views and ideas of all of the attendees, even if they appear reluctant at first. This can stretch your interpersonal skills to the limit, but there is little point in organising a workshop if its attendees fail to engage in the debate. Table 7.9 presents the key responsibilities and tasks of a facilitator.

It is important to remember at all times during a requirements investigation workshop that you should not be an active contributor and should remain unbiased at all times. The purpose of the workshop is to gather information, not to sell your ideas. Later on in your project you may use workshops as a tool to present and refine solutions, in which case you as the facilitator will have a slightly different set of objectives, which may include communicating the benefits of your solution. Nevertheless, the workshop will still primarily be held to encourage the true views of participants to come out, rather than to sell your system in the face of genuine concerns.

In most workshops you will use a variety of devices for capturing the proceedings, including handwritten notes, flipchart sheets, OHP acetates and whiteboards. You may also be able to use more technically sophisticated tools such as video cameras or laptop computers. However, you must be sure that such tools will not interfere with the workshop process, and that you or your scribes

Table 7.9 Responsibilities and tasks of a workshop facilitator

Task	Comment
Control the agenda	You should steer the workshop so that it sticks to the subject matter of the agenda. However, you must allow for some divergence as important asides may come up, and to close debate down prematurely may risk missing significant new facts. If you stick too rigidly to your planned timings, you may also fail to explore some issues in the depth that they deserve. This will also risk disrupting the momentum of the workshop. The agenda should include regular breaks, as workshops can often get quite intense, and you need to avoid workshop fatigue. Frequent breaks also provide attendees with an opportunity to make telephone calls and to pick up messages.
Maintain momentum	Your objectives will include maintaining the flow and momentum of the workshop. However, if you feel the workshop is becoming bogged down or

Table 7.9   (*Cont'd*)

Task	Comment
	sidetracked, you may need to call an unscheduled 'time-out', in order to break out of the topic, and to give you a chance to rethink how to get the workshop back on track. You should think in advance about what to do if you start to fall badly behind schedule. It is far better to drop less important questions than to try to rush your interviewee's answers.
Coach and encourage participants	The two most common problems with regard to participation are the dominance of one individual, and the reluctance of attendees take an active part in the workshop. If one person is dominating the workshop, then you need to address the issue during a break. For example, by asking them for help in drawing other people into the debate. If you notice that an individual is not really engaging in the discussions, then encourage them by directing some easy questions at them, or refer to one of the points that they have made earlier.
Identify key issues and conclusions	As soon as you identify significant new ideas you should clarify that you understand them fully, and ensure that they are noted by your scribes.
Identify new leads	While you need to guard against the workshop being sidetracked unnecessarily, you should also be open to new ideas or issues that you had not anticipated.
Aid communication	In some circumstances you may be dealing with a system that will introduce unfamiliar terminology to some of your attendees. You may also need to discuss some technical issues in terms that are not commonly used within the business. You must explain all such terminology and ensure that your attendees have understood it.
Mediate in disagreements	Attempt to resolve misunderstandings. Where genuine disagreement exists, then you may be unable to guide the debate to a point of total agreement. In this case you should not allow the workshop to degenerate into an argument. Instead, if one person is clearly 'outvoted' by the others you should try to encourage that individual to accept the needs or views of the majority. Alternatively, you should make a note of the unresolved issue on a flipchart sheet entitled 'parked issues'. You should then revisit the parked issues before each break. In most cases you will find that parked issues can be resolved quite quickly in the light of further information that has been uncovered since the original debate, and once the heat has gone from an issue. If you are left with any unresolved issues at the end of the workshop you should follow them up outside the workshop, in interviews or via e-mail or the telephone.
Capture, summarise and present information	You should take care to note all of the main points that arise, and to keep them on prominent display, if possible by sticking completed flipcharts to the walls of your workshop room.
Guide the group to conclusions	You should do this by asking the group to come to their own conclusion by asking questions such as 'is there a consensus on this issue?' You should not attempt to prejudice conclusions by imposing your own views of which idea is best.
Organise and manage the workshop facilities	It is the responsibility of the facilitator (backed up by other members of the project team) to make sure that the workshop room is properly fitted out, that refreshments are available, etc. Once the workshop is under way there may be requests for additional facilities.

are able to operate them effectively. Typing notes directly into a laptop computer is more difficult than you might think, especially if a lot of the information is being generated using brainstorming techniques. People are often put off if video cameras are used, and the analysis of video recordings is also very time consuming. So if you plan to use a video camera you must check in advance that your attendees are comfortable with this, be sure that you really will benefit from its use, and set it up carefully.

The discussion process (GRAS)

For each of the major items on your workshop you should consider adopting the following process:

1. **<u>G</u>enerate ideas.** Invite your participants to contribute ideas or views on the topic, perhaps using brainstorming techniques (see Box 2.1), such as pasting Post-it™ notes on the wall, or by asking each participant to call out in turn. Do not attempt to filter or analyse the ideas as they are generated, as this will stifle the creative process. At this stage you are looking for as many views and thoughts as possible, however 'off the wall' or contentious they are.

2. **<u>R</u>ationalise.** Examine the ideas *briefly*, and eliminate any duplicates by asking your attendees if they believe them to be the same, not by imposing your views (unless the wording is identical). Try to ensure that each idea is worded so that everyone can understand it. Group the ideas into themes, so that you can analyse them in similar batches.

3. **<u>A</u>nalyse.** Take each idea and discuss it so that you understand its meaning and the entire group has had the opportunity to add their views to it. You should guide the group into a discussion about the validity of each idea, whether any can be combined, and what their priority is. Some ideas will emerge with the support of everyone and with a high level of significance attached to them. You should ensure that these are documented prominently, both in your notes and on a visible flipchart sheet. If the ideas or views relate to existing systems, your attendees may be able to provide you with examples of relevant documents.

4. **<u>S</u>ummarise.** As you finish the discussion of each major topic, you should quickly summarise what you believe has been concluded by the group. This gives your attendees the chance to add any final comments, and acts as a check that you have understood the information correctly.

The GRAS model has been tried and tested in countless professional workshops, and has the benefit of ensuring that a degree of rigour and discipline is imposed on what is essentially a creative and free-flowing process.

Following up a workshop

Workshops are quite different from other investigative techniques where notes can usually be analysed directly. The results of a workshop will usually be documented

Table 7.10 Checklist for planning and conducting a workshop

- ☑ Set objectives, ensuring that a workshop is most appropriate information-gathering technique
- ☑ Identify potential attendees from across the organisation
- ☑ Check that the culture of the organisation will enable all potential attendees to contribute fully (e.g. are at a similar level, or are from a non-hierarchical organisation)
- ☑ Consider whether to hold more than one workshop (beware of the time involved in doing so)
- ☑ Make appointments with all attendees well in advance
- ☑ Identify and book a suitable location and facilities
- ☑ Create an agenda and send a copy to all attendees, together with details of where and when the workshop is to take place
- ☑ Enlist the help of other students as note-takers (non-group project)
- ☑ Practise and rehearse holding a workshop with fellow students
- ☑ Set up the room with appropriate seating and tools, such as flipcharts and whiteboards
- ☑ Start the workshop with introductions (possibly including an ice-breaker) and a broad discussion topic that encourages full participation
- ☑ Adopt the GRAS process for exploring each of your major topics
- ☑ Write up and review your notes as soon as possible after the workshop
- ☑ Send copies of the output to all attendees, and clarify any outstanding issues

in several different forms, such as flipcharts, Post-it™ notes, whiteboard photographs and written notes. In order to make sense of them, you will need to bring them together in a single document. This can be quite a lengthy and intensive process, and should be done as soon as possible after the workshop (preferably on the same day), while the verbal discussions are still clear in your mind.

Once you have written up the notes, you should circulate a copy to your attendees, so that they can correct any misunderstandings, or add to points that they feel have not been fully captured during the rough and tumble of the workshop.

Table 7.10 provides a checklist for planning and conducting a workshop.

7.8 Defining and recording requirements

In any system development project you will need to produce a definition of requirements that will act as a comprehensive statement of what the new system is required to do, and to what level it will need to perform. If, as in most projects, you are replacing an existing system, or mimicking some of an existing system (this is often the case in an academic project where there is not a real client, but where you are basing your application at least in part on systems that have been developed elsewhere), your requirements definition will consist of two parts:

1. A textual description and/or models of the functions and data of the existing system.
2. A description of the required improvements, features and performance characteristics that the new system will need to deliver in addition to those provided by the existing system.

In the requirements definition you are not primarily concerned with how the requirements are to be satisfied, although during your investigations you will inevitably have given some thought to how the requirements might fit together into a coherent system, and about how certain problems might be overcome.

The need for requirements definition

A requirements definition document or statement is a feature of every system development approach (what vary from method to method are the techniques used to produce it), and for good reason. To develop a system or application without a clear idea of what it needs to do will inevitably lead to a system that is unfit for its intended purpose. It rather like setting out on a journey without a clear destination.

The definition of requirements will be critical to the success of your project, as it will provide the foundation for your entire system, so it is important not to just pay lip service to it. Sadly, many students fail to realise that without a proper statement of requirements there is no way that they or anyone else, including their assessors, can be confident that the software they develop is fit for anything, other than to prove that they can use a programming tool.

Note that your aim in defining requirements is *not* to justify some prechosen solution or a piece of software that you have already produced. To base a system development on an assumption that you already know implicitly what the software needs to do displays an ignorance of the system development process. If you try to use your requirements definition in this way, it is certain to be detected in a viva voce examination, and will invalidate your system development approach, leading to possible failure. Just as importantly, it will deny you the opportunity to experience and learn from the application of a proper and considered development process. Remember too that you are likely to receive a much higher mark for a simple application that has been developed in a rigorous manner to meet well-thought-through requirements, than for a piece of software developed on a whim, however flashy it looks.

Types of requirement

There are two types of system requirement, both of which you will need to define fully in order to produce a complete picture of what your development will need to deliver:

Functional requirements

Functional requirements define in some detail what the system needs to do, and cover the following areas:

- **Data.** Data lie at the heart of any information system. You need to capture details about what data the system will need to store and process, ensuring that you have understood fully their meaning, structure and source. Data items are rarely as simple as they might first appear from the high-level view that comes across from interviews and casual observation. At first you will concentrate on the major items of data, which will reflect the key concepts that support the business. As you begin to investigate more deeply, you will uncover large numbers of lower-level data items, often in the form of status, financial control and classification or descriptive attributes.

- **Processing.** Processing requirements will describe most of the things that the system will need to do with the data. This covers the processes that create, update and delete data, as well as those that enquire or report on the data. In many systems the number of enquiry processes will outnumber the update processes. It is important to capture enough detail to make it clear to users that you have understood *fully* what your system will need to do. This means gathering a lot more detail than a bland and generic functional heading, such as 'register new members'. The issue of what details you should record is discussed in detail in the next two sections.

- **Facilities and features.** You will also need to record any special facilities and features that your system will need to provide, including tools such as calculators and/or message boards and user interface features such as customisable tool bars.

- **Algorithms.** Your system may need to make use of specialised or prespecified algorithms, such as those that estimate sales demand for products, or carry out tax calculations. This may involve making use of commercial software components.

- **User interfaces.** The precise layout and full specification of user interfaces is usually completed as part of the design phase. However, users are often able to explain their interface requirements most clearly using physical sketches or samples (which is why prototyping is such a powerful tool). Your requirements definition may therefore include some suggested designs as part of specifying their processing requirements. At the very least, your requirements definition should contain information on the data content of user interfaces.

- **System interfaces.** Student projects all too often focus on user interfaces to the exclusion of almost everything else. However, in most commercial projects system-to-system interfaces are just as significant, if not more so. While it is true that student projects are more likely than commercial projects to involve the development of a stand-alone system, many will need to provide or receive data from other systems. If you are unable to request or make changes to the systems you need to interface with, you will need to document precisely what those systems require from you or can provide for you. If changes to other systems are possible, then you need to record at an early stage the required content, format and timings of the interfaces, as any changes will need to be agreed well in advance with the relevant system owners.

Non-functional requirements

Non-functional requirements describe the performance and constraints that your system should meet. Most non-functional requirements apply to one or more specific functional requirements, and provide information that will inform the way in which you design and build the necessary system support. The most common of these requirements cover the following:

- **Capacity or volumes.** Some of the biggest factors in deciding how a system function or database component is designed are the volume of data, number of users and frequency of access or update. For example, if your system needs to report on an item of data with just a dozen occurrences once a day, your solution may be very different from a solution for reporting on a data item that occurs many thousands of times and is accessed hundreds of times a day.

- **Speed.** Response times are another factor that will influence your solution to a specific requirement. For example, an on-line query that will be used when answering customer service calls over the telephone will need to run quickly, and therefore will need to be carefully optimised, whereas a daily report that is used for occasional reference purposes throughout the day may run more slowly, or even as a background off-line task that completes in time for the start of work each morning.

- **Usability.** Some processes and interfaces will need to be easy to use without any formal training, such as web pages that are accessed by the customers of a website. Others, especially those that are used day in and day out by expert users, can be built with efficiency rather than ease of use in mind. For example, if you are designing a screen that will be used by people to enter large volumes of data all day, you should not design it to step them through the process window by window with lots of descriptive text and pictures. Instead you should design it so that users can enter the data with the minimum number of keystrokes or mouse clicks, and with as little unnecessary text and clutter on view as possible. Where possible, usability requirements should be specified in terms that can be measured and tested in some way, for example 'must be usable with 90 per cent success rate by an average operator after 1 hour of training'.

- **Availability.** Some areas of the system may need to be available for longer periods or at different times to others. For example, a month-end accounting report may be needed on-line by 9am on the first day of each accounting period, while access to an order-tracking query might be needed from 8am to 8pm on Mondays to Fridays, except for Bank Holidays.

- **Access.** Access to some processes and data items will be restricted to certain types of user. You should aim to document these access restrictions at an early stage.

Try to be as precise as possible when defining performance-related requirements. It is all too easy to slip into the habit of attaching the same bland statements to each functional requirement, such as 'must be easy and efficient to use, capable of handling large volumes and have a short response time'. This is the kind of thing that many users will say in interview, and this should not surprise us, as in a perfect world this is just what we would like to produce. However, the reality is that in many circumstances these aims are mutually exclusive, and even if they were not, you would not have the time or budget to achieve them in all but the highest priority cases. By establishing what is really needed you should be able design solutions that are appropriate for the performance needs of each requirement.

The second group of non-functional requirements applies to the system or development as a whole:

- **Technical constraints and requirements.** Your project may need to meet specific infrastructure requirements, such as making use of specific hardware, software or suppliers. For example, you may be asked to reuse existing equipment, or build your system to run on a particular version of an operating system, or make use of a specified database management system (DBMS) or GUI.

- **Design constraints.** These may include design standards, such as a corporate look and feel for user interfaces, or required deliverables such as training materials or operating instructions.

- **Organisational constraints.** For example, you may need to take existing organisation structures into account in designing how to structure your system. You may also need to document particular training needs and constraints (such as standard methods or facilities). In many projects there will be organisational policies that will also drive certain elements of the system, such as standard credit arrangements (e.g. all invoices to be paid in 30 days).

- **Project constraints.** Your project will almost certainly have overall time and cost constraints, but it may also have restrictions on such things as when you will be able to implement your system. For example, few organisations are likely to allow system implementations during their busiest trading periods.

- **Transitional requirements.** Where you are replacing an existing system, you need to think about how you are going to get the data from the old system into your new system. It is rare for the data to be in an identical format in both systems, and you may need to design some conversion programs or manual translation procedures. These will need to be rigorously tested, as any errors in converting data will cause the new system to fail from the outset. You will also need to consider how to wind up the old system while introducing the new one. For example, in a system that deals with orders, you may decide that any existing orders should be completed using the old system, while any new orders are taken with the new one. Alternatively, you may decide to convert all existing orders over to the new system as soon as it goes live.

- **Security and back-up.** Surprisingly few students consider security and back-up requirements in any depth, if at all. If your project involves the development of a business information system it is an essential requirement to protect the data from unauthorised access. It is also important to build in a system for backing up and restoring the system and its data, for use in the event of system failure or data corruption.

The reasons for requirements

When identifying and analysing requirements it is helpful to consider why they arise:

- **Problems requiring resolution.** Such as software bugs, capacity constraints, and outdated process or data support. In a commercial project, most requirements will usually relate to the solution of existing problems.
- **New or changed functionality.** For example, to support new business processes and ventures, to fill existing data and process gaps, or to respond to changed organisational policies and structures.
- **Improvements.** Such as improved efficiency, increased availability, improved ease of use (and reduced training requirements) and streamlining of existing processes.
- **Technical issues.** Such as out-of-date hardware and software that is no longer supported, lack of reliability and poor performance.
- **Cosmetic changes.** For example to support new corporate standards, logos or marketing position.
- **Redundant features.** Such as support for data and processes that are no longer required by the business.
- **Interfacing system changes.** Changes that are necessary to support the implementation of a system that interfaces with yours (and may for example require new data or system interface procedures).

In many projects there will be an overriding reason for the development as a whole. For example, if a business makes a strategic decision to move into e-commerce it will need a project to develop and implement appropriate systems. However, within this project there will be a range of user requirements, some of which will be essential to the basic functioning of the system, such as support for passenger data in a flight booking system, and many more that are optional (i.e. the system could function without), such as city guides in the flight booking system.

It is important to analyse and document the reason for each functional requirement, even if this consists merely of a statement that the requirement is 'essential' for the system to function. Most requirements in real-world system will not, however, be essential in the strictest sense, but will be requested as they offer some benefit to the business. For these requirements you will need to define the benefit (ideally in financial terms), so that it can be taken into account when justifying the costs of meeting them.

What to record

A requirements definition document should consist of two things, both of which are essential to create a complete picture of what the system should

Table 7.11 Contents list for a requirements definition document

Item	Outline description
Overview	A short textual description of the scope and objectives of the system development. You may include a list of the key business processes that your system will cover, and an outline of its benefits.
Requirements summary	A prioritised list of system requirements. This will act as an index to your full Requirements Catalogue.
Requirements Catalogue	A detailed description of each requirement.
System models	Models of the existing system that you will be replacing (if there is one), plus high-level models of new system components. Detailed modelling of the new system is usually created only after the requirements that the new system will meet have been agreed with all interested parties. Models may include data and process models, Use Case diagrams and class models, depending on the approach being used. May also include prototypes.
Appendices	Any other significant documents, such as workshop output, related business studies.

deliver. Firstly there should be a textual description of the system requirements, and secondly there will be a set of models and diagrams, which may also include some early prototypes (models and prototypes are considered in Sections 7.9 and 7.10). The following pages cover suggestions about what you should include in your requirements definition document, while Table 7.11 provides a suggested contents list.

Many students are reluctant to use text as a way of capturing and communicating requirements, largely because of the focus that most courses place on modelling techniques. However, the reason for this focus is *not* that text is unimportant, but that modelling is conceptually difficult and unfamiliar to students. Modelling also requires a depth of theoretical understanding and intellectual rigour that needs to be carefully developed within the classroom, in a way that is unnecessary for text.

In reality, however, text is an essential tool for defining requirements in a way that is easily understood and commented on by people outside the analysis team. It is also the best (or only) mechanism for capturing non-functional requirements, problem descriptions, requirements justifications, subjective opinions, business policies, cost information and a wide range of constraints. If the reader has knowledge of the problem domain, text also needs little training beyond an explanation of technical terms and acronyms. For all of these reasons text is a powerful tool, and one that, despite the drawbacks of relying solely on text, still predominates in the real world; one study conducted in 1992 suggested that up to 80 per cent of requirements definition documents use text alone (Bray, 2002).

Models are vitally important to the definition of requirements too (see Section 7.9), especially as part of an academically rigorous project. But they should be viewed as an *essential supplement* to the textual descriptions, and not as a substitute for them.

Requirements Catalogue

The term Requirements Catalogue has been borrowed from SSADM in order to differentiate it from the overall requirement definition document. In other methods the Requirements Catalogue may be known by different names, such as requirements definition, requirements list and so on. However, regardless of what you choose to call it, the items recorded in a Requirements Catalogue will be similar to those listed in Table 7.12. In academic projects, such as those that involve complex programming, the number of requirements will generally be smaller, and you will not need to record some of the more business-oriented items, such as benefits.

While the format of the Requirements Catalogue is secondary to its content, you should still put some thought into how to structure it, ensuring that it is easy to read, logical and above all consistent. Figure 7.3 illustrates a 'one page per requirement' format. This is a fairly common approach in large commercial projects, where there will large numbers of fairly complex requirements, which are easier to organise in this way. It is also the format that most CASE tools use when printing the catalogue.

Figure 7.4 shows a tabular approach to organising a Requirements Catalogue. This is more suitable for smaller development, and is ideal for most student projects (your supervisor will certainly thank you for presenting requirements in a more space-efficient manner). Note that you still need to cover all of the information in Table 7.12, so you will need to merge some items (such as issues and description), rather than listing them in separate columns, as you might with a 'one page per requirement' format.

As well as a full Requirements Catalogue you should produce a simple summary or table listing all your requirements, as shown in Figure 7.5. The summary will act as an index to the full catalogue, but will also be a useful document in its own right, as it will be far easier to refer to in discussions with users and your supervisor than a long and necessarily wordy document. Do not feel tempted, however, to produce the summary alone, as it does not contain anywhere near enough information to base the design of the system on.

How much detail do you need to record?

One of the most common questions that students ask in some form or other is 'how much detail do I need to record?', to which the tempting answer is always 'how long is a piece of string?' The reality is that there is no easy answer to this question. Each project will have different needs, depending on its complexity, size and the state of the existing systems. For instance, if there is an existing

Table 7.12 Contents of a Requirements Catalogue entry

Item	Description
Identifier	It is useful to give each requirement a unique number, as it will make it easy to refer to them elsewhere.
Name or short description	A single sentence only.
Full description	The full description may consist purely of text, but it may also include formulae, pictures, flowcharts, or even subsets of system models.
Issues and outstanding questions	At any one time you are likely to have a significant number of requirements that you still need further information about. You may also have questions about the real benefits, validity or priority of a requirement.
Priority	An indication of whether the requirement is essential, desirable (i.e. important, but the system would be viable without it), or nice to have (i.e. useful, if it can be delivered with little cost or impact on the overall project). You need to be a little careful when assigning priorities as people have a natural tendency to classify all requirements relevant to themselves as essential.
Source	A description of where the requirement came from, such as a specific interview, company document, literature source or workshop.
Owner	The person responsible for agreeing that the requirement has been properly defined (and subsequently delivered). In a student project the same person (such as the supervisor or client contact) will often be responsible for agreeing all of the requirements, so this item will be unnecessary.
Non-functional requirements	A list of any non-functional requirements applicable to this requirement, e.g. volumes, response times.
Benefits	It is not necessary or feasible for every requirement to have an individually identifiable benefit or justification. Some will be needed for the system as a whole to function properly and therefore deliver the overall benefits of the project. Where requirements are not strictly essential for the operation of the system, you should try to provide a justification for their inclusion in the final solution. If possible the benefits should be measurable (ideally they should have a financial value), but this is often not possible.
Suggested solutions	Any ideas that you or others have for satisfying the requirement should be noted down as they are suggested, as too many good ideas are lost by neglecting to record them. This may include a manual solution, or keeping a component of the existing system.
Related documents	These may include documents such as your notes, sketches of report or screen layouts, formal system models (e.g. data and process models, class models and Use Case diagrams), and current system documentation. If the functional requirement relates to data, then the best approach is to provide a summary of the data requirement in the Requirements Catalogue together with a link to a data dictionary or to entity descriptions.
Resolution	Notes on how the requirement was satisfied. This may consist merely of a comment that the requirement was met in full by the system, or it may name the system component (such as a particular report or querying facility) that satisfied it. If you subsequently decide that the requirement is not to be implemented, or its implementation is to be deferred to another project, you should record the reason.

Requirements Catalogue Entry	
Requirement number	2
Requirement name	Register new member
Description	Potential members apply for membership using a standard form (sample attached). The system should record the details using a simple on-line form.
	The system should check that the applicant has not been barred previously. It should also suggest other services and facilities that the applicant might be interested in.
	If the applicant has made a previous enquiry their name and address details should be called up from the database.
	The system will not be expected to process payment directly (this will still be done using the till).
	Once details have been entered a confirmation page should be printed for the new member (current layout produced by word processor is attached).
Priority	Essential
Source	Interviews with head receptionist, admin clerk and junior receptionist (C. Hodge). Examination of current forms and procedures.
Owner	Club manager (TS)
Non-functional requirements	Required on-line from 8.00 until 22.00, Monday to Saturday, and 8.00 until 20.00 Sunday.
	Average is 12 new members per week.
	Must be designed for fast data entry.
Issues and outstanding questions	Clarify where historical data on barred members is held.
Comments/suggested solutions	Needs to be on a single screen, and mirror the layout of the paper form completed by the applicant in order to aid data entry.
Benefits	Mandatory requirement – records core system data. New members can also be fully processed on the spot. Currently the member's details are typed into a spreadsheet in batches at the end of the day, and confirmation letters produced by a mail merge and then posted.
Related documents	Application form (to be retained in current form) and current confirmation letter – both attached.
Resolution	TBC

Figure 7.3 Entry from Requirements Catalogue for sports centre membership system

#	Pri	Owner	Name	Description	Non-functional Requirements	Benefits/Suggested or actual solution
1	D	TS	Record membership enquiry	The system should record the details (names, addresses, telephone numbers and e-mail addresses) of people who request membership information (as per the attached handwritten form – sample 1).	Required on-line from 8.00 until 22.00, Monday to Saturday, and 8.00 until 20.00 Sunday.	Benefits: Will speed up new member registration. Enables follow-up of enquiries.
2	E	TS	Register new member	Potential members apply for membership using a standard form (sample 2 attached). The system should record the details using a simple on-line form. The system should check that the applicant has not been barred previously. It should also suggest other services and facilities that the applicant might be interested in. If the applicant has made a previous enquiry their name and address details should be called up from the database. The system will not be expected to process payment directly (this will still be done using the till). Once details have been entered a confirmation page should be printed for the new member (current layout produced by word processor is attached – sample 3). Source: Interviews with head receptionist, admin clerk and junior receptionist (C. Hodge). Examination of current forms and procedures. Note: Clarify where historical data on barred members is held.	Required on-line from 8.00 until 22.00, Monday to Saturday, and 8.00 until 20.00 Sunday. Average is 12 new members per week. Must be designed for fast data entry.	Benefits: Mandatory requirement – records core system data. New members can also be fully processed on the spot. Currently the member's details are typed into a spreadsheet in batches at the end of the day, and confirmation letters produced by a mail merge and then posted. Solution: Needs to be on a single screen, and mirror the layout of the paper form completed by the applicant in order to aid data entry.
3	D	TS	Weekly new members report	The system should automatically print a report every Sunday evening listing new members from the previous week (possible layout in sample 4).	Overnight (off-line report).	Benefits: Aids monitoring of trends and success of advertising.

Figure 7.4 Tabular Requirements Catalogue format

Requirements Summary			
#	Pri	Owner	Name
1	D	TS	Record membership enquiry
2	E	TS	Register new member
3	D	TS	Weekly new members report
4	E	TS	Full membership report - on-line and printed
5	E	TS	Membership renewal reminders
6	D	TS	Membership enquiry follow-up report

Figure 7.5   Requirements summary extract

system and much of the functionality will be replicated in the new system you will be able to capture many of the details of the required functionality by modelling the current system. Your Requirements Catalogue will then need to identify what is to be replicated, and provide more detailed information on what is to be added or improved.

The purpose of the Requirements Catalogue is to capture a complete picture of what is required, and to a level of detail that enables your client and/or supervisor to be confident that you are in a position to begin designing and building a suitable solution. One indication of that you have reached the necessary level of detail is when you find yourself adding information that is really related to *how* the system will be built, rather than *what* it will need to do.

A test that you can apply to your requirements definition as a whole is to ask yourself (or your supervisor) the following question:

> 'If I gave this requirements definition, complete with my system models, to another student, would they be able to use it to begin the design of an appropriate system?'

Sadly, a significant proportion of the requirements documents produced in student projects are woefully inadequate. In many cases they list a small number of requirements, which barely cover the scope of the project, and to a level of detail similar to that of the requirements summary in Figure 7.5. No business system is so simple that its requirements can be defined on half a sheet of A4 paper (as is the case in a surprisingly large number of student projects). When asked to list her requirements for a birthday party, my 8-year-old daughter managed twice this level of detail.

Some students suffer from the opposite problem, and find it hard to call a halt to the process of adding detail to the Requirements Catalogue. It is always possible to make adjustments and improvements to your textual descriptions, even if these consist merely of improved grammar or formatting. The best solution to this problem is to impose a timebox on the requirements definition process. In order to get the most out of the timebox you should then attempt to balance your effort equally across all areas of your investigation, rather than perfecting one area at the expense of others. The management of timeboxed activities can be quite tricky, so this is an area you should discuss in detail with your supervisor.

Box 7.3

Example of poorly defined Requirements Catalogue

The following example is taken from a real-life student project concerning the development of a booking system for a boat hire company. The student in this case submitted a Requirements Catalogue that consisted of a list of ten high-level features that the system needed to support. Taking just one of the listed requirements, it is quickly apparent that this level of detail is nowhere near sufficient to act as the basis for the design of the system.

Requirements Catalogue:

1. Process boat hire requests using a PC-based system.
2. Produce reports of most popular types of boat.
3. Print invoices for boat hires.
4. Capture payment details.
5. Allow customers to cancel boat hires and process refunds.
6. Produce reports detailing regular customers.
7. Manage the fleet of boats, with details of which are available and which are not.
8. Print sheet of bookings for day ahead.
9. Print summary of bookings for week ahead.
10. Print mailing lists of past customers.

Every one of these requirements raises more questions than it answers about what the system needs to do. For example, looking at requirement 1, a number of questions immediately come to mind, such as:

■ How will requests be received?
■ Will the system cover advanced bookings, on the spot bookings, or both?
■ What data should be captured?
■ Will confirmation details be printed or reference numbers given to the customer?
■ How many requests will be received each day?
■ What time periods will hires be made for?
■ Can hire requests cover more than one boat or time period?
■ What customer details will need to be captured?
■ If customers hire a boat in person do they need to provide any details?
■ What payment methods will be accepted?
■ Is a deposit necessary for advance bookings?
■ How will repeat bookings be handled for existing customers?
■ Are there discounts for bulk hires?
■ Will business bookings be handled differently?
■ What equipment in addition to boats will customers be able to hire, if any?

And so on. A properly constructed Requirements Catalogue should provide the answers to all of these questions and more. It could do this through greatly expanded descriptions of the high-level requirements listed above, or by listing a much larger number of low-level requirements. The format is secondary; what matters is that the amount of detail captured is sufficient to start detailed design of the new system.

The final version of this Requirements Catalogue listed over 120 requirements, many of which included associated non-functional requirements and considerably more detail than shown above.

7.9   Modelling system requirements

In Section 7.8 we discussed the need to describe requirements in textual form as an essential aid to communication, and to capture details that are difficult to model using diagrammatic techniques. However, text on its own has a number of significant drawbacks, for example:

- Text is highly ambiguous, and open to different interpretations.
- It is difficult to show relationships between components of a system, such as objects, data items and processes.
- Text becomes very unwieldy once you need to describe logic, structure or flows, and is more difficult to modify than diagrams.
- Text usually requires careful reading of large amounts of text, even to gain a high-level view of system requirements.
- Developing textual descriptions is an open-ended and imprecise activity.

The two main approaches to overcoming these difficulties are to use models (based on diagrammatic notation) and to build system prototypes (see Section 7.10).

Regardless of the method or approach you have decided to adopt for your project, there will be a minimum set of models that you will need to develop at each stage of the life cycle. This book does not attempt to describe how individual models should be developed; it is assumed that you will have covered this during your studies, and there are other textbooks dealing with the detail of development methods (see the Bibliography). This section offers instead some general guidance and words of caution on applying models within the investigation phase of a student project.

Your use of system models must be consistent with the academic objectives of your project. You should try to explore fully the application of the method and techniques that you specified in your PID (or proposal). This means applying the techniques in a rigorous and relatively formal fashion. Many experienced and skilled analysts are instinctively able to modify established techniques in fairly radical ways to suit the needs of an individual project. As a student you are unlikely to have the experience and depth of understanding to do this. Indeed, one of your objectives should be to start the process of developing this understanding through a critical evaluation of the techniques and tools that you have used during your project.

While you may decide not to use a particular model or technique on the basis of detailed research and consultation with your supervisor, it is quite unacceptable to jump to conclusions in advance of developing a particular model, based on nothing more than gut feel or your limited experience of coursework. Many students report that their project is the first time they have appreciated the true purpose and worth of formal system models, as it is the first time they have applied them in a realistic context.

Current system models

Analysis models can be used to describe both the existing system and the required system. While few would argue with the need to model the required system in detail, there is a growing tendency for students to dismiss the use of current system models, possibly because of a mistaken belief that they have no place in projects using a RAD approach (see Table 7.13 below), or perhaps because of a natural desire to get on with the development of the required system.

Some authorities advocate the dropping of current system analysis, mainly because they believe it leads to a risk that the design of the new system will be constrained by current system design and practice. They are, however, outnumbered by those who believe that, if used with care, current system analysis has a number of benefits that will improve the efficiency and effectiveness of an investigation. These benefits include the following:

- Many of the functions and features of the existing system will need to be carried forward in the new system, albeit in a different physical form. Models are an extremely efficient and unambiguous way of capturing the underlying picture of what the current system does.

- Most new requirements will refer to problems or restrictions with the current system that need to be overcome. Users will usually express such requirements in terms of 'I want something just like this, but with the following changes . . .'

- Much of the data required by the new system will need to be imported from the old system.

- Complex algorithms or data structures are sometimes used but not well understood by users. Analysis of the current system documentation or source code will often enable you to model these elements fairly quickly, rather than attempting to reinvent them from scratch.

- An understanding of the current system will help you to understand the problem domain and to communicate with users during your requirements investigation.

- If you are undertaking a client-based project it is likely that your system will need to interface with other existing systems. By modelling current interfaces you will understand many of the requirements of your system-to-system interfaces.

- Some parts of the current system may need to be retained, particularly if you find that they support the business adequately at present.

While it is important to model current systems as part of your analysis of requirements you must never lose sight of the purpose of your project, which will usually be to implement new or improved system support. You should therefore aim to restrict the amount of time you spend on current system models by limiting the level of detail in some areas (notably those that you will be changing substantially in the new system), or perhaps by using timeboxes as discussed in Section 7.8.

Applying techniques during requirements analysis

The best approach to using models during your investigation is to begin to sketch them out as soon as you start to get a picture of how the current and/or required systems operate. Although they will be rough and ready at first, system models provide an excellent tool for highlighting areas that you need to look into further, and are in any case easier to modify as you go along than they are to draw from scratch towards the end of your investigation. For example, if you are following a structured method you should start to develop a high-level process or activity model using the findings of your initial document analysis or opening interview. As you try to complete the models you will discover gaps or areas that you are unable to resolve without further information. These gaps will then need to be covered in your next round of fact-gathering. You will also be able to use your initial models to confirm the scope of your project, to identify problems with current system support and to provide a structure for your subsequent interviews or observations.

At first you may prefer to draw your models by hand, as this will undoubtedly be quicker than using a CASE tool or flowcharting package while the changes you make from one version to another are fairly drastic. Very soon, however, your models will begin to stabilise and you will need to produce an electronic version, as they will be far easier to modify and manage in this form. If you have access to a CASE tool you can also use it to check the completeness and validity of your models. Few supervisors will be happy to mark hand-drawn models as part of your final report, as they are difficult to read and almost by definition will be over-simplified (otherwise they would be virtually impossible to maintain).

As mentioned above, you should think very carefully before deciding which models or product you are planning to use or to drop from your chosen development method, and you should always consult with your supervisor before committing yourself. There are two approaches that you can adopt with regard to specific models:

1. Research the applicability of the model to your type of project, and only use it if your research indicates that it is directly suitable.
2. Develop the model and subsequently evaluate its applicability or benefits to your project. This will be the most effective approach for most development projects.

Whichever approach you choose to adopt should be reflected clearly in the academic objectives of your project.

Table 7.13 lists the principal requirements analysis models (in addition to the Requirements Catalogue) from SSADM, UML and RAD approaches, which you should think long and hard about before dropping, regardless of the nature of your project.

One area that all students need to address is how to record the textual information that supports their diagrammatic models. Most textbooks present a picture of what should be recorded in a large commercial project. The layouts and contents that they recommend are therefore tailored to projects with

Table 7.13 Core requirements analysis models

Method/ approach	Technique/ product	Comments
SSADM	Business Activity Model (BAM) or functional decomposition	Both of these models are easy to produce and are readily understood by users. They provide an excellent way of confirming the scope of the project in terms of its high-level activities as perceived by the users, and of establishing a common frame of reference for everyone involved in the project (including your supervisor). Try to keep the number of activities in a BAM down to a maximum of 12. Otherwise you will be modelling tasks, and will not be adding to the effectiveness of your BAM.
	Logical Data Model (LDM)	The LDM is the single most important model that you will produce during your development. It is invaluable as a means of understanding the content, structure and meaning of the data that lies at the heart of an information system (current and required). At first it will consist of just the Logical Data Structure diagram, but towards the end of the investigation phase you will need to describe the data more fully using entity descriptions (see example box below). The LDM is a rigorous product with a mathematical underpinning. The number of entities that you identify will be determined by the complexity of the data in the problem domain, and not by the judgement of the analyst. It is therefore impossible to give guidance on how many entities you should model, but you should be suspicious if the number falls much below ten. Even a simple business scenario will generate well in excess of this number (unlike some of your coursework scenarios).
	Data Flow Model	In many projects the Data Flow Model will serve a useful purpose in capturing a snapshot of how the current system's data and processes interact, particularly when analysing system documents and the results of observations. However, in some projects (especially where there is no current system) their role is less clear, as BAMs and the Requirements Catalogue are more easily verified by users, and DFMs serve little purpose in specifying the system (this role is taken by function definitions). In any event, for most student projects you should consider producing level 1 DFDs only.
UML	Use Cases	Use Cases are not in themselves object-oriented, and can be used with any type of method (I would always recommend that my students produce Use Cases regardless of the method they are following). They provide an excellent means of documenting and communicating the main functions of a system as the users see them, and of who does or will interact with it. Use Cases can be used for the current and required system, but the level of detail included in the Use Case description will be greater for the required system as it becomes a specification model. They can be developed at a high level in the early stages of analysis, and refined and enhanced as your understanding increases. Your Use Case diagram should probably be restricted to around 12 Use Cases during the analysis stage, but you may decide to break them into smaller Use Cases as you begin to specify the system.
	Class diagram	In a similar way to the LDM, the Class diagram lies at the heart of UML. All other UML models feed into the Class diagram in some way, so it is important to start drawing the class model at an early stage.

Table 7.13   *(Cont'd)*

Method/ approach	Technique/ product	Comments
		At the analysis stage you will develop a fairly high-level view of the system that you can use to explore system concepts and requirements. As your project progresses you will gradually refine the Class diagram until it becomes the basis for program design. As with the LDM it is not possible to give advice on how many classes you should model, but again you should be suspicious if the number is less than ten.
RAD/DSDM	BAM/Use Cases	It is important to keep in mind that a RAD approach is not an excuse to 'escape' the need for system models, with the exception of some user interface and intermediate design products. The principal analysis models will all be necessary in order to ensure that the system is built on firm foundations and can be maintained once live. What differs from a more conventional approach is the way in which you develop the system models and the products that you use to supplement your Requirements Catalogue and models (such as screen and report samples). DSDM is not proscriptive regarding the analysis products you should use, but you should be consistent in the type of notation that you adopt. A BAM and/or a Use Case diagram will be an essential output from the business study depending on your chosen notation.
	Data/Class diagram	Started during the business study you will develop LDMs or class models, which you will then enhance in parallel to the prototyping process during the Functional Model iteration.
	System architecture definition	While not being a system model in the conventional sense, it is essential that you define (using infrastructure diagrams where appropriate) the target technical architecture during your business study. You should do this as soon as you have established high-level requirements (functional and non-functional), as you will need a suitable infrastructure to be in place to support the prototyping process during the Functional Model iteration. You will then refine the system architecture definition as you add more detail to your Requirements Catalogue during the Functional Model iteration.

significant complexity and data/user volumes. Many of the things that such textbooks suggest that you should record, or the ways in which they suggest you should record them, are there to assist in managing change control and communication processes across large teams. Few student projects will need this type of information. Instead, you should examine what information you need to support the specific needs of your development, and eliminate those items that will serve no useful purpose.

The example that follows contrasts the sort of documentation you might need for recording entity descriptions in a large SSADM project (Figure 7.6) with what might be needed for a typical student project (Figure 7.7).

Entity Description				
Entity Name *Member*				
Description *A member is an individual who has paid at least a monthly subscription to one or more sports. Details of individuals who take out day membership are not recorded.*				

Attribute	Primary Key	Foreign Key	Mandatory /Optional
Membership Number	*Yes*		*M*
member Surname			*M*
Member First Name			*M*
Member Initials			*O*
Member Address1			*M*
Member Address2			*M*
*Etc.			

must/may be	either /or	Link Phrase	one & only one /one or more	Entity Name
must be		*subscriber to*	*one or more*	*Sport*
may be		*purchaser of*	*one or more*	*Sports Product*
*Etc.				

Entity Volumes: Max. 450 Min. 400 Average 420	
User	**Access**
Admin Clerk	*Read, Create, Delete, Modify*
Manager	*Read*
*Etc.	

Growth Rate: *15% per year*
Archiving *Members should be archived 2 years.*

*Etc. has been used to keep the example to a manageable size

Figure 7.6   Entity descriptions from commercial project

Entity List			
MEMBER	**SPORT**	**SPORTS PRODUCT**	
Membership Number M	Sport Name M	Product Number M	
Member Surname M	Sport Description M	Product Description M	
Member First Name M	Annual Subscription Fee (adult) O	Cost Price M	
Member Initials O	Annual Subscription Fee (OAP) O	Selling Price M	
Member Address1 M	Annual Subscription Fee (Jnr) O	Etc	
Member Address2 M	Etc.		
Etc.			

Entity Descriptions					
Entity Name	**Short Description or Comments (optional)**	**Min Volume**	**Max Volume**	**Ave Volume**	**Growth Rate**
Member	*Numbers rise following Wimbledon*	*400*	*450*	*420*	*15%*
Sport		*15*	*15*	*15*	*5%*
Sports Product	*Products for sale to members*	*300*	*350*	*325*	*5%*

Figure 7.7   Entity descriptions from a student project

Attribute Name	Short Description or Comments (optional)	Domain	Length
Membership Number	Automatically generated by system	Integer	6
Member Surname		Text	24
Joining Date		DDMMYYYY	8

Figure 7.8   Attribute descriptions from a student project

In Figure 7.6 all the information regarding an entity is recorded together (sometimes duplicating the information recorded elsewhere), resulting in at least one page of documentation for each entity. In a large data model it is helpful, if not essential, to have all this information available in one place, rather than having to pull together information from a number of sources.

In a student project, with its greatly reduced complexity and size, it is relatively straightforward to cross-reference different models and diagrams, and the level of detail that needs to be recorded is also reduced. For example, it is not necessary to record relationship details within the entity descriptions, as this is readily available and visible in the data model diagram. One approach to documenting entity and attribute descriptions in a student project is to use a tabular format, as in Figure 7.7. This type of format will reduce the levels of paperwork in your project and make your requirements definition easier for you to use and for your assessors to read. Note that with either of the entity description formats shown above you will also need to provide attribute descriptions, which for a student project are again best presented in a tabular form such as that shown in Figure 7.8.

Before committing yourself to a documentation format (all of which should be electronic), you should discuss the format with your supervisor.

7.10   Early prototypes

Early prototypes can be a useful tool for investigating requirements, as long as you use them sensitively. During requirements analysis your prototypes will tend to be fairly crude and should not confused in your or your users' minds with the kind of prototypes that you might produce during the specification stages of your project.

Prototypes used for investigation purposes should be seen as illustrations or sample layouts that will help you to capture ideas and to draw out requirements. By showing a user a mock-up or sketch of a report or a screen dialogue you may be able to engage them in a way that is difficult using words or models alone. You should, however, be wary of using prototypes that look like a finished product, *unless* you are planning to implement a preselected package, in which case it makes sense to use the default screens and reports that the package provides as the basis for requirements discussions. In most projects your analysis prototypes should be nothing more than sketches or outlines (either hand drawn or produced rapidly in a graphics package or word processor), and should be easy to amend.

In contrast, specification or design prototypes (such as those produced during the Functional Model iteration of DSDM) will represent early versions of the system that you ultimately intend to implement. These prototypes will consist of functioning system components, rather than static 'pictures', and will be refined and supplemented as the project progresses to form the basis of the new system.

If your analysis prototypes look too much like the finished article, you run the risk of encountering one or more of the following problems:

- **False expectations.** One of the most common issues with prototypes in general is that they can create the impression that the system is nearly finished and about to be implemented. This may well be the case if you are in the later stages of your project, but at the investigation stage this impression can seriously undermine your project when implementation does not then occur within a short time frame.

- **Railroading of users.** If you present a polished prototype at the analysis stage it may appear to users that you have designed the system before you have consulted them fully on their requirements.

- **Premature design decisions.** If your analysis prototype looks convincing you may find yourself being drawn into discussions about design issues rather than requirements. If your prototype is clearly just an illustration, you will find it much easier to focus on what the system needs to do, rather than what it looks like.

- **Wasted effort.** Polished prototypes take a long time to produce. You do not have sufficient time within the constraints of a student project to put a lot of effort into what is really a throwaway product. Even the crudest of pencil sketches or hand-annotated current system layouts are just as effective at illustrating requirements (when as an attachment to your Requirements Catalogue) as the most polished of prototypes, so save your design energies for later in your project.

7.11 Investigating potential solutions

Once you have a clear understanding of the requirements of the system, you need to make some decisions about how you are going to approach the design and construction of the system. The main questions that you need to answer are the following:

- **Which requirements will the system satisfy?** Your project is by its very nature timeboxed. It is unlikely that you will be able to implement even a prototype system that meets all of the requirements you have documented, whether or not they can be justified on commercial or academic grounds. A similar situation will arise in almost all projects, but in student projects the time constraints are especially tight. You will therefore need to prioritise your requirements and identify a subset that you will be able to implement on time (assuming your university will require you to deliver some software).

One way of prioritising requirements is to classify them using the MoSCoW acronyms suggested by the DSDM Consortium (Stapleton, 1997):

- **M**ust have. These requirements are essential for the system to operate in any form.
- **S**hould have. These requirements might be regarded as essential if you were not severely constrained by time, but are such that the system will function without them.
- **C**ould have. These requirements could be justified on business or academic grounds, but are not central to the effectiveness of the system.
- **W**ant to have in the future. These are important requirements, but ones that can wait until a later software development.

Any software that you produce must include the 'must haves', whereas the 'could haves' may be left out if you believe that you will be unable to develop them in time. Take care to examine the 'could haves' properly, rather than dismissing them as low priority, as you may find that that some of them can be satisfied with little effort or impact on your timescales. It is important to plan ahead in order to identify which requirements you will be able to meet, rather than setting out with an infeasible scope and either running out of time or dropping requirements as your deadline approaches.

■ **How am I going to meet the requirements?** There are likely to be a number of ways in which you can meet the system requirements, including package solutions, bespoke development and modifications to the existing systems. If your project includes explicit academic objectives requiring the application of specific programming skills, then your choices will be constrained, but options will still exist as to how you shape and construct your solution.

In many projects you will be faced with the alternatives of creating a functional prototype for a significant part of the system scope or implementing a full solution for a smaller subset. To a large extent your choice will be driven by the objectives of your project or the requirements of your university, but if you have an external client their needs may also influence your decision. In any event you should spend some time discussing these issues with your supervisor.

■ **How am I going to approach the remainder of the development?** Once you have decided which requirements you intend to satisfy and what your strategy is for building the system, you need to plan the remainder of your project. It is possible or even probable that you will have uncovered things during your investigation that mean you need to review or question your original plan. You may even need to reconsider your development approach or methodology. For example, you may have discovered that the system-to-system interfaces are far more complex than you had envisaged, meaning that you will need to devote more time to the design of these components, and adopt a more formal specification method than you had anticipated.

■ **What technical infrastructure and tools am I going to need?** Now that you understand the non-functional requirements of the system, you should start to specify the technical infrastructure that will be needed to build and run the system. At this point your specification should be fairly high-level, as information may emerge during the design stage that will influence the detail of the infrastructure, e.g. more accurate data volumes.

■ **Are there any changes to the objectives of my project arising from my requirements analysis?** Some of your objectives may have been based on assumptions about the requirements of your system, which have not been confirmed on closer inspection. For example, you may have planned to use a programming tool, but have found that the user interface needs to be of a type for which that tool is inappropriate.

It is important that you make time to think these questions through properly and consider a full range of solution and technical options. No project is so constrained that there are no alternatives to or within your chosen solution. You must avoid the temptation to jump to an 'obvious' solution, or to adopt the solution that is most convenient for you. In some cases this may mean implementing a system with reduced scope, because of the time you have taken to explore suitable solutions or learn new skills. However, you will get far more credit for a well-considered solution that fully meets a subset of requirements, than a hastily constructed one that covers the full scope poorly.

Once you are clear about the way forward you should produce a *short* textual overview of your chosen solution, accompanied by a Requirements Catalogue and system models that have been updated to reflect the decisions you have made.

7.12   Summary

1. Investigation is at the heart of all system development projects. Before you can embark on the specification, design and construction of your application, you need to be clear about what your system needs to do. This will require you to obtain information about a potentially wide range of subjects, such as: new requirements, current problems, system objectives and success factors, existing systems and infrastructure, potential solutions, organisational or cultural factors, existing policies and procedures, and internal politics.

2. For academic projects the main sources of information will include: literature search, lecturers, businesses and their customers, fellow students and personal contacts.

3. If you are developing a system for an external client information sources may include: company representatives and system users, company documents and the workplace. Company documents to be analysed include: previous project outputs, existing system and procedure manuals, change request and problem logs for existing systems, training materials, forms and reports, memos and other correspondence.

4. Interviewing forms the backbone of most requirements-gathering exercises in student projects. In order to get the most from the interviewing process you will need to

make use of three types of question: open questions, closed questions and probing questions. You should try to use a combination of all three types of question.

5. As well as considering the individual questions that you wish to ask in an interview, you need to decide on how you are going to conduct the interview. There are three main types of interview: structured interview, unstructured or open interview, and guided interview.

6. Observations can be one of the most effective techniques available for gaining a rapid insight into current practice and problems in a workplace situation, in a way that reveals what people are really doing, rather than what people or documents say should be happening.

7. Questionnaires, while being an extremely useful tool for research, are of limited use in investigating requirements. In certain circumstances they can be of some use as a supplement to other techniques. The main function of questionnaires in a development project is to clarify issues or points that have been raised during your requirements analysis.

8. Workshops can be an extremely effective and rapid way of identifying and investigating system requirements. For this reason, they are regarded as fundamental to the success of many RAD projects. In a well-run workshop a number of interested and informed parties are brought together and encouraged to discuss, exchange and debate their views and ideas.

9. You will need to produce a definition of requirements that will act as a comprehensive statement of what the new system is required to do, and to what level it will need to perform, rather than with how the requirements are to be satisfied. There are two types of system requirement: functional and non-functional requirements.

10. In every development method there is a minimum set of models that you will need to develop at each stage of the life cycle. Your use of system models must be consistent with the academic objectives of your project. You should try to explore fully the application of the method and techniques that you specified in your PID (or proposal). This means applying the techniques in a rigorous and relatively formal fashion.

11. Current systems analysis has a number of benefits that will improve the efficiency and effectiveness of your investigation, including: many of the functions and features of the existing system will need to be carried forward in the new system; most new requirements will refer to problems or restrictions with the current system that need to be overcome; much of the data required by the new system will need to be imported from the old system; understanding the current system will help you to understand the problem domain and to communicate with users; your system may need to interface with other existing systems; some parts of the current system may need to be retained.

12. In a student project, with its greatly reduced complexity and size, it is relatively straightforward to cross-reference different models and diagrams, and the level of detail that needs to be recorded is also reduced.

13. Early prototypes can be a useful tool for investigating requirements, as long as you use them sensitively. During requirements analysis your prototypes will tend to be fairly crude and should not confused in your or your users' minds with the kind of prototypes that you might produce during the specification stages of your project.

14. The main questions that you need to answer before starting system design are: Which requirements will the system satisfy? How am I going to meet the requirements? How am I going to approach the remainder of the development? What technical infrastructure and tools am I going to need? Are there any changes to the objectives of my project arising from my requirements analysis?

8 System design

8.1 ## Introduction

The aim of this chapter is to provide guidance on issues and activities that are common to the system design stage of a wide range of development projects.

In the design stage your chosen development approach will determine the activities you will carry out to an even greater extent than in the analysis stage. As you move through the development life cycle, the tasks that you undertake will become increasingly specific, as the number of factors that are unique to your project increases. During the analysis stage your project will have had its own context, business problem and organisational factors that you needed to adapt to. During the design stage you will also need to consider a unique combination of implementation, technical and environmental factors.

Nevertheless, there are a number of underlying principles and issues that will apply to all student projects, even if the way in which you address them differs greatly, and it is these that form the basis for much of this chapter.

As with the analysis activities discussed in Chapter 7, a number of the issues discussed in this chapter are covered only in a theoretical context within many system design courses. A project is often the first real exposure you will have to the practical questions that need to be answered during system design. The issues you are likely to encounter are similar in many respects to those of a commercial project, but on a greatly reduced scale. The guidelines that follow are therefore tailored to reflect the circumstances of a range of typical student development projects.

Learning Outcomes

After reading this chapter, you will be able to:

- Understand the need to produce a conceptual system design within a student project

- Understand the key principles and activities involved in user interface design

- Apply a four-stage prototyping approach to application prototyping, tailored for student projects

■ Appreciate the need for data design optimisation

■ Understand the requirements of infrastructure design within a student project

8.2   Conceptual specification and design

It is tempting, once you have a picture of what the system is required to do, to start building the system right away or, failing that, to produce designs that provide details of how you are going to use the tools that are immediately at your disposal to build a solution. However, these approaches miss out an important stage, for both practical and academic reasons.

Before you commit yourself to a particular physical implementation of the required system, you need to think carefully about how the system should behave and how it needs to interact with the outside world (in the shape of users and other systems). If you leap straight from a picture of what the system is required to do to a fully functioning system it is likely that your system will be built on nothing more than assumptions regarding business rules and logic, together with constraints imposed by your limited knowledge of the implementation environment. This approach invariably leads to a substandard system that fails to function correctly, and whose design has been driven by the implementation tool rather than system requirements.

Student projects that are hurried into construction are characterised by missing functionality, poor structure and faulty logic. Instead, you need to establish in some detail how your system should support the business rules, and how it should behave in response to events. This can be done in many ways, using techniques that range from iterative prototyping to sophisticated system modelling using CASE tools. Only when you have confirmed the specification of your system should you finalise the physical specification and implementation of the solution.

From an academic standpoint, a system that has been implemented without a proper design process indicates an ignorance of accepted systems theory and a lack of rigour. It also denies you the opportunity to explore and understand the application of design techniques in a real-world context. I always encourage my students to develop formal design models for at least some elements of each part of their system, even when they are totally convinced they will be of no practical use. By developing formal design models for some components and informal models (if any) for others they will then be able to evaluate and contrast the outcomes of the different approaches, in a way that is impossible through coursework.

In a RAD project it may appear to the novice that conceptual design can be bypassed, but it is just this kind of misunderstanding that led to the poor reputation of early RAD implementations. It is now widely accepted that RAD techniques such as prototyping can be invaluable in accelerating the design process. They are even able to drive the conceptual design for certain types of system or component, such as the GUI (see Section 8.4). However, even in the most GUI-based of systems there will still be many components (such as system-to-system interfaces, complex algorithms and housekeeping tasks) that cannot be prototyped effectively, and so will need to be specified fully before being constructed. In addition, conceptual design models should be used to validate and document the underlying logic for the physical system that is being developed iteratively through the prototypes.

All widely used system development methods provide techniques and models for assisting with and capturing the logical design of your system. Some of the key specification and design techniques for SSADM and UML projects are listed in Table 8.1. Note that in a RAD (DSDM) project you will use techniques from other methods and notations, such as SSADM and UML.

Table 8.1 Core conceptual design models

Method/ approach	Technique/ product	Comments
SSADM	Logical Data Model (LDM)	The LDM remains at the centre of the project throughout the design stage, where you will need to ensure that the model captures all of the details of the required data, and is fully normalised. Towards the end of the design stage you will need to map the LDM onto a physical database design (see Section 8.5).
	Function definition	The processing or functionality of the system in an SSADM will be based on the concept of functions. Each function represents a meaningful and complete unit of work, carried out in response to a business or system event. The complete set of functions, when taken together, will represent all of the processing that the system needs to carry out, whether user or system initiated. It is essential therefore to create a complete set of function definitions. At its most basic, a function definition will consist of a textual description (in as much detail as you feel is necessary to make the purpose and logic of the function clear). As you develop other products, such as entity life histories (ELHs), effect correspondence diagrams (ECDs), GUI designs, GUI prototypes and program specifications, you will need to cross-reference these with your function descriptions. It is the sum of all of the products that together define a function that constitutes a completed function definition.
	Entity behaviour modelling (entity life histories, enquiry access paths and effect correspondence diagrams)	Entity behaviour models are some of the most powerful tools within SSADM for ensuring that you have understood and documented fully the interaction between data and processing. However, they are labour intensive to produce and for simple interactions add little to the textual descriptions of functions. In a student project many of the interactions will be fairly straightforward and so behaviour models may not be of any value in many areas (instead you should consider using a create, read, update, delete (CRUD) matrix. However, unless your system is extremely simple, there will still be some entities that are complex and so should be modelled using ELHs, and some complex functions that should be modelled using ECDs. It is unlikely that you will need to use enquiry access paths (EAPs), unless you are designing a decision support system where there may be some very complex enquiries.

Table 8.1 *(Cont'd)*

Method/ approach	Technique/ product	Comments
	Data Flow Model	I do not recommend that my students produce a DFM for the required system, as it will not get carried forward into the later stages of the design process (the DFM is superseded by function definitions). A DFM also tends to drive an internal system design that is not based around events (and that, unless you are careful, will closely resemble the old system). Some students find the DFM useful for providing an overview of the system, and it is undeniably useful in this regard. However, I recommend that students produce a Use Case diagram for this purpose, as it is more readily understood by users, and feeds directly into function definition (you may even choose to replace function definitions with Use Cases) and system test planning.
UML	Use Cases	The Use Cases you produced during your analysis should have covered the entire scope of the system. You will now need to add more detail to them, by expanding their descriptions and developing scenarios or paths through their processing. There are no standards within UML for Use Case descriptions (in their most refined form when linked to behavioural models they are sometimes referred to as behaviour specifications). You may choose to present unstructured text, include flowcharts, pseudo-code or a semi-structured description showing user actions in one column and system responses in the other of the process, e.g.:

Actor	System
1. Enters membership number	Shows details of member and confirms expiry date of membership Shows renewal options and prices
2. Selects renewal option	Confirms cost and prompts for payment

Your Use Case descriptions may also cover alternative valid paths, each of which will support a particular scenario, and references to the other models that will further specify system behaviour and implementation.

| | Class diagram | As with the LDM in SSADM, the Class diagram remains at the core of your system design.
Towards the end of the design process you will need to map your Class diagram onto a physical database, which will often mean converting it to a set of normalised tables. |
| | Behaviour models | Behaviour models are, like the entity behaviour models of SSADM, powerful ways of specifying complex business processes (sequence and collaboration diagrams) or complex data objects (statechart diagram). Behaviour models operate at a low level of detail, and are most often used in student projects to complete the behaviour specifications of complex Use Cases. For simpler Use Cases a textual description is a more efficient means of specifying behaviour, given your time constraints, but you should still attempt to explore the application of formal behaviour models in some areas.
In a student project many of the interactions will be fairly straightforward and so behaviour models may not be of any value in many areas (instead you should consider using a CRUD matrix as described in the next section). |

		Entities		
		Customer	Product	Sales Order
F	Set up customer	C/U		
u	Receive sales order	R	R	C
n	Despatch sales order	R		U
c	Sales order enquiry	R	R	R
t	Sales order report	R		R
i	Overdue despatch report			R
o	Receive returns	R	R	U
n	Receive payment	R		U
s				

Figure 8.1 CRUD matrix extract showing functions and entities

Regardless of which method or notation you are using it is essential to cross-reference each of your models with your Requirements Catalogue, to ensure that each requirement has been considered, and that you can trace each model back to the requirement that it is intended to meet.

One product that lies outside most methods, but that can be used to great effect to supplement other formal products, is the CRUD (Create, Read, Update, Delete) matrix. In a student project, where the lack of complexity can make it hard to justify the creation of behaviour modelling products (unless it forms part of your academic objectives), a CRUD matrix can be especially useful. Its main uses are to summarise how processes and data interact, or how objects interact, and to provide a checklist that ensures you have accounted for all necessary interactions in your more detailed behaviour models. While a CRUD matrix does not describe the full nature, sequence or control of complex interactions, it may be all that is needed (in conjunction with products such as the Requirements Catalogue, Function Definitions, Use Cases and Class/Logical Data Models) to capture straightforward interactions, which is what predominate in most student projects.

Figure 8.1 shows part of a CRUD matrix for a SSADM style project, where it is used to indicate which functions interact with which entities. The letter entered into each cell will denote whether the function is creating, updating, reading or deleting one or more occurrences of an entity. If you have entities that do not have at least one function that creates occurrences and one that deletes them, it means either that you have not identified a compete set of functions or that you have modelled entities that are in reality out of the scope of your system. Similarly, if you find entities that do not have at least one update or read function you have almost certainly overlooked one or more functions, as data that are created and deleted without ever being used serve no useful purpose whatsoever.

8.3 User interface design

The design of the user interface can be one of the most enjoyable and creative parts of a system development project. This is largely due to the ease with which GUIs can be 'painted' in most development environments.

The immediate satisfaction and sense of productivity that GUI builders provide lead many students to jump into user interface design before they have necessarily thought about what the interfaces are required to do, how they should be designed and which is the most appropriate form of user interface. The ease with which existing technical features (such as animation and graphics) can be built into a GUI, whether they are needed or not, can also lead students to produce user interfaces that are not fit for purpose, but are undeniably interesting.

To help in overcoming these issues, there are three guiding principles that you should always keep at the front of your mind when designing user interfaces:

1. **Keep it simple.** Any unnecessary clutter, features or distractions in your user interface designs will interfere with their efficiency. You should focus your attention on the task that the user interface is required to support, and design the user interface to support this task in the most straightforward manner possible. If that means using plain and technically unchallenging interfaces, then that is what you should do. You will get more credit for a simple, clean design that supports a function in an efficient manner, than one that demonstrates your technical brilliance but stands in the way of efficient performance.

2. **Design for your users.** You must ensure that you have understood the type of user you are designing your user interfaces for. In the Internet age, when surrounded by web pages designed for occasional use or novice users, it is all too easy to forget that in a commercial or academic situation many of your users will be experts. If your system is to be used primarily by novices, or you are developing some functions that will be used only occasionally, you will need to build user interfaces that take people carefully through the process, accompanied by explanatory notes. If, however, you are developing a system or functions that will be used day in and day out by expert users, you will need to design your user interface with efficiency in mind, involving the minimum of interaction and explanation (experts are more than happy to use shortcut codes, tabs and abbreviations without the need for reassurance or explanation). This does not mean that your user interfaces should be difficult to use, but that they do not need to provide as much on-screen assistance.

3. **Be consistent.** All of your user interfaces should use the same conventions, terminology and navigation schemes. Do not feel tempted to make every screen and report different, in an attempt to appear creative or to demonstrate your technical ability (unless your project includes a specific academic objective that requires comparisons or demonstrations of different user interface design techniques).

The user interface design process

While most system development methods have clear and well-documented processes for internal design, few provide much guidance on user interface (external) design. What follows is the outline of a generic process that could be applied to a range of projects. It is beyond the scope of this book to provide detailed guidance on the user interface design process, but there are a number of textbooks that cover this area well, some of which are listed in the Bibliography.

Establish user interface standards

Before diving into the process of user interface design it is useful (perhaps even essential) to establish standards or 'rules' for how you will implement common features and functions across all user interfaces. These standards should cover such cosmetic issues as your use of colour, logos, text styles and icons, as well as more technical features such as navigation schemes (e.g. drop-down menus and navigation bars) and user help. In a group project it is essential that the standards are understood and adopted by all team members, otherwise your system will appear inconsistent and confusing. In SSADM these user interface standards are an example of what are termed style guides.

Create user interface structure

Using your Function Definitions, Use Case descriptions or an equivalent product, you should develop a structure diagram that illustrates how you plan to group your functions and how they will be presented in menus. Some notations for documenting user interface structures (e.g. organisation charts or tree diagrams) do no more than show a hierarchy of user interfaces, while others (e.g. Window Navigation Models from SSADM) illustrate how users will navigate between and within user interfaces. In practice you may decide to document the overall structure of your user interfaces using organisation chart notation, while developing detailed navigation models for your most complex user interfaces.

Design your individual user interfaces

Once you have decided on how your user interfaces will be structured you can begin their detailed design. For each user interface there will be a number of fundamental questions to be answered:

- **Should the data be input in batch?** For some processes it is much more efficient to collect data together for input in batches, rather than in real time, one transaction at a time.
- **Should query results be presented on screen or on paper?** If a significant amount of data needs to be displayed (more than will fit on a single screen) it will almost certainly be necessary to provide the option of printing the query results on paper, even if you have formatted the output for optimum display on screen. For multi-page reports it will be best to design the query with paper printing in mind, and provide an option to preview the report before printing.
- **Numbers in tables or graphs.** If you are reporting on trends or comparisons between large sets of data, you should consider whether to present the data in graphs as well as or instead of tables.

For most user interfaces the answer to these questions will be fairly obvious, but for some there will be genuine choices, in which case you should make a note of the reasons behind your design decisions, so that you can justify them if asked to do so by your supervisor.

The best way to format your user interfaces is to document the most common scenarios or sequences of events for each function or Use Case (if you have produced behaviour models then you should use them as the basis for drawing up your scenarios), and structure the user interface so that it reflects the flow of actions associated with those scenarios. Other tips for refining your user interface designs are given in Table 8.2.

I always recommend that my students sketch their user interface designs on paper before moving on to produce and demonstrate user interface prototypes (see Section 8.4). This sketching process is fast and the results are far easier to modify than any software prototype. Screen- and report-painting tools are increasingly easy to operate, but they still require a lot more time and effort than a pencil and paper. If you use a screen painter to create your initial designs you will feel less inclined to change them or accept constructive criticism than if you have produced rough pencil sketches.

Design input validation

Once you have created your user interface designs you need to consider what input validation is needed. Students often underestimate the effort needed to design and implement effective input validation that both prevents invalid data entering the system and helps users to correct it. This is because the focus of their studies will usually have been on developing solutions to tightly defined problems, rather than considering the range of invalid actions and data that characterise real-world systems. You need to cater for the following kinds of things in your designs:

- **Invalid data types.** If a user enters the wrong type of data (e.g. a text string instead of a date), you need to highlight this immediately so that the user can correct their input.

- **Incorrect values.** Some fields within your user interface will have restricted ranges of acceptable values, e.g. dates of birth must be in the (relatively recent) past.

- **Incomplete data entry.** All user interfaces will have a minimum set of data items that need to be entered. For example, in an ordering screen the names, addresses and payment details of customers will usually be mandatory, whereas mobile phone numbers will be optional. The user interface should identify missing data items and assist the user to correct them.

- **Conflicting data.** The handling of conflicting data can be slightly trickier to design, as it is by its nature more complicated than the other types of input validation mentioned above. A simple example would be the entering of an outward journey date that is later than a return journey date in a travel system.

Table 8.2 User interface design tips

Objective	Tips
Keep it simple	Never add complexity or time to the processes you are supporting by including unnecessary features in your user interface designs. Always remember that (in the vast majority of cases) you are designing a functional system not a work of art. Stick to plain colours (if in doubt use black on white/pale grey). Only use graphics and animations where they add true value (or are a requirement of your course, such as in some multimedia projects), and ensure that all text is a minimum of 10 point.
Design for ease of learning	If designing for novice or infrequent users keep the density of information on the page relatively low (40–50%), but not so low as to require multiple screens or scrolling. Add explanation and/or easy to access help facilities for all user interface elements. Use on-screen prompts to lead users through lengthy processes.
Design for efficiency	If designing for expert or frequent users you can use much higher densities (up to 80–90%). Allow users to enter shortcut codes directly (not necessarily via drop-down lists or look-ups), and design for tabs and keystroke data entry rather than mouse clicks. Keep on-screen explanations, graphics and labels to the absolute minimum (consider using abbreviations and acronyms wherever possible).
Make it easy	All of your user interface design should follow the natural flow of the processes they support. If they do this you will minimise the number of mouse clicks or tabs the user needs to perform.
Prevent mistakes	Radio buttons, drop-down lists, look-ups and checkboxes all help users to pick from valid data and reduce the risk of incorrect data entry.
Provide consistent and clear navigation	Use the same menu structures, navigation bars and shortcut codes throughout your system. Avoid the use of 'clever' but obscure navigation schemes, such as those that rely on users having an understanding of obscure icons or technical terms, or that require the user to hover a cursor over them to activate them. Keep the navigation scheme compact but prominent.
Do not reinvent the wheel	Use familiar layouts, symbols and terminology. For example, if the current system has a screen or form that is well liked then copy it. There may also be more general conventions that you can adopt, such as search box layouts, standard icons (e.g. the shopping basket), and words such as 'help', 'more' and 'cancel'.
Do not be technology led	Avoid using technical features and tools just because they are novel or exciting. Your objective should be to deliver a system that meets requirements, not one that uses flashy but ultimately pointless technology. Do not treat the user interface as a showcase for your technical prowess, unless this is one of your explicit project objectives. To use a well-worn phrase, 'form should follow function'.
Project the right image	Ensure it is businesslike and consistent with corporate image. If in doubt stick to black on white/grey.
Reduce clutter	Cut out unnecessary 'noise', such as animations, graphics and backgrounds. Keep text to the minimum necessary.

It is much better to carry out these types of validation within the user interface than rely on database processing, as this will tie up system resources, be slower and you will often have to put in a lot of effort to make the error messages as slick as they can be if coded within the user interface.

8.4 Application prototyping

Prototypes are pre-production versions of part or all of your system, and may vary in sophistication from paper sketches to near complete systems. If your project is adopting an RAD or iterative development approach (such as in the spiral or spiral design life cycle models), your early prototypes will be steadily evolved into the final system by refining and adding to them in the light of user feedback and testing, and by building operational-level capacity and resilience into the final versions.

If your project is using a non-iterative approach (such as in the spiral GUI life cycle model) then some elements of the system may be delivered iteratively, while others are delivered using more traditional methods. Alternatively, prototypes can be used to develop what is in reality a visual or animated model of requirements, which is then used as a design specification for the final system that may be built in a different technical environment from the prototypes.

Many student projects will aim to deliver a prototype application, as they do not have sufficient time to produce a fully operational system covering the entire scope of their project. The prototypes in these cases will consist either of a subset of the full system that is close to production, or an earlier but still working prototype of the full system. In few cases will a non-working or static prototype be acceptable to your university. To be academically acceptable your prototype system will normally need to include at least the following features:

- **User interfaces.** It is possible that only a subset of your user interfaces will be fully operational. In this case you will need to identify clearly those elements that are working and those that are static.
- **Database integration.** A stand-alone GUI prototype will rarely be acceptable on its own, unless your project is a multimedia project that delivers innovative or groundbreaking interfaces. A set of user interfaces that does not interface with an underlying database is likely to be far too simplistic to meet the requirements of your university, or to meet the system requirements defined during your analysis.
- *Tested* functionality. Including input validation and database error handling. All components of your prototype that you identify as operational should be properly tested.
- **Recognisable subset of requirements.** If possible, your prototype system should provide complete support for a self-contained set of requirements.

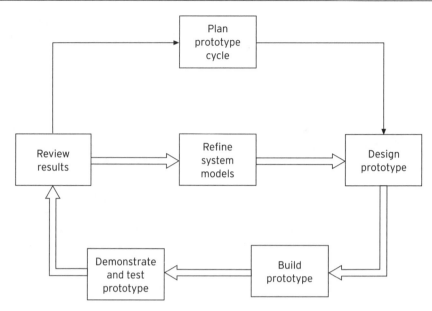

Figure 8.2 Prototyping cycle

This will enable your assessors to judge how well your software meets its requirements. If instead your prototype supports a scattering of requirements from different areas of the full system it will be difficult to establish how well your design hangs together.

A general picture of the prototyping process or cycle is shown in Figure 8.2 (note that the cycle can be applied to the entire system or just some elements of it).

In theory you should move through enough of these cycles to produce a system or interface that is entirely acceptable (but perhaps not perfect) to your users. However, in a student project the constraints of time will may mean that you will be able to complete only a restricted number of cycles. In some cases, if your prototypes are in the form of working software, you may be able to complete only a single cycle followed by one revision. If you find yourself in this situation you should ensure that one of your reviewers is your project supervisor. Otherwise you run the risk of producing a final piece of software that does not meet academic assessment criteria, and that you could have modified had you demonstrated it to your supervisor during the proto-typing stage.

If your initial prototypes are unsophisticated, you will be able to complete a greater number of cycles than if you develop a working prototype from the beginning. This is the main reason that I recommend the use of pencil sketches, as they will almost certainly enable you to fit in at least one additional cycle. In most student projects you should be able to complete three or four cycles if you adopt a 'low-tech' approach for the early versions, as in Table 8.3.

Table 8.3 Four-cycle prototyping approach

Cycle	Prototype	Description
1	Paper rough	Create some rough designs for your key functions or Use Cases. You should concentrate on producing sketches that support the structures and content of your more formal models and specifications, rather than the presentation of your roughs. Try to create one or two different layouts.
2	Paper revision	If there are significant issues with your first set of roughs you may need to produce another set for review before committing yourself to producing software prototypes.
3	Static software prototype	Your first software prototypes should be static screens and reports, with limited real functionality, rather than working software components. You may choose to demonstrate your prototypes using presentation software, such as Microsoft PowerPoint.
4	Working prototype	Your final prototypes should consist of working software that includes validation and error handling (it is important to prototype your error messages and processes as well as 'normal' functionality). Following your final review, you should aim to carry out one final set of revisions to your software, which you will not usually have time to take through another cycle. Note that (in line with the principles of DSDM) if you are using an iterative development approach you need to test your prototypes as you produce them, with a particular focus on database integration.

8.5   Data design

In student projects you will rarely have a great deal of choice when selecting the database for your implementation. Most students will be restricted to those offered by their university, although you may have been directed towards a specific database if your project is for an external client. If you are in a position to choose between different databases you will need to balance the optimum choice for the requirements of your project with the time that will be needed to learn them. For most students, the best option will be to stick with the database they have learned during their studies, unless their project has specific objectives that include exploration of a different database or database type.

The main types of database used by modern systems are as follows:

- **Relational.** This is by far the most common type of database in use in industry and in universities. Relational databases can be adapted to most types of application, from transaction processing to decision support. Older relational databases provide support for simple data types only, but most of the market leaders (e.g. Oracle, Informix and Microsoft SQL Server) now provide support for more complex data types, such as multimedia objects. Relational databases are stable and utilise well-established skills and tools. They are the most 'open' of all types of database, in that most hardware and development environments are able to support them. There is a large choice of vendors; the database management software is widely available and relatively easy to install.

- **Object-oriented.** The market for object-oriented databases is much smaller than for relational databases, although their presence is growing, albeit slowly, in academia and in commercial systems that require the manipulation of complex data types. Their progress has been hampered to some extent by the support for objects provided by leading relational databases.

- **Multidimensional.** Multidimensional databases are specialised products used for decision support systems, and in particular for Executive Information Systems (EISs). In the vast majority of cases they will be fed from an underlying relational database that is the repository for the transactional data that is summarised and aggregated in the multidimensional database. They are rarely used in student projects, unless the project is an EIS project, as decision support systems can be built very effectively using relational databases (indeed many specialist decision support software applications and tools have been developed to interface directly with relational databases).

The vast majority of student projects will be implemented using relational database management systems (RDBMSs), even if they have been designed using object-oriented techniques, such as UML. If you have used an analysis and design method that is not based on relational theory, you will need to map your designs onto a normalised relational data model (such as an LDM or entity relationship diagram) before carrying out physical database design.

Once you have created a relational data model it is possible to construct a database that mirrors your model more or less exactly, using SQL or the data design tools that come with your chosen RDBMS. If your application is a prototype system, or involves limited amounts of data or users, you may need to do no more than implement your data model using a simple RDBMS such as Microsoft Access. However, if your system involves substantial amounts of data, or will be used by more than a handful of users, you will need to use a more powerful RDBMS such as Oracle, Informix or Microsoft SQL Server, and will need to optimise your database design. Even if you are implementing a limited prototype, and will be doing so in a simple RDBMS, your project should include a plan for the migration to a more sophisticated implementation, again including plans for data design optimisation.

The areas that you should consider in optimising your database design are covered in Table 8.4.

Table 8.4   Database design optimisation techniques

Technique	Explanation
Denormalisation	If your system is biased towards querying *large* volumes of data (such as in decision support systems), rather than updating or accessing small quantities of data, then you may need to consider denormalising your database in some areas in order to reduce the number of joins your queries will need to make. Otherwise performance may be unacceptably slow. A denormalised database will introduce redundancy, increase update times, and risk the kinds of update anomalies that normalisation aims to eliminate. You should therefore denormalise data *only* when there is a real need (demonstrated by verifiable database performance estimation or volume testing).
Derived values, summary tables	If your system is designed to report on trend or highly summarised data (again, a characteristic of some decision support systems or EIS functions) you may need to create summary tables or store derived data values in order to avoid calculating these in real time when queries are submitted. In large systems summarisation (often in aggregate tables in a 'star schema') can lead to big increases in database size. It also leads in all cases to slower update times and to problems of having to recalculate or restructure previously summarised data as new values are input into the database, or as the catgories around which the summarisation has been calculated are changed.
Query optimisation	Most RDBMSs include automatic query optimisation features. However, some optimisation may still need to be carried out manually for complex or high volume queries.
Disk placement/ clustering	Data items, rows or tables that are frequently accessed together can be clustered or placed near each other on the physical storage devices in order to improve performance.
Indexing strategies	To improve data access performance you may be able to build multiple indexes on top of your database tables. The downside to indexes is the overhead in maintaining and rebuilding them.
EIS/data marts	If your system is largely transactional, but includes a decision support subsystem you should consider building data marts (smaller separate databases that hold a subset or summaries of the main operational database) or EISs that are fed from the transactional database. This will leave you free to concentrate on tuning the different databases for their individual needs without compromising the performance of the others.
Multi-user access	Your data design should include careful consideration of how you will deal with multiple users trying to update the same items of data at the same time. In most cases you will do this using record locking at some level within the database.
Back-up and recovery	Any system can be subject to failure, for example through hardware faults. Your system design must therefore include consideration of how you will take back-ups of the system and its data, and how you would restore the system following a failure. In a production system you will need to test these procedures.

One final consideration, which is not a design issue for the final database itself but is a critical issue for the implementation of that database, is how you intend to populate the new system with data from any existing systems. The conversion and migration of data from one system to another are notoriously difficult and complex processes that are all too often overlooked in student projects. In particularly complex cases data conversion can require the development of sophisticated programs that cleanse the old data items, convert them to new formats, add new data and then update the new database. You may also need to consider how to handle data that relate to transactions that are in progress, e.g. do you wait until orders that have been partly delivered have been completed before moving them across, or do you convert them part way through their life cycle? The answer in this case will be partly determined by whether the new order process is the same as the old. If it is not, then part completed orders in the old system may be in a state that would be invalid in the new system.

8.6   Infrastructure design

In a commercial project the design of the physical infrastructure is just as critical to the success of a system implementation as the design of the applications that will run on it. If the infrastructure design is substandard then the performance of the system will be impaired and it may have insufficient capacity and resilience to cope with business demands. It may also be difficult to manage and maintain, or have issues regarding security.

Student projects rarely involve the installation of the kind of substantial new production environments that are a feature of many commercial projects. It is more likely that you will be faced with setting up a small-scale infrastructure in order to implement a limited prototype, or that you will use an existing environment with minimum modification. If you are developing an academically based application in which the technical demands are low, you will probably use the university's development infrastructure in a fairly standard configuration.

While this may mean that the amount of effort you need to devote to the design of your project's actual implementation infrastructure is greatly reduced, you will still need to spend some time specifying how you plan to configure and use the infrastructure. Furthermore, if you are implementing a prototype of part of a more substantial system, then you also need to produce designs for the ultimate fully sized production environment, even if you do not plan to install it.

Infrastructure components

In most projects you will need more than one technical environment, together with procedures for migrating software from one environment to another. A common configuration consists of three environments:

1. **Development environment.** This is where you carry out your programming tasks and store your software components while they are being developed.

2. **Test environment.** Once you have completed the development of a software component it is helpful to store it in a separate environment where it can be tested and integrated with other completed components. In a large development or group project the separation of development and test environments is essential. If your development is relatively small you may be able to combine the development and test environments, but only if you have a version control mechanism in place (e.g. using separate directory structures or version numbering) to identify completed software.

3. **Live environment.** The live system must of course be kept isolated and protected from other environments. Software components should be added to the live environment only once they have completed rigorous testing procedures.

Commercial project may have additional environments, to cater for activities such as user acceptance testing and volume testing, while in an academic project you may have just a single environment as there is no concept of a 'live' system.

There can be no firm rules governing the configuration of different environments, as the needs of different projects and organisations vary widely. The important thing from an academic perspective is that you can demonstrate that you have made a considered and logical decision about how to set up your technical infrastructure. Given the size and complexity of a typical student project it is of course possible to muddle through with just about any configuration. However, your work will be more efficient in the long run if you do set things up properly, and will help to demonstrate to your assessors that you have worked in a methodical and professional manner.

For each of the environments that you plan to set up or to use you will need to create a hardware architecture design, which could potentially include the following:

■ **Client–server architecture.** As well as deciding how the different components of your application and system management software will be distributed, you need to consider what types of client you plan to support, such as PCs, personal digital assistants (PDAs), fax machines and mobile telephones.

■ **Input and output devices,** such as printers, scanners, bar code readers and cameras.

■ **Data storage.** You may need dedicated database servers, optical storage devices and back-up drives.

■ **Communications,** including hubs, routers, network cabling, modems.

In most projects the majority of your hardware architecture will already be in place, in which case you will need to specify which elements you plan to make use of, rather than what you plan to install. The best way to document your architecture design is to draw a network diagram of the type shown in Figure 8.3, supplemented with a table describing how many of each device you plan to use.

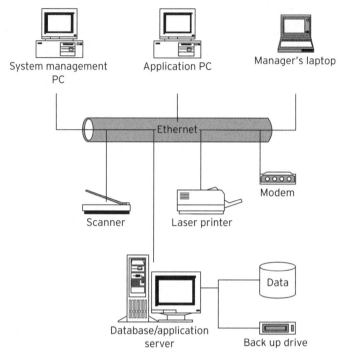

Figure 8.3 Simple 2-tier architecture design

Note that in a student project the underlying architecture of each environment is often the same, so you may need to document the architecture design only once.

The final area of the infrastructure that you need to consider is the software. In addition to the software you create, you may need to acquire and install other software components, such as:

- development tools;
- operating systems;
- application packages and plug-ins;
- database management systems;
- web server software;
- security or anti-virus software;
- communications, interfacing or networking software;
- system management utilities;
- hardware drivers.

Infrastructure specifications

The selection and specification of each component within your planned infrastructure should be based on the non-functional requirements you identified during your analysis, together with any technical constraints imposed by your

Table 8.5 Infrastructure requirements and selection factors

Requirement	Comment
Capacity	Capacity requirements may refer to data volumes, transaction volumes or numbers of users.
Performance	Including on-line response times, batch run-times and print speeds.
Availability	If long availability times are required (up to 24×7), then hardware and support costs are likely to be high.
Integration and compatibility	Software and hardware components may need to interface with or be used to support existing systems.
Platform strategy	If your project involves an external client, they may have a platform strategy that constrains or dictates your infrastructure specification.
Costs	Including the costs of purchase, licensing, support, technical training, upgrades and installation.
Suppliers	The reliability of suppliers may be an important factor, especially if your infrastructure is innovative in any way.
Security	Special or complex security requirements can significantly constrain your technical options.
Back-up and recovery	All systems that process or store valuable data will need reliable back-up and recovery facilities. This will be less of an issue for more academic/problem-solving projects, but you should still ensure that your source code is well protected.
System management	If your architecture is complex or high capacity you will need to think about how the system will be managed to ensure optimum use of resources.
Scalability	If your system will be used on an ongoing basis you need to specify how it will cater for future growth. If technology prices are falling you may decide to build minimum capacity now, and plan for upgrades later. If they are stable (and low) you may decide to install spare capacity now in order to avoid upgrade installation costs later.
Future proofing	You need to balance the attractions of adopting cutting edge technology against the risks of choosing components that may fail in the market (the VHS versus Betamax syndrome). In many cases you will be better served by adopting stable, but still current, technologies.

university or client. Table 8.5 summarises some of the main requirements that your infrastructure specification will need to take account of. If you are planning to use an existing infrastructure then your specification will not need to have the same level of detail as it would if you were implementing new components.

In this case it is essential only for you to check that the existing components have sufficient capacity and performance to support your needs.

8.7 Program specification

There are numerous ways of specifying how your conceptual designs are to be transformed into physical software components, depending on your development method and on the programming tools you are using, including:

- logical design models (such as Update Process models in SSADM);
- method specifications;
- pseudo-code;
- structured English;
- structure charts and diagrams, etc.

		Functions						
		f1	f2	f3	f4	f5	f6	f7
Software Components	**User interfaces**							
	UI1	x						
	UI2		x					
	UI3							
	UI4	x						
	UI5			x				
	UI6			x				
	UI7					x	x	
	UI8							
	UI9					x		
	UI10						x	
	Reports							
	R1	x						
	R2			x				
	R3						x	
	R4							
	System interfaces							
	SI1				x			
	SI2				x			
	SI3							x
	SI4							x
	Program/objects							
	P1					x	x	
	P2			x				

Figure 8.4 Extract of implementation matrix

It is possible that you are using a CASE tool that will generate software specifications or physical components automatically. You may also be using a development tool that is self-documenting to an extent.

In many projects it will be appropriate to use different ways of capturing your specification depending on the nature of the component concerned. For example, you may choose to complete formal text-based program specifications (supplemented perhaps by structure diagrams) for complex off-line components, but use self-documenting application generators for simple user interfaces.

The important things in specifying software components are that your specifications cover all the components you need to implement the system, that they satisfy your conceptual design (and therefore your system requirements), and that all your software is documented to a level that will enable it to be maintained in the future.

In order to ensure that your software specification and set of physical components is complete, it can be helpful to complete an implementation matrix that maps each element of your conceptual design onto one or more physical components (each of which may in turn be used to implement more than one conceptual component). The example in Figure 8.4 shows an implementation matrix that maps functions (the basic unit of processing in an SSADM conceptual design) to the software components that implement them.

8.8   Summary

1. Before you commit yourself to a particular physical implementation of the required system, you need to think carefully about how the system should behave and how it needs to interact with the outside world. Student projects that leap into construction are characterised by missing functionality, poor structure and faulty logic.

2. The design of the user interface can be one of the most enjoyable and creative parts of a system development project.

3. There are three guiding principles that you should always keep at the front of your mind when designing user interfaces: keep it simple, design for your users and be consistent.

4. While most system development methods have clear and well-documented processes for internal design, few provide much guidance on user interface (external) design. A generic process that could be applied to a range of projects consists of four steps: establish user interface standards; create user interface structure; design individual user interfaces; and design input validation.

5. Many student projects will aim to deliver a prototype application, as they do not have sufficient time to produce a fully operational system covering the entire scope of their project. To be academically acceptable your prototype system will normally need to include at least the following features: user interfaces, database integration, tested functionality and a recognisable subset of requirements.

6. If your initial prototypes are unsophisticated, you will be able to complete a greater number of cycles than if you develop a working prototype from the beginning. In

most student projects you should be able to complete three or four cycles if you adopt a 'low-tech' approach for the early versions: paper rough, paper revision, static software prototype and working prototype.

7. If your system involves substantial amounts of data, or will be used by more than a handful of users, you will need to optimise your database design. The things that you should consider in optimising your database design are: denormalisation, derived values, summary tables, query optimisation, disk placement/clustering, indexing strategies, data marts, multi-user access, and back-up and recovery.

8. Few student projects will involve the installation of the kind of substantial new production environments that are a feature of many commercial projects. While this may mean that the amount of effort you need to devote to the design of your project's implementation infrastructure is greatly reduced, you will still need to spend some time specifying how you plan to configure and use the infrastructure.

9. A common configuration for student projects consists of three environments: development environment, test environment, live environment. For each of the environments that you plan to set up or to use you will need to create a hardware architecture design, which could potentially include the following: client–server architecture, input and output devices, data storage and communications.

10. The selection and specification of each component within your planned infrastructure should be based on the non-functional requirements you identified during your analysis, together with any technical constraints imposed by your university or client.

11. There are numerous ways of specifying how your conceptual designs are to be transformed into physical software components, depending on your development method and on the programming tools you are using, including: logical design models (such as Update Process models in SSADM), method specifications, pseudocode, structured English, and structure charts and diagrams.

9 System construction and implementation

9.1 Introduction

The aim of this chapter is to address the issues that confront many students when they come to construct and implement their system.

Few students will come to their project with previous experience of implementing a piece of software. They are therefore unaware of the considerable practical challenges that may face them when they implement their software in a live environment. Much of the material presented in this chapter is intended to provide guidance in implementing a system for real, even if it is a limited prototype. However, other parts are relevant to the final construction stage of any software development.

Learning Outcomes

After reading this chapter, you will be able to:

- Understand how to manage the production of software objects

- Appreciate the importance of the different forms of testing

- Complete appropriate levels of system and user documentation

- Understand how to plan and execute system installation, conversion and change management

- Appreciate the need to plan for system maintenance

9.2 Software programming and production

Programming or software generation (if you are using some sort of application generator or are configuring a package) is the activity that most students focus their energies on during the construction phase of their project. This is not surprising as it is the most visible and obvious element of the system construction process. In a complex programming project, it may legitimately be the largest single activity of the entire project. However, in most student projects, programming tasks should account for less than half the time they spend on the construction phase, and in many projects it should account for less than a third. The majority of your time should probably be devoted to activities such as testing (often the largest single task), hardware installation, documentation, user training, and data set-up or conversion. All of these activities are covered in Sections 9.3 to 9.5.

One thing to be especially careful about is starting to program your software too soon. You may well be prototyping some elements of the system, but many other elements, including some of the algorithms that may be used by your prototyped components, will be unsuitable for prototyping and should wait until their design and specification is complete. Even if you are using a RAD approach you should remember that all RAD methodologies provide guidance on which elements or systems can be and which should not be prototyped. The time and effort involved in constantly reworking complex software components can be huge, and it will be much more efficient and effective to think your designs through carefully, and only once this is stable to begin production of the software.

One of the biggest problems encountered by students in the construction phase is managing their software objects, particularly as they produce different versions of the same component. The solution is usually quite straightforward, but it does mean setting up and sticking to the simple housekeeping procedures listed in Table 9.1.

Figure 9.1 shows an example of a configuration management log. In a group project the log should be accessible to all members of the team, so that they can update it whenever they are making changes to, or need exclusive use of, a system component.

In most projects the construction phase marks the point at which user requirements and the resulting system design are baselined. Without imposing some kind of freeze on requirements the final build stage can become chaotic, resulting in scope creep or in applications that lack consistency. This does not mean that changes cannot be made to the design or to requirements, but that you need to examine any such changes carefully to establish whether it is really necessary to make them right now, or whether they could be delayed to a future software release. If changes do need to be made, you must have a process in place for documenting the changes in a change control log (see Figure 9.2), and for assessing fully their impact on your designs and project timescales. As well as making practical sense, a change control log will help you in completing your critical evaluation of the execution of your project, as it will provide valuable information on how effective your analysis and design process was in delivering a stable system specification.

In a group project the responsibility for managing the change control log should be given to one person, whose responsibility it is to communicate the changes to other team members, and to ensure that all proposed changes are discussed fully.

Table 9.1 Software component management procedures

Procedure	Description
Adopt meaningful names	If your operating system allows you to, then you should try to make the names of the files containing your physical software components consistent with those of your design components. For example, Member_ Update_Window1 or UI1 (if you are using a more numerical system of identifiers as in Figure 8.4).
Use version numbers	As you develop a software component you will normally produce several versions. This could be because you need to make changes following testing feedback, or in reaction to changes in requirements, or because you want to try more than one way of solving a particular problem. Each time you produce a new or amended version it is sensible to add a numeric suffix to your component's name, e.g. UI1_v1, UI1_v2.
Set up folder or directory structure	You should set up a structure of folders or directories that mirrors your strategy for development, testing and production environments. As a minimum, you will need one directory for development, one for testing and one to hold the final versions of your software. In addition, you may need further directories such as system testing, user acceptance testing, volume testing, pre-live (components that are fully tested and ready to go live) and live.
Track your components	As the number of components grows it becomes increasingly difficult to assess what state your software is in by browsing through your directories. This problem is much greater if you are working on a group project, where it can be difficult to keep track of who is working on what, leading to problems with some people believing a component is finished, while someone else is still making changes to it. The answer is to set up a simple configuration management log, such as the one shown in Figure 9.1 (a template for this log is available on the companion website).

Component Log						
Software Component	Status	Current Version (full path)	Date Out	Reason	Person	Date In
User interface U11	ST	h:\stmemsys\systest\U11_v5	12/04/2003	System testing	AS	
User interface U12	Dev	h:\stmemsys\dev\U12_v4	10/04/2003	Unit testing	FD	11/04/2003
Report R4	Dev	h:\stmemsys\dev\R4_v3	11/04/2003	System test corrections	MK	

Figure 9.1 Extract of a configuration management log

Change Control Log					
Date	Status	Description of change	Impact of change	Priority	Date Resolved
14/04/2003	Proposed	Member's report to include full address details	Significant redesign and coding of member's report (1 day)	3	
21/04/2003	Accepted	Member renewal letters do not include all subscription fee options	Add fee calculation to letter minor modification (1 hour)	1	21/04/2003
24/04/2003	Accepted (next release)	Daily task log to automatically print overnight	New scheduled batch job (1/2 day)	2	25/04/2003

Figure 9.2 Extract of a change control log

9.3 Testing

Testing is critically important to the success of any project that aims to deliver working software. Unless your implementation is simply an early design prototype (in which case your software is really just an animated storyboard), you will lose marks if your software fails to work when you are asked to demonstrate it during a viva voce examination. Your assessors may be quite happy to accept an application that represents a limited subset of your full design, but they will not be happy if that subset falls over or fails to meet its limited set of requirements. The way to ensure that this does not happen is to adopt a systematic approach to the testing of your software.

There are many types of testing, grouped under the categories listed in Table 9.2. While some of these will rarely be needed in a student project, others, such as unit, integration and system testing, will be necessary in almost all projects.

To plan your tests you should carry out a simple step-by-step planning process, as follows:

1. List the things that you need to test. Document these as objectives or scenarios in a test plan using a form such as that shown in Figure 9.3 (a template for this form is available from the companion website).

Test Plan					
Test Objective/Scenario	Test Cases (input data)	Script/Steps	Expected Results	Actual Results	Test Date

Figure 9.3 Blank test plan document

Table 9.2 Types of software testing

Test type	Purpose
Unit testing	To test that individual software components or modules are error free, and conform to their specification.
Integration testing	To test that the components integrate with each other, and that data and control flow correctly between them.
System testing	To test that the system (or subsystem) as a whole meets its requirements and conceptual design. In a group project, someone who has taken a lead analysis role should carry out system testing.
User acceptance testing	If your project is being undertaken for a client or academic sponsor, they should test the acceptability of the system and its user documentation before signing it off as complete.
Volume testing	To test whether the system is able to meet its performance requirements when used with large volumes of data, and/or by large numbers of users. The emphasis in volume testing is on the number of users, size of database or number of transactions, rather than on how the system responds to different events or data combinations.
Operational testing	If someone else will ultimately be operating or managing your system, they should test its operational suitability before you hand it over.

2. Decide what test data you will need to set up in order to test all the relevant conditions. Some of the data will be input data, and some will need to be the database before the test. Each set of data, designed to test one or more test conditions, is known as a test case. It is impossible to test every condition, or combination of data conditions, but as a minimum you should attempt to test valid data that are well within the normal range, invalid data and data that are on the boundary. For example, if in a unit you were testing the input of data into a field with a valid range of 1–10, you should probably test something like 0, 1, 5, 10 and 11.

3. Produce a script for each test, detailing the steps that you will need to carry out.

4. Define the expected results.

5. Set up the test data. At this point you should *always* take a copy of the data, so that you can restore data and re-run the tests as necessary. It is inconceivable that all your tests will be successful first time (indeed, if your testing is rigorous, the majority will probably fail). If you do not take copies of your test data, you will have to set the data up from scratch every time you re-run the tests. Test data can be generated in spreadsheets, input manually, or

imported from existing systems (this is a particularly good way of creating volume test data, assuming that conversion to the new system is straightforward, and it will also help to test your data migration programs).

6. Conduct the tests, and document the actual results.

9.4 User and system documentation

Depending on the nature of your system, you may need to produce two distinct sets of documentation as part of your final deliverables. The first is user documentation, which is designed to help people use your system. The other is system documentation, which is designed to explain how the system works or how it should be managed and maintained. If your project involves end users you will need both types of documentation, while if your project is more academic in nature, you may need to produce a limited set of system documentation only.

It is tempting to leave documentation to the last minute. This is partly because it appears on the surface to be a mechanical task that can be fitted in once the 'real' development work is over. The other reason often cited by developers for delaying the production of documentation is that until you have completed your testing you will be 'aiming at a moving target', as the software will be subject to continual change.

The problem with leaving documentation until the very end of the project is that it is *always* much more time consuming than you expect, and will itself need to be thoroughly tested before the system is put live. It is far more efficient to develop documentation as you design and build the software. Most system documentation is produced as part of the analysis and design process, but other parts, such as back-up instructions, will be produced during the construction stage. User documentation is also produced mainly during the construction stage, as it is only at this point that the user interfaces are relatively stable and complete. If you produce documentation at the same time as you complete other related construction tasks, the results will be more tightly integrated with the software than if you produce it later. You will also produce it more efficiently, as the information required will be at the front of your mind.

With all types of documentation you will have a choice of presenting the material on paper or on-line. On-line documentation has a number of benefits:

- It is easier to keep up to date than multiple copies of paper documents.
- It can be indexed and searched with great flexibility and speed.
- It can be made interactive, and presented in the context of the system feature it is describing (e.g. by using a pop-up window).
- It always available to any user at any time.
- It can always be printed off if people prefer to read instructions on paper (a common need for tutorials, for example).

There are of course some disadvantages, mainly associated with the time and cost of developing it in the first place, as a fully functional on-line help system is a sophisticated piece of software in its own right. For this reason you may not have time to set up a full on-line help system, even for a relatively small subset of your system. The best solution in this case is to produce paper-based documentation, together with a few on-line examples of each that will demonstrate to your assessors how you would plan to implement the full on-line help system.

User documentation

In most student projects, you will normally plan to produce just a sample of the final user documentation, as you will not have time to document your entire implementation. You should not, however, ignore the issue of documentation, as it is a vital component of any real-life project, and your assessors will normally expect you to demonstrate some experience of designing and implementing it. The four main types of user documentation that you need to consider are summarised in Table 9.3.

In a commercial project members of the development team often produce reference materials, while users may produce the more training-oriented materials, usually as part of user acceptance test planning. In a student project you will normally produce all the user documentation, although in some rare cases your client may provide some user resource to help with testing, documentation and training tasks.

The style that you adopt for your user documentation will be determined by the needs of the users that you are writing for. However, there are a few tips for writing effective user documentation that will apply in almost all cases:

Table 9.3 Types of user documentation

'Getting started' guides	These provide overviews of the system, together with step-by-step instructions for carrying out basic system functions.
Tutorials	Tutorials provide lessons on how to use the system, function by function, with plenty of examples designed to build the knowledge of the user in a steady fashion.
'How to' guides	These provide detailed guidance on specific tasks or functions of the system. They are usually structured to match business activities, processes or use scenarios as established during the analysis stage.
Reference materials	Reference materials provide short explanations of terminology, input and output fields, and individual functions, features or components of the system. They are usually indexed alphabetically, often in an on-line help system.

■ **Be brief.** Provide your users with short instructions and explanations, preferably in bulleted or numbered paragraphs.

■ **Write short paragraphs.** Do not force your users to wade through long sections of text to find what they need.

■ **Use simple and consistent terminology.** Avoid the use of technical terms, and remember that user documentation is not an opportunity to demonstrate your literary prowess. Above all, use terminology consistently and do not be afraid of over-using a term if it is the right one.

■ **Do not assume any prior knowledge.** Write for people who have little or no previous experience of your system or its predecessor. Test your documentation on your peers.

■ **Use an active voice.** Always use the active voice, especially when providing step-by-step instructions. For example, when explaining how to print a copy of an order using the active voice, you might say 'To print a copy of the order, press F3'. This is far more direct than it would be when phrased in the passive voice, such as 'A copy of the order can be printed by pressing F3'.

System documentation

You will produce most of your system documentation as part of the analysis and design process. This is the material that will describe what the system does and how it does it from a technical perspective. In addition, you should always add comments to your program code, including specification extracts inserted next to relevant pieces of code, in order to explain how the program works. Program comments will help your assessors to understand why you have developed your components in the way that you have. In a client-based project they will also assist people who may be required to maintain your software once your project has finished. Program code without explanatory comments is difficult to interpret and time consuming to maintain. All your program code should therefore be properly commented.

The other main type of system documentation is the set of instructions that describes how to manage and operate your system. This will include:

■ installation and set-up instructions;

■ back-up and restore procedures;

■ disaster recovery procedures;

■ housekeeping task instructions (e.g. data archiving procedures);

■ operating instructions, describing what actions need to be taken to start and shut down the system, what external system dependencies exist, how to respond to error messages, etc.;

■ capacity constraints.

As with user documentation, you may not have sufficient time to produce a complete set of system management documentation, so should aim to write a representative subset (covering some of the parts that you have implemented).

9.5 System implementation

The main activities of a system implementation can be grouped under three headings: installation, conversion and change management. The nature of your project will determine the extent to which you need to consider these activities. For example, in an academic project that involves the development of complex algorithms, you may not need to carry out any of these activities, while in a client-based project they may prove be some of the trickiest activities of your entire development.

Hardware and software installation

It is unusual for student projects to involve the installation of significant amounts of new hardware, but many do make small changes to an existing infrastructure, such as the addition of new PCs or printers. If your project requires any new hardware, you should order it as soon as you are clear on what you need. While new software can usually be purchased and delivered quickly (often using downloads), hardware lead times are notoriously unpredictable, as they are dependent on production cycles and the capacity of physical distribution operations. To be safe, you should order early, as without the necessary hardware you will not get far in implementing your system.

Once your hardware has arrived and been physically wired in (sometimes a complex task in its own right), or you are ready to implement your system in an existing production environment (or pseudo-production environment for viva voce demonstration purposes), you will need to carry out the following tasks:

1. **Install and configure system software.** This may include hardware drivers, browsers, operating systems and communications software.

2. **Install and configure third party applications and utilities.** This may include spreadsheets, database management systems and browser plug-ins.

3. **Transfer your application software.** Once the production environment is in place, you are in a position to transfer your application software from its development or testing environment.

4. **Conduct operational testing.** In many cases there will be small differences between your development and testing environments, and the production environment, often because of contention with other applications. For this reason, you should schedule some time to carry out operational testing using some of your system test data.

Once you have completed these tasks you have what is essentially an 'empty' system, ready for data population.

System conversion and data population

There are a number of tried and tested models for cutting over to a new system, as summarised in Table 9.4, which also includes some of the pros and cons of each model.

Table 9.4 System cut-over models

Cut-over model	Description	Pros and cons
Big bang	The new system is made live in all locations for all users at the same time. Any existing system is shut down simultaneously.	Simplest model, with lowest costs and shortest timescales. High risk, as the fall-back position is often complex if things go wrong. The most common model in student projects, due to the limited scope, low business risk and stand-alone nature of many projects.
Parallel running	The new system is implemented as in the big bang model, but the existing system is left running in parallel until the new one is judged to be running smoothly.	Low risk, as the fall-back position is simple and easy to enact. Can be labour intensive to run two systems. May not be technically or organisationally possible to run both systems at the same time. Typically found in student projects that are intended to automate manual systems.
Pilots	The new system is implemented in one location. Once this is stable, and any changes resulting from experiences during the pilot have been applied to the software and change management procedures, it is rolled out to other locations.	The only way to implement many geographically dispersed systems. Large timescales and roll-out costs may be a consequence. A rare model in student projects owing to long timescales.
Phased implementation	The system is implemented in a series of 'chunks', where each one contains a functional subset of the whole system, e.g. customer ordering functions first, followed by customer service, and finally by purchase ordering.	Inevitable if using the incremental development life cycle model. May simplify organisational changes within a business. Can be technically difficult or impossible to achieve.
Production prototype or trial	A trial system is implemented in one location or function. The results are reviewed, and requirements adjusted, before an amended version of the system is developed and implemented using one of the above models.	Low cost and risk. Beneficial when requirements are difficult to establish or justify without full field tests. Involves long timescales, and may be costly if trial results are poor. A significant number of student projects deliver trial systems.

As part of switching over to the new system you will need to plan and execute the population of the database. You will need to set up three types of data:

1. **Reference or 'master' data.** This refers to entities such as products, customers and places. While reference data are far from static, they change far less than transaction data, and in most systems need to be in place before a system goes live in order for transactions to be processed efficiently. For example, can you imagine implementing a tool hire system without first setting up details of the tools that are available for hire? If data were not set up in advance you would need to enter basic data about each item before it was hired out for the first time; a process that would be impractical.

2. **Transaction data.** This refers to entities that record the actions and events that take place within a business, such as orders, sales, appointments and bookings. If you are replacing an existing system (even a manual one) you will need to populate the database with details of historical transactions and potentially of transactions that are partially complete (in a parallel running implementation you may choose to complete all such transactions in the old system before copying them across to the new system).

3. **Control data.** This refers to data that control the operation and management of the new system, including such items as user names, passwords and user access parameters.

Control data are usually entered into a system manually by using the standard data maintenance facilities within your system. Reference data may also be entered manually in projects where there is little or no current system support, or where new reference data are required that are not present in the current system.

In projects where there is an existing system, the bulk of the reference data and all transaction data will typically be transferred from existing databases to the new system using a combination of automated conversion programs and spreadsheets. The process of data conversion is rarely straightforward, as in most projects there will be issues of data incompatibility and restructuring that will require careful handling if the new system is to avoid problems of data corruption and lack of integrity. Some of the most common data conversion issues are summarised in Table 9.5.

To overcome these issues data conversion usually consists of a three-stage process:

1. **Data extraction.** Selected data are extracted from the current system using query programs. In most systems the tables will contain control data or other items that are not required by the new system, so you will need to exclude these from your extracts.

2. **Data cleansing and manipulation.** Extracted data are rarely in a form that can be uploaded without some manipulation into the new system. If changes are relatively straightforward (e.g. format changes) they may be applied as part of a combined extract/upload program. More often the extracted data will be placed in a holding area (often a spreadsheet) and a succession of changes

Table 9.5   Data conversion issues

Issue	Description
Changed data formats	Data format may change between old and new systems even where the meaning of the data remains the same. For example, date formats may change from DDMMYY to MMDDYYYY. In other cases the changes may be more fundamental, with numeric formatting changes, new data types and changes to data item lengths (increases and reductions).
Data corruption	Existing systems invariably contain data that have become corrupted because of system bugs, or that will be invalid in the new system because of changed validation rules.
New data item values	Some data items will have different value ranges (domains) in the new system, e.g. an existing system might classify customers as being 'trade' and 'retail', while the new system may classify them as 'commercial', 'government' and 'public'.
Additional data items	The new system is almost certain to have new data items that need to be merged with existing system data before they can be uploaded. This may be relatively straightforward, such as additional address details, but may be more complex, particularly if new keys are involved.
Status conflicts	If data are being extracted from more than one existing system then the same entity may have different or even conflicting statuses in each system. In addition the existing systems may differ from the new system in how it establishes the status of an entity. For example, in the existing system a product may be classified as 'new' until a customer orders it, whereas in the new system it may classified as 'new' until it has been on sale for one year.
Restructuring	Data models rarely, if ever, remain unchanged between old and new systems. For example, data items that existed as attributes in an existing system may have multiple values and therefore be tables in their own right in the new system.
Data redundancy	The existing system will almost certainly contain data that are not required by the new system.
Referential integrity	The new system may have new rules for how tables relate to each other. For example, previously optional relationships may have become mandatory.
Derived data	Derived data in the old system may have been created using different calculations from those required by the new system.
Work in progress	Any transaction data relating to partially competed business transactions will need to be handled carefully, as processes may have changed radically, and so may need to be completed in the old system or manually in a spreadsheet before being uploaded to the new system.

applied to 'cleanse' or restructure the data before uploading into the new system. Data cleansing can be carried out using update programs or manually within a spreadsheet.

3. **Data upload.** Once data have been cleansed they can be inserted into the new database. In doing so, you need to be conscious of mandatory data items, table relationships, etc. so that referential integrity is maintained.

If corrupted or invalid data are transferred into the new system the success of your entire project will be put at risk, so it is essential that all data conversion programs are carefully designed and rigorously tested before being used for real.

Change management

Change management is an important and complex subject that is covered well by a number of excellent textbooks (see Bibliography). It is difficult to over-emphasise its importance within a commercial project, as it does not matter how elegant a piece of software is, it is entirely pointless if it is not used.

If your project is client-based, you must make time to consider the issues associated with change management; otherwise you will have ignored the opportunity to explore one of the most important success factors in a commercial project. You are most unlikely to have the time or opportunity to put change management procedures into effect, but you must be able to demonstrate that you have considered the issues and developed a change management strategy.

To the uninitiated it may appear that 'all' you need to do in order to have your system accepted and adopted by its target users is to develop a user-friendly system that meets some real organisational requirements. Then everyone will look at the system and jump at the chance to get started with it. Sadly, the real world is not at all like this. In many cases there is great reluctance or resistance to adopting a new system, even when an existing one is removed. There are a number of genuine reasons for this resistance, including the following:

- Users may feel threatened by the new system. This may be due to fears about redundancy or loss of status acquired through knowledge of the existing system. It may also be caused by concerns about their ability to learn new ways of working.

- Some users are unsettled by change of any kind. They are rarely resistant to change, but do not willingly accept it.

- The benefits of the system may not be obvious to all users. Indeed for some there may be no direct benefit, but they will still need to change the way they work in order to facilitate improvements elsewhere in the organisation.

- The training offered in how to use the new system may not have been adequate.

- Users may already be working at full capacity and so find it difficult to make time to train and become effective in using the new system.

- Some users may be resentful about not being directly consulted or involved in the development of the system, and so seek to undermine its implementation.

■ Users may be poorly trained in the use of computer equipment in general, and therefore feel uneasy about adopting a computer-based system.

■ The system may not be as easy to use as you think.

A number of these issues are particularly associated with projects that have a significant effect on the ways in which people work, while others (such as those associated with poor training and communication) could apply to any project, including a student project.

There are many techniques for addressing change management issues, the most obvious one being the creation of appropriate training materials (see below). Detailed discussion of these techniques is beyond the scope of this book, but they might include:

■ information and education programmes, including internal marketing and system training;

■ operational procedure manuals and checklists developed by users, and published widely;

■ adequate (and possibly additional) resourcing for the changeover period;

■ visible sponsorship and leadership from senior managers;

■ early communication of the benefits and impact of the system;

■ adjusted or new reward schemes;

■ comprehensive user acceptance testing, involving key influencers from the user community;

■ active user involvement at all stages of the project;

■ co-opting of respected users into the project or training team.

User training

Possibly the most widely applicable and critical factor in achieving widespread adoption of a new system is the quality of the system training offered to users. Training is an area that you as a student should be able to relate to. It is also one area of change management that you should be able to develop a realistic approach for, even if you get few opportunities to put it into practice.

There are three main delivery methods for system training:

■ **Classroom training.** Classroom delivery is an effective way of delivering training relatively quickly to a number of individuals at the same time. This is probably the most widely used training method. It can be tailored to the needs of groups of users, who then have the opportunity to share their learning experience and to learn from each other. By creating a classroom environment away from their normal place of work, it is also a method that is free from distractions. With small to medium sized user populations it can be the cheapest method of delivery, as the set-up costs are lower than with some methods (such as self-study), and delivery costs are reasonable if the number of groups is low.

- **Face-to-face training.** Training that is delivered on a one-on-one basis can be tailored to meet the needs of one specific user. It also allows the trainer to respond directly to the concerns of the individual and to ensure that they have understood fully all of the material. Face-to-face training is expensive to deliver, so it can be used only for small user populations or for a handful of key individuals.

- **Self-study.** Self-study materials can either be paper-based or more commonly (and effectively) computer-based. Computer-based training (CBT) can be extremely expensive to develop, but the cost of delivery can be correspondingly low, as there is no need to provide a trainer. As self-study material can be used at any time, it is easier to schedule its use than it is to coordinate the attendance of groups of people for long classroom sessions. Conversely, because self-study often takes place in a work setting, the risk of distraction is high. CBT is more effective at presenting short topics or covering relatively simple concepts. It can also be effective in providing training in more complex systems, but only in situations where the users are highly computer literate; a fact that leads some computing students to believe wrongly that CBT is the answer for all training needs. Owing to its ease of distribution CBT is used extensively where the user population is large and widely dispersed.

9.6 Planning for maintenance

In a student project it is clearly not feasible for you to experience the maintenance phase of your system. In many ways this mirrors the situation found in many commercial projects, where one team will develop the system and another group will then take over responsibility for its maintenance.

In a student project the software produced is often 'disposable', and so will not pass into a maintenance phase. However, in projects that involve the delivery of software that is intended for ongoing use, or that simulate the delivery of such software, you will need to plan for the maintenance phase, even though you will not be responsible for managing it. This again mirrors the role of commercial development teams.

Your maintenance plan will need to consider the following:

- **System support.** Once a system is up and running there need to be procedures and people in place to deal with requests for help, and to solve problems that arise. For a large system this will usually involve a help desk of some kind, backed up by 'second-level' support staff (system experts) who know how to tune the system, who understand in great detail how it works, and who have administration privileges that will allow them to fix corrupt data. Procedures should cover such things as the contacting of support staff, problem logging and prioritisation, and system administration.

- **Application maintenance and bug fixing.** Any problems that cannot be fixed through system administration procedures are usually down to bugs in the software. Change control procedures are needed both to manage and track bug fixes, and to process user requests for system changes. In a small system the roles of the help desk, second-level support and program maintenance may be carried out by the same individuals.

■ **Software and hardware upgrades.** Procedures are also needed for applying system software and hardware upgrades. No operating system, network software, browser or plug-in remains current for long, and will need to be upgraded before the manufacturers withdraw support for them. Likewise, as databases or transaction levels grow there will almost certainly be a need to upgrade hardware.

■ **System tuning.** Most systems are implemented in a way that is optimised for the current levels of usage. These levels will not remain constant, as most businesses have cycles that place different demands on the system at various points in those cycles, and most will also be subject to longer-term trends in transaction volumes and user numbers. The tuning mechanisms within a system should be well documented so that they can be used as necessary in the future.

In a typical student project, where you will have little or no experience of system maintenance (in a commercial project maintenance plans are usually developed jointly by the development team and the maintenance/operations team), your plan will inevitably be high level, but should at least demonstrate to your assessors that you have thought about the issues, and have produced a system that could be maintained given the development and implementation of appropriate procedures and roles.

9.7 Summary

1. Programming tasks may account for less than half the time spent on the construction phase, and in many projects it should account for less than a third. The majority of your time should be devoted to activities such as testing (often the largest single task), hardware installation, documentation, user training, and data set-up or conversion.

2. Managing the production of software should be straightforward if simple housekeeping procedures are set up and followed.

3. Testing is critically important to the success of any project that aims to deliver working software. There are many types of testing, and while some of these will rarely be needed in a student project, others such as unit, integration and system testing will be necessary in almost all projects.

4. Depending on the nature of your system, you may need to produce two distinct sets of documentation as part of your final deliverables. The first is user documentation, which is designed to help people use your system. The other is system documentation, which is designed to explain how the system works or how it should be managed and maintained. The main types of user documentation that you need to consider are: 'getting started' guides, tutorials, 'how to' guides and reference materials.

5. In addition to system models, development documents and program specifications, the main type of system documentation is the set of instructions that describs how to manage and operate your system. This will include: installation and set-up instructions, back-up and restoration procedures, disaster recovery procedures, housekeeping instructions and operating instructions.

6. The main activities of a system implementation can be grouped under three headings: installation, conversion and change management. There are a number of tried and tested models for cutting over to a new system, such as: big bang, parallel running, pilots, phased implementation and production prototype or trial.

7. As part of cutting over to the new system you will need to plan and execute the population of the database. The three types of data that you need to set up are: reference or 'master' data, transaction data and control data.

8. The most widely applicable and critical factor in achieving widespread adoption of a new system is the quality of the system training offered to users. The main delivery methods for system training are: classroom training, face-to-face training and self-study.

9. You will need to plan for the maintenance phase, even though you will not be responsible for managing it. Your maintenance plan will need to consider the following: system support, application maintenance and bug fixing, software and hardware upgrades, and system tuning.

Project completion

10 Analysing your results

10.1 Introduction

The aim of this chapter is to provide guidance on the analysis of the results and outcomes of your project. This will cover both the analysis of data and information that you have gathered through your research activities, and the evaluation of your success in meeting the objectives of your project.

Learning Outcomes

After reading this chapter, you will be able to:

- Understand the importance of analysis and evaluation within a student project
- Write a literature review
- Apply a range of techniques for presenting and interpreting data
- Understand the scope of the critical evaluation of your project

10.2 What are analysis and evaluation?

In any student development project there are two principal components. The first and most obvious is the development of a piece of software to fulfil a stated purpose. The second is an academic component in which you are expected to demonstrate your understanding of the theory that is relevant to your development, and to analyse and evaluate the results of your project. In many projects the emphasis will be on the system development process, while in some it will be on the academic component. In the most academic of projects you will use system development activities as research tools, as opposed to using research to inform your development.

In order to satisfy the academic component of your project you will need to analyse your execution of the development process, gather data on its outcome and evaluate the results. If your project has a research bias your plans will have placed great significance on these activities, and much of your time will have been devoted to them. If your project has been dominated by the development of a piece of software, however, you may not have given them much thought or time. This is hardly surprising, as developing a system is a time-consuming and intensive activity in its own right, and this fact is recognised in the assessment criteria and expectations of many universities.

However, you must remember that as a student the academic component is still of major importance, and is in many cases what distinguishes a good project. At the undergraduate level your conclusions may not necessarily be of wider academic significance, but should *at the very least* provide evidence that you have gained deep personal insights into the development process and operated as a 'reflective practitioner'. If you neglect the academic aspects of your project you will almost certainly be imposing a 'cap' on your final mark, no matter how well you have developed your software.

There are three basic stages to the analysis and evaluation process in a development project:

1. **Gathering data.** In most projects you will have undertaken a literature search as part of setting up your project (see Chapter 4). As your project passed through its development stages you should have gathered further data in your project diary, plans, meeting minutes and issue logs. You may also collect primary data either as a central part of your project or as part of an end of project review (see Section 10.5).

2. **Analysing the data.** Once you have gathered the data, you will need to collate them, place them into groups and search for significant features, associations or patterns. You may be looking for evidence that relates to specific research objectives and theories (the deductive approach to research), or attempting to provide an analysis on which to base the development of theories and conclusions (the inductive approach).

3. **Evaluating the results of your analysis.** It is not enough to present the results of your analysis without an evaluation of their significance. Far too many students present a final report that lists various facts and figures relating to their development, with little by way of informed discussion. It is important to reflect on the results of your analysis, and to draw conclusions and make judgements. This may lead you both to challenge or confirm existing theory and the hypotheses you developed during the initiation of your project.

10.3 Writing a literature review

Literature reviews can be written at various points within your project. For example, you may be required to produce an initial review at the start of your project as part of its selection, while for most projects the main literature review will be presented as part of your final report. Even in cases where a single literature review is required at the end of your project, you should have carried out much of your search during the early stages of your project, as the information gathered will have been invaluable in setting up your project. You may also have chosen to complete some early drafts of sections of your review while the search was still fresh in your mind. The final draft of your literature review should, however, be left until you are nearing the end of your development, as your project is likely to have thrown up issues that have led to further targeted searches, and the results of your development will provide valuable insights that will add to the quality of your review.

Most literature reviews in development projects are presented in a combination of two formats:

1. A separate section in your final report.
2. Paragraphs embedded in your final report in places where they relate directly to the material presented.

Before writing your literature review it is worth reflecting on what you need it to do. You should not view it merely as an academic deliverable that needs to be 'ticked off'. A well-written literature review has a number of direct contributions to make to both the execution of your project and the presentation of your results, such as:

- to establish the academic context of your project, and provide readers of your final report with an introduction to your area of work;
- to increase and demonstrate your understanding of current thinking and theory;
- to assist you in developing and justifying your project, by identifying best practice, gaps in current research, emerging technologies and theories, etc.;
- to provide an academic underpinning for your conclusions.

Your literature review should include only discussion and evaluation of materials that are of direct relevance to your project, i.e. that are linked directly to the context of your project, or to specific research objectives or development activities within your project. It should on no account be used as a survey of all that has been written on subjects associated with your project, or to provide a 'shopping list' of all the books and articles you have read. While your background reading may have helped you in some indirect way during your project, the literature review should focus on direct contributions only. Your literature review should also be tightly focused on your project, and not be used as padding or to avoid expressing your own ideas. A literature review that merely presents a succession of quotations from the literature, with little by way of original evaluation or conclusions, will attract criticism from your assessors.

In a development project the literature review may be fairly brief. I have read reviews that have occupied no more than three or four sheets of A4 paper, but that have summarised and evaluated the relevant literature very successfully. Conversely, I have read reviews that have fallen into the 'catalogue of quotes' trap, and have dragged on for many pages without presenting anything that links directly to the project concerned. Some of the things that make a real difference in constructing a successful and readable literature review are as follows:

- **Authoritative and recognised sources.** Refer back to Section 4.7 for details of how you should evaluate potential sources. The important things are that you distinguish between unsubstantiated opinion and well-researched fact, and that your sources are properly referenced.

- **Balanced conclusions.** You should not ignore sources that contradict your hypotheses or approach. Instead you need to cover both sides of the argument and explain the differences. It is important to demonstrate that you have considered the evidence and made logical judgements. If you are challenging published theory you should be able to draw on other studies that have informed your views. Try to support your evaluation of the literature by highlighting gaps, lack of clarity, areas of consensus and apparent contradictions between sources.

- **Summarisation in your own words.** Only include block quotes where it is impossible to express the ideas more succinctly or where the quote has particular power. It is also entirely acceptable to present short tables of figures or graphs as they appear in the literature, as long as you acknowledge the source. Any block quotes should be directly linked to and discussed in your own conclusions, and not inserted to pad out your review.

- **Informed conclusions.** It is critically important, when presented as part of your final report, that your review is informed by the experience and results of your project.

- **Coherence and consistency.** Your literature review must be coherent, and not read like a list of disjointed paragraphs. Try to group the material around high-level concepts, topics or ideas. Do not group your review around the articles or authors you are citing. Your review should also be consistent, in that your conclusions must back each other up and link together.

There are no hard and fast rules for constructing a literature review, but many of my own students have used the 'funnelling process' suggested by Saunders *et al.* (2003) with some success:

1. Start your review at a more general level before narrowing down to your specific research and development objectives.
2. Provide a brief overview of key ideas.
3. Summarise, compare and contrast the work of the key writers.
4. Narrow down to highlight the work most relevant to your project, and emphasise those theories that have directly informed the conduct of your project.
5. Provide a detailed account of the findings of this work.
6. Highlight those issues where your project will or has provided fresh insights.
7. Lead the reader into subsequent sections of your project report that explore these issues further.

10.4   Analysing data

The complexity and volume of 'research' data collected during system develop-ment projects is usually fairly limited, and is most often used for descriptive purposes, rather than to test or develop complex theories. The emphasis in this section is therefore on the presentation and straightforward exploration of data, and not on the more challenging areas of data interpretation, such as the testing of relationships, which are rarely relevant to a development project. There are many good textbooks dealing with the subject of data analysis and quantitative research, some of which are listed in the Bibliography.

The process of analysing data breaks down into three stages:

1. **Preparation.** The raw data that you have collected need to be checked for errors and omissions, collated and formatted for input into a spreadsheet or analysis tool.
2. **Presentation.** Data can be presented in a variety of ways, using tables and charts, in order to paint a picture of your findings and to help you to explore their significance.
3. **Interpretation.** Interpreting your data may involve looking for relationships, differences, trends, groupings, patterns and significant facts.

Preparation

The first step in preparing your data is to check for omissions, ambiguities and errors. It is very difficult, if not impossible, to design a foolproof method of data collection. Regardless of whether you have gathered your data using question-naires, interviews or documentary analysis, there will inevitably be items of data that are unclear, contradictory or missing. You need to examine your data and remove any such anomalies.

If you find that certain of your questions have a high error rate, you may need to exclude those questions from your analysis entirely. Likewise, if you have produced a questionnaire and have received some returns that are riddled with errors throughout, you may need to exclude them from your results. How-ever, you should *never* attempt to exclude responses on the grounds that they do not agree with your theories or assumptions.

If you have gathered data from a number of different sources, such as a batch of returned questionnaires, you will need to collate all the data items, and translate them into a form that can be input into spreadsheets for analysis. A common way of doing this is by using matrices. Table 10.1 shows how a matrix might be used to summarise a range of responses to questions within a question-naire, taking one question at a time.

Table 10.2 provides an extract of a matrix that has been used to summarise a number of questions at the same time. This is useful when dealing with large numbers of questions, particularly if they have a limited range of responses. In

Table 10.1 Summarisation matrix extract (single question)
Question – Number of applications using HCI types

	Browser	Windows	Character	Other
Company 1	2	12	4	1
Company 2	3	3	0	0
Company 3	6	30	12	2
Company 4	0	8	6	0

Table 10.2 Summarisation matrix extract (multiple questions)

	Q1					Q2					Q3				Q4		Q5	
	1	2	3	4	5	1	2	3	4	5	1	2	3	4	1	2	1	2
Company 1	✓						✓				2	12	4	1	✓			4
Company 2		✓					✓				3	3	0	0		✓		2
Company 3	✓								✓		6	30	12	2	✓		1	
Company 4				✓		✓					0	8	6	0	✓			1

order to make the matrix manageable it is useful to devise a coding scheme to represent the range of responses, e.g. using the number 1 to represent 'browser', 2 to represent 'windows'.

The way in which you choose to summarise your data depends on a number of factors, such as the number of questions and the range of responses you are analysing, as well as your personal preferences. The key thing is that you summarise your data in a way that will feed into your analysis and is consistent.

As part of summarising your data, you will need to consider how the data should be categorised. Some of your questions will have precise numerical responses, such as 'what is the annual IT expenditure of your company?', while others will be more descriptive in nature, such as 'which operating systems do you currently support?' Numerical data will often need to be categorised into bands or ranges in order to identify patterns or relationships. For example, for the above expenditure question, you may need to group responses into bands such as £0–9,999, £10,000–19,999. In a well-designed questionnaire, you would have presented these catgories as part of the question, but in analysing less structured data, such as documents and interview transcripts, you may need to do this at the data analysis stage.

Exploration and presentation

Once you have collated and summarised your data, you will need to decide on how you plan to present the data in your final report, and to facilitate your exploration of the results. While it is perfectly possible to quote numerical results as part of a normal paragraph of text, or to study the summary matrices mentioned above, the use of charts and tables will add enormous value and impact to your final report, and make it far easier to spot trends and patterns in your data.

There are many tools available to help you in presenting your data, ranging from standard spreadsheet packages (which were used to produce all of the following examples) to specialist statistical analysis packages, such as SPSS and SAS. For a large number of development projects all that you will need is a simple spreadsheet tool.

The most commonly used forms of data presentation include the following:

- **Grids.** Grids or tables are ideal for listing precise numerical values, or presenting small pieces of text (such as those gathered using short open questions).

- **Bar charts.** Bar charts are useful for emphasising the differences in values of different categories, and in presenting the way in which values are distributed across a population. While tables have the benefit of accuracy, they do not in any way highlight how the values in each category relate to each other, nor do they help you to identify patterns quickly, in the way that bar charts do. Figure 10.1 illustrates how a simple bar chart can capture the profile of a group of questionnaire respondents at a glance. Figure 10.2 shows a variation on the bar chart, called a stacked bar chart. This is an ideal way of exploring how two variables might relate or compare to each other.

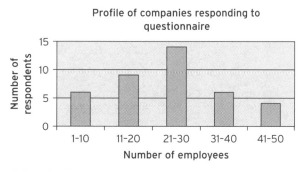

Figure 10.1   Simple bar chart

- **Pie charts.** Pie charts are most frequently used to show what proportion of a population belongs to each category. In order to make pie charts easy to interpret, it is useful to convert your data into percentages before translating the figures into a pie chart, as in Figure 10.3. Pie charts are most effective where there are relatively few categories (no more than six).

- **Line graphs.** Line graphs are particularly useful for showing trends in data. Figure 10.4 shows how two variables (IT expenditure and Turnover) have

Figure 10.2 Stacked bar chart

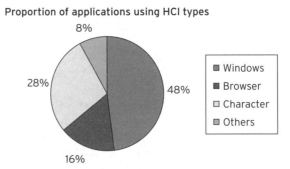

Figure 10.3 Pie chart

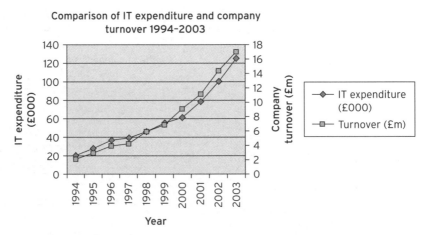

Figure 10.4 Line graph

changed over a period of ten years for a single company. By using two different *y*-axes, it is also possible using a line graph to compare trends in two distinct sets of data that have widely differing scales.

■ **Area graphs.** An area graph is a variation of the line graph. As well as showing trends in the overall value of a variable, an area graph can also help to highlight trends in the proportion belonging to two or more categories within the overall total. For example, Figure 10.5 shows how the proportion of total IT resource hours has increased during a 13-year period for a particular company. It also shows how an increasing proportion of those resource hours is being devoted to system maintenance.

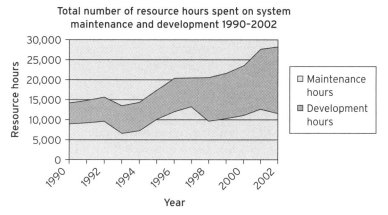

Figure 10.5   Area graph

■ **Scatter diagrams.** Scatter diagrams can be helpful in identifying relationships between variables. For example, the pattern of the plots in Figure 10.6 suggests that there *may* be a relationship between expenditure on user training and the satisfaction of users with the implemented system. However, you need to be careful in leaping to such conclusions, as there may be other factors that are responsible for this apparent relationship that are not represented in the diagram (for example, in Figure 10.6 the improved user satisfaction could be due to a more user-focused approach to the entire development, resulting in a better quality analysis of requirements).

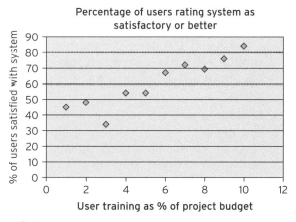

Figure 10.6   Scatter diagram

Note that whichever style or chart you choose to use, you must ensure that the axes are clearly labelled, that the chart has a meaningful title, and that you provide a legend where appropriate.

Interpreting data

In a system development project you are likely to carry out fairly simple and straightforward analysis and interpretation of your data, usually limited to the presentation of facts and the identification of simple trends, associations and patterns. It is quite common in a system development project for the interpretation of data to be restricted to a comparison of your findings with other data that you have reviewed in the literature.

Sophisticated statistical analysis of data is a highly sophisticated process, which utilises techniques that are well outside the scope of this book. You are extremely unlikely within the confines of a development project to have the time to conduct such analyses, so you must take great care when claiming to have identified relationships of significance within your data. You will not have the time or resources needed to validate or to follow up any radical assertions, so should probably content yourself with noting the presence of potential relationships, and present these alongside possible actions and questions needed to investigate them further.

While complex statistical analysis will be beyond the vast majority of development projects, there are some basic statistical measures that will be of use in virtually all projects in presenting your findings. The first group of measures is one that you should certainly be familiar with, and is used to describe the central tendency (i.e. a representative value) of your data:

■ **Mean.** The mean value of your data is what is commonly termed its average. It can be used only where your data have true numerical meaning, and not when numerical codes have been assigned in place of category descriptions (e.g. where you have used '1' to represent 'yes', '2' to represent 'no' and '3' to represent 'don't know'). The mean value will take all of your data into account, and therefore may be skewed towards extreme outlying values. It may be more appropriate therefore to use the **median**. For example, assume that you wish to provide a measure of the central tendency for a range of activities of the following lengths: 5 days, 8 days, 11 days, 12 days, 14 days, 20 days and 140 days. The mean length of activity would be 30 days. This could hardly be described as representative of the group, as only one activity lies above this value, with more than two-thirds being less than half of the mean.

■ **Median.** If you were to list all of your data values in order from the lowest to the highest, the median value would be the one that lies at the halfway point in your list, i.e. the middle value. The median is not affected by extreme outlying data values in the same way as the mean. In the example above, the median length of activity would be 12 days, which is much more representative than the mean of 30 days.

■ **Mode.** The mode is the most common value, and is most frequently used where the data involved are not quantifiable. Indeed, for descriptive or category-based data it is the only meaningful measure of the central tendency. For example, in the pie chart depicted in Figure 10.3 the modal group is 'Windows'.

The second group of basic statistical measures is concerned with giving an indication of the spread of values within your data:

■ **Range.** This is the simplest measure of how spread out your data are, and is the difference between the lowest and highest values. The higher the range, the more spread out your data. For example, take the following short lists of values:

    i   20, 40, 60, 80, 100
    ii 58, 59, 60, 61, 62

Both of these lists have a mean and median of 60. However, the first list has a range of 80, while the second has a range of just 4, reflecting the very different spreads of the two lists.

■ **Inter-quartile range.** The inter-quartile range is usually used in conjunction with the median, and represents the difference between the value that is one-quarter of the way up your ranked list of values (known as the lower quartile) and the value that lies three-quarters of the way up (known as the upper quartile). In other words it tells you the range that the middle half of your values lie within. As with the median, the inter-quartile range gives a measure of spread that is not unduly skewed by extreme values.

■ **Standard deviation.** The standard deviation provides an indication of the average amount by which your data differ from the mean value. If your data are well spread out then on average they will deviate by a large amount from the mean, whereas if your data are grouped more tightly around the mean they will on average deviate less.

The standard deviation can be calculated as follows:

    i   Subtract the mean from each value in your data set.
    ii   Square each of the resulting figures.
    iii Add up all of the squared differences.
    iv   Divide the resulting sum by the number of values in your set minus one.
    v   Take the square root of the result.

Table 10.3 illustrates this process for two small sets of values representing the user satisfaction scores with two different systems. While both have the same mean score, the standard deviation tells us that the views of users are far more variable for system one than for system two. For large sets of data, where spreads are less apparent from visual inspection, the standard deviation is an important statistical measure of the distribution of your data.

Fortunately, all modern spreadsheets include a function for calculating this value for you, but it is important to have an understanding of where the standard deviation comes from and what it means.

Table 10.3 Calculation of the standard deviation

Data set 1	Difference from mean (= 9.7)	Difference squared	Data set 2	Difference from mean (= 9.7)	Difference squared
1	−8.7	75.69	4	−5.7	32.49
4	−5.7	32.49	7	−2.7	7.29
6	−3.7	13.69	9	−0.7	0.49
7	−2.7	7.29	9	−0.7	0.49
9	−0.7	0.49	10	0.3	0.09
12	2.3	5.29	11	1.3	1.69
13	3.3	10.89	11	1.3	1.69
13	3.3	10.89	11	1.3	1.69
15	5.3	28.09	12	2.3	5.29
17	7.3	53.29	13	3.3	5.29
Sum of squares:		238.1	Sum of squares:		56.5
Divide by number of values minus one (10−1 = 9):		26.46	Divide by number of values minus one (10−1 = 9)		6.28
Square root of result (standard deviation):		5.14	Square root of result (standard deviation):		2.5

10.5 Evaluating the success of your project

One thing that distinguishes an academic development project from a commercial one is the evaluation of its execution and outcomes. In a commercial project you will be encouraged to carry out some kind of post-implementation review, in order to assess whether the business objectives of the project have been met, and to identify any lessons that have been learnt for future development projects. In a student project you will need to carry out a similar assessment, but in addition you will also need to reflect on your own personal development and to focus in more depth on the development process itself.

Analysing and evaluating the development process

In a student project the manner in which you carry out your development is as important as the software that you deliver. It is vitally important therefore that you take the time to reflect deeply on what you have done, and the way in which you have, or could have, done it. This involves carrying out two activities. The first activity involves the recording and analysis of data and information on the execution of your project. If you have been diligent in updating your project diary and project plans then you will have a lot of this information ready to hand, and in a form that captures the details of events as they happened. You should aim to supplement the data with information gathered at the end of your project on the views of others involved in your development, such as your supervisor, fellow team members and sponsoring clients.

The best ways to collect this information are through brief questionnaires and interviews that ask for views on success or otherwise of activities, deliverables and your personal performance. If you have been experimenting with specific techniques during your project you will need to ask focused questions about these areas. Try to use a mix of open questions that invite comment and suggested improvements, and closed questions that record the perceived success of elements of your project (see Sections 7.4 and 7.5), for example:

- Do you feel that your involvement in the JAD workshop encouraged a sense of ownership of the final system (please circle one number)?

    Not at all   1   2   3   4   5   A great deal

- Do you have any comment about how the workshop could be improved?

The second activity is a critical evaluation of the execution of your project, using the data you have gathered and analysed. The kinds of thing that you need to consider in your evaluation include:

- **Things that went well.** You should not be afraid to 'blow your own trumpet', but you must do more than merely list successful activities. For example, if you undertook an activity where you had a choice of approaches, you should attempt to include some discussion of why your chosen approach was successful, how your experience contrasts with or confirms reports in the literature, and what the implications might be for other projects that you undertake.

- **Things that went badly.** In any project there will be activities that do not go as well as you had planned or anticipated. You must be careful to consider these activities in some depth, and not just report that an activity overran 'because it was more complicated than I expected'. You need to consider the underlying reasons for issues, overruns and unsuccessful outcomes. You also need to reflect on how your experience contrasts with the literature, and establish the knock-on effects of problems that you encountered.

- **Discussion of problems encountered and decisions made.** During your project you will probably have encountered several significant problems that you had not anticipated. You should single these out for discussion.

- **Summary of changes to original scope or plans.** You should discuss the reasons and implications of any changes to your original scope or plans.

- **Potential improvements.** Throughout your project you are likely to have compromised on how or whether certain activities were carried out, owing largely to the constraints you were operating under. You should reflect on what the implications were for the execution of your project, if any, and how you might have undertaken these activities had you been operating under different circumstances.

- **Next steps and follow-up actions.** In most student development projects your deliverables are likely to be incomplete in some way. For example, you may have delivered a prototype of a full system, or have carried out superficial research into the application of certain techniques. Your critical evaluation should include discussion of what your next steps might be in delivering the full system, or what actions would be necessary to confirm your findings.

- **Key messages for future projects.** In every development project there will an element of uniqueness that will deliver some insights that have not been fully explored elsewhere, either because the context differs from previous projects or because you have executed it in a different way. This should lead to insights that could be applied to other similar projects in the future.

- **Reflections on alternative approaches.** Even if your project has been largely successful in meeting its objectives, there will inevitably have been realistic alternatives to the way in which you approached it. Your critical evaluation should include some reflection on whether your chosen approach was the optimum one, or whether on reflection these alternatives might have delivered some benefits to your project, e.g. through reduced costs, issue avoidance or improved software quality.

In reality, while it may well reveal lessons that can be applied in the future to projects of a similar nature, your critical evaluation is unlikely to deliver any momentous insights that will challenge established systems theory. However, it will provide evidence of your personal development and academic understanding, and demonstrate that you can operate as a reflective practitioner.

Review of project objectives

In your PID or project proposal you will have defined a number of specific objectives for your project. You may also have set out certain hypotheses that you wished to test. The nature of these objectives will vary enormously from project to project, but regardless of how you have phrased them or what specific tasks you have carried out, you need to examine the extent to which you have met them.

To do this you take your project objectives one by one, and write a few paragraphs reflecting on the results and outcomes of your project. You must include *all* your objectives, even if you have not been entirely successful in meeting them. It is extremely rare for a project to meet all its objectives, so you should not attempt to obscure those objectives that you have not met in full. Instead, you should explore the reason for not meeting them, many of which you could not have anticipated in advance, but others of which you may have identified in your risk assessment. Your assessors will always give you credit for a thoughtful exploration of the issues that affected the outcome of your project, but will certainly penalise you for attempting to hide them.

In evaluating the results of your project, you will clearly need some measures of how well your software meets its requirements, together with evidence to back up your academic conclusions. This should be an integral part of the data-gathering and analysis mentioned above. You should also examine the assessment criteria of your university to ensure that your analysis covers all of the main points that your project is required to address.

Note that the analysis and evaluation of your project objectives will feed directly into the conclusions section of your final report, and as this is one section that is certain to be read by your assessors, you must not rush or skip over it.

Personal development

The final part of your project evaluation concerns your own personal development. In selecting the topic for your project you should have taken into account what you hoped to get out of it on a personal level.

It is important once you have completed your project to reflect on what you have learnt, which areas you need to concentrate on in the future, and how your project has affected your personal career or academic objectives.

10.6 Summary

1. In a student development project there are two principal components: the development of a piece of software to fulfil a stated purpose and an academic component in which you are expected both to demonstrate your understanding of the theory that is relevant to your development and to analyse and evaluate the results of your project.

2. In a student project the manner in which you carry out your development is as important as the software that you deliver. It is vitally important therefore that you take the time to reflect deeply on what you have done, and the way in which you have, or could have, done it.

3. There are three stages to the analysis and evaluation process in a development project: gathering data, analysing the data and evaluating the results of your analysis.

4. The final draft of your literature review should be left until you are nearing the end of your development, as your project is likely to have thrown up issues that have led to further targeted searches, and the results of your development will provide valuable insights that will add to the quality of your review.

5. Most literature reviews in development projects are presented in a combination of two formats: a separate section in your final report, and paragraphs embedded in your final report in places where they relate directly to the material presented.

6. Your literature review should include only discussion and evaluation of materials that are of direct relevance to your project. Some of the things that make a real difference in constructing a successful and readable literature review are: authoritative and recognised sources, balanced conclusions, summarisation in your own words, informed conclusions, and coherence and consistency.

7. The complexity and volume of 'research' data collected during system development projects are usually fairly limited, and such data are most often used for descriptive purposes, rather than to test or develop complex theories. The process of analysing data breaks down into three stages: preparation, presentation and interpretation.

11 Presenting your results

Introduction

The aim of this chapter is to describe the ways in which you can present the results of your project. This may consist of much more than just a final written report. For example, it could include presentations, software demonstrations and viva voce examinations. The writing of your final report is, however, an important part of your personal development, as well as being a major requirement in most universities. It is therefore covered in some detail.

Most universities provide a project handbook that will give details of their specific requirements regarding the format and broad content of project reports. This chapter is intended to act as a substantial supplement to university handbooks. It provides detailed guidance on what to include in the reporting of your results, and on how to prepare and produce your materials.

Learning Outcomes

After reading this chapter, you will be able to:

- Prepare interim project report and poster presentations

- Understand what should be included in your final written report

- Create a final report structure

- Apply a range of techniques and a structured process to the writing of your final report

- Prepare and deliver a software demonstration or formal presentation

- Prepare for a viva voce examination

Interim reports and poster presentations

Many universities require students to submit an interim report at some point during their project. The timing of the interim report varies quite a lot, with some universities asking for a report early on in your project, as a way of ensuring that you have set out on the right track, while others use the report as a midway progress check. Another increasingly common way of reporting publicly on progress is the poster presentation, which is covered later in this section.

Interim report contents

Interim reports are usually around 1000–1500 words in length, and often include the following information (in summary form):

- **Confirmation of the objectives of your project.** You should not attempt to duplicate the background information that you included in your PID, but it is worth restating the overall aims and objectives of your project. If there have been any alterations to your objectives, you should provide an outline of the changes together with the reasons behind them.
- **High-level literature review.** If you have completed your literature search, your interim report should include a high-level review in order to further establish the context for your project. In some universities, your full literature is a required element of an interim report.
- **Progress and achievements.** You should summarise the activities that you have completed to date.
- **Interim deliverables, results and conclusions.** If you have already produced some of your final deliverables or key development products, you should include an outline of them, together with any high-level diagrams that will help to explain them. You will generally be discouraged from presenting full details of your deliverables.
- **Up-to-date project plan.** As well as a copy of your latest project plan, you should provide explanations for any major changes to your original plan.

Poster presentations

Poster presentations are similar in form to public exhibitions. Each student is asked to prepare a 'poster', usually consisting of between six and nine pages of A4 paper, which provides an interesting and stimulating overview of their project. The posters are then displayed around the walls of a room, for viewing and comment by members of the academic staff and fellow students.

Most poster presentations take place at a similar time to the interim report, so their contents need to be consistent with each other. The kind of information you need to include in a poster is also similar to an interim report, but in a very different format. The audience for your poster is likely to know little about your project, so in a few words and pictures you need to get across a flavour of the purpose and content of your project, together with a summary of what you have done so far and what you plan to do next.

There may be a large number of projects on display during the poster presentation, so the competition for attention will be quite intense. Your poster therefore needs to be attractive, attention grabbing and informative. Above all, your poster must be readable from several feet away. Do not fall into the all too common trap of copying sections of text from your interim report. Instead, you should use a combination of short statements and clear diagrams, and include only the most significant facts and figures from your project.

Things that can really enliven a poster include:

- boldly coloured text or backgrounds (but *only* if it remains easily readable);
- diagrams, photographs and screen shots;
- large sans serif fonts;
- corporate images and logos (for projects with an external client or that are using proprietary technology);
- short bulleted or numbered lists;
- quotations (in moderation);
- matt paper (glossy or laminated paper may be unreadable if room lighting is strong).

A poster presentation is an ideal opportunity to pick up advice on how to conduct the rest of your project. If you have been successful in attracting people to your poster, than as well as answering their questions, you should ask for guidance on how to address issues and tasks that are coming up.

11.3 Final report contents

It is often stated that it is impossible for a good report to rescue a poor project, but it is entirely possible for a poor report to wreck a good project. So it is important that you take the time to prepare and construct a well-written report that truly reflects the content, execution and results of your work.

Many students focus enormous amounts of attention on their final report, almost to the exclusion of everything else. This is not surprising, as it is the report that will provide some of your assessors with their only exposure to your work. Your supervisor will be able to provide outside assessors with some background information, but the evidence in your report will form the basis of their marks.

However, you must not fall into the trap of confusing form with function. The purpose of your report is to present the substance of your work, not to substitute for it. Its main function is to show what you have done, not to impress assessors with your desktop publishing skills or your ability to regurgitate lecture material. It is important therefore to produce a report that presents your deliverables in a concise, coherent and readable form, rather than to produce a verbose theoretical essay or a personal diary.

In a group project, each student will be required to produce an individual report that makes it clear which elements of the project were carried out by themselves, and which were carried out by others or as a group.

Structure

Each university and course will have different requirements for the layout of project reports, but most will share a broadly similar list of contents. Table 11.1 provides an overview of the structure of a typical project report; each entry is then presented in more detail in the subsequent pages. The section lengths in Table 11.1 are based on averages from a collection of around 50 development project reports from the University of Westminster, which in common with many other universities suggests a report length of around 60 pages, excluding appendices. The lengths of the individual reports varied enormously, according to such things as the nature of the development and the balance of research activities.

Title page

The title page of your report will almost certainly need to conform to the standard layout specified by your university. It will typically be required to detail your name, the name of your supervisor, the title of your project and its submission date.

Acknowledgements

While most student projects are carried out either as individual pieces of work or by teams of students undertaking a group project, it is likely that you will have received some support from individuals outside the university. This could include clients, interviewees, sponsors and commercial contacts. It is important to recognise the support that you have received, partly as a matter of courtesy, and partly to give your assessors a feel for the context of your project.

Contents

Try to resist the temptation to break your report down into sections that are little more than a paragraph in length. Word processing packages will enable you to generate a table of contents, which will also provide hypertext links to relevant pages within your report. The ease with which you can number sections and produce contents pages may lead you into the trap of numbering everything. The result, in a document the size of a project report, is a long list of

Table 11.1 Typical final report structure

Section	Description	Length in pages
Title page	The title page will need to conform to the precise requirements of your university.	1
Acknowledgements	This is usually an optional section giving you the opportunity to thank fellow team members or individuals who have provided support to you during your project.	1
Contents	A single page of contents will be sufficient, listing the top two or three levels of headings within your report.	1
Abstract/summary	A *brief* summary of how you conducted your project, and what it delivered. Always less than one page in length, and usually the last section to be written.	1
Introduction	The introduction provides a full description of the problem your project was designed to solve and of your objectives.	5
Literature review	The literature review should summarise the current state of knowledge and practice within your problem domain, and support the selection of your overall project approach.	8
Method and execution	This is the main body of the report, and will describe in detail the method that you adopted for your project, how you applied that method in practice and the development products that your project delivered.	25
Analysis of results	The results of your project should be presented in summary form, with detailed tables of results included in the appendices.	5
Critical evaluation	The results and execution of your project should be critically evaluated, as discussed in Section 10.5.	8
Conclusions	The conclusions section will provide readers with a high-level summary of the key outcomes of your project, and a discussion of your success in meeting the original objectives of your project.	3
References and bibliography	References should be provided for all articles and books that you have referred to in your report. Your university may also require you to provide a bibliography listing all sources that you have consulted during your project.	1
Glossary	An optional section, defining all technical terms used in your report.	1
Appendices	Full details of items referred to in your report, such as program listings, test scripts, Requirements Catalogues and system models.	

low-level subsections that serves only to obscure the overall structure of your report. The best tables of contents usually break chapters into just one level of subsections (as in the contents pages of this book).

Abstract/summary

Abstracts (sometimes referred to as synopses) are brief summaries designed to convey the essence of what your project was designed to do, how you did it, and what the key outcomes were. An abstract should never exceed one page in length, and in some universities you may be required to fall within a word limit of 100 or less. Your abstract should not attempt to act as a guide to the structure of the main report, as this function should be fulfilled by a combination of the contents page and the introduction.

In most cases the abstract is the last section of the report to be written, as it is only at this point that you will have a complete picture of what your report will say. The following box contains an example of a project report abstract that was limited to a word count of 100.

Box 11.1

Example of 100 word abstract

This project implemented a trial system for capturing sales estimates by consultants operating in the field using Personal Digital Assistants, for the installation of building security systems. Research was carried out into appropriate development approaches, resulting in the selection of a package-based solution. Detailed requirements analysis was conducted followed by system design, configuration and implementation. A number of additional software modules were constructed for use alongside the base system in order to meet user requirements. Finally, the development process was evaluated in some detail, leading to recommendations regarding future projects utilising similar package-based solutions and technologies.

Try to avoid the use of technical terms or acronyms in your abstract, as your aim is to provide an easily readable piece of text. Your abstract should also be self-contained (i.e. make sense on its own without the need to refer to other material in your report or to outside sources).

Introduction

Your introduction should aim to place your project in context, and to provide readers with an understanding of what your project and your report contains. The main items that your introduction will need to include are:

- purpose, scope and objectives of your project;
- background and context to the project, including information on your client if appropriate;

- justification for undertaking the project;
- description of the problem (essentially a summary of your requirements analysis);
- outline of the method that you adopted and of the plan that you followed;
- summary of what you delivered;
- description of any major changes to the scope of your project as defined in your PID;
- project organisation, including descriptions of team roles;
- summary of what is contained in the remaining sections of your report.

Much of this information will have been presented as part of your PID, so can be paraphrased quite simply for inclusion in your introduction. Some students insert an unabridged copy of their PID in the introduction to their final report, but it is far better to attach the full version as an appendix and refer to it in the main report, as it tends to break up the flow of your text otherwise.

Literature review

Your literature review will provide the academic context for your project. It should not be used as a catalogue of all that has been written on your subject or to demonstrate the extent of your reading. While you may start to draft your literature review at an early stage in your project, you should not complete it until the end of your project in order to ensure that you place the results, and not just the subject, of your project in context.

It is normal for the main part of your literature review to be presented in a chapter of its own. It is also quite acceptable to break your review up into sections that are presented alongside relevant material throughout your report, perhaps with a high-level review as part of your introduction. There can be no hard and fast rules about which is the best way of presenting your review, as it will depend largely on the nature of your project and on university guidelines. If you are in any doubt about which approach to take, you should discuss it with your supervisor.

Literature reviews are covered in detail in Section 10.3.

Method and execution

The main part of your report will concern the planning and execution of your system development, and any related research activities.

In a project where the selection and adaptation of your development method were straightforward or even mandated by your university, the section that describes your approach will be very short, and may even be included in your introduction. Conversely, in a project that was designed to test or explore approaches to development, or that applied techniques in an innovative way, the section covering your development method may well require a chapter of its own. For most projects, however, you should begin the description of how you executed your project with a discussion of how you selected your approach, the ways in which you then adapted it, and your reasons for rejecting alternative approaches.

Once you have provided your readers with an explanation of your planned approach, you will need to step them through the project stage by stage, covering both your development and research activities. You should explain how you executed each step in your plan, comparing planned versus actual timescales, and present the main products of each activity.

You are highly unlikely to be able to present the details of every design product, system model and software component within the body of your report without making it unreadable. Instead you should aim to include all the core products, such as your requirements catalogue and data or object models, some of which will need to be summarised or presented at a high level, together with links to the full set of detailed deliverables in your appendices. It is a good idea to include examples of some of your lower-level products within the report in order to illustrate your descriptions of the relevant activities. For example, if you have a large Requirements Catalogue, you might include a requirements summary (see Figure 7.5) in the main report, together with one or two samples of full catalogue entries that demonstrate the level of detail that you have captured, and attach the full catalogue in an appendix.

The best way to structure the discussion of your project is to break it into subsections that reflect the stages of your project, such as analysis, design, construction, testing and implementation.

Analysis of results

Most projects will need to present data of some sort. This may have been collected by a range of project activities, such as the research component within your project, your post-development review, requirements analysis questionnaires, or merely as a by-product of project management (e.g. actual duration of tasks versus planned duration of tasks).

You will need to think carefully about how to present the data, and how to highlight things of significance. This will usually mean summarising your results in a chart, where there are a lot of data, with the full set of results shown in an appendix. Alternatively, if the volume of data is not too great, you may choose to present the detail in a table, especially where the precise values of the data are important, rather than overall trends, patterns or distribution. Data presentation and analysis are covered in detail in Section 10.4.

Critical evaluation

As discussed in Section 10.5, your critical evaluation should cover the development process that you followed, your success or failure in meeting your project objectives and your personal development. While it is rarely one of the longest chapters in your final report it is one of the most important as it is here that you should demonstrate to your assessors that you have developed a deeper understanding of systems theory and practice.

Conclusions

The conclusions chapter draws together everything that your project has delivered. It should act as a summary of your major findings and deliverables, and provide an overall evaluation of the success of your project.

The conclusions section should also draw attention to the limitations of your work (it is inevitable within the constraints of a student project that there will be some), and make recommendations for further development of your software or for additional research projects.

Finally, you should take the opportunity to discuss how well you believe you have performed during the project, and to summarise your key personal achievements and lessons learnt. You should also be prepared to admit to any shortcomings in your performance (accompanied preferably by discussion of how you might have done things better), as your assessors will be aware of these in any case, and are more likely to be impressed by an element of self-criticism than by attempts to cover up your mistakes.

References and bibliography

The references chapter will list all of the articles and books that you have referred to within your report. It is extremely important that you include every source that you have referred to, and that the references are complete. This will enable the readers of your report to understand where you obtained the information you have used, and to find it for themselves should they wish to do so. See Section 4.8 for a detailed discussion of references.

Some universities or supervisors also require that you include a list of all of the other sources that you have consulted during your project, even though you have not referred to them directly in your report. You do this by listing the sources in a bibliography, using the same format as for your references.

Glossary

If your report includes a large number of acronyms or specialised technical terms, it may be helpful to your readers to include a glossary.

Appendices

The body of your report should be written so that it can be read by a suitably educated reader in a logical and fluent fashion. If you include large blocks of detailed information in your report, such as tables, forms or listings, these will break it up and make it difficult to follow your arguments and discussions. The solution to this is to provide summaries and extracts of large documents in your report, and then to point your reader to the detail in an appendix, should they need to look at it. The sorts of thing that you might consider including in full in an appendix include:

- source code listings;
- screen shots;
- test plans and results;
- project plans;
- Project Initiation Document;
- questionnaire and interview samples;
- Requirements Catalogue;
- system models;
- infrastructure diagrams;
- technical specifications;
- meeting minutes and workshop notes;
- significant correspondence;
- project control documents;
- user guides and manual;
- detailed tables of results.

11.4   Report writing

Just as you have done with the rest of your project, you must think about how and when you are going to write your report, and produce a plan that leaves you sufficient time to allow for problems with printing and so on. If you have followed the advice in some of the preceding chapters, you will already have most of the material you need to write your report ready to hand, and may even have produced drafts of some of your chapters. If not, you will probably need to spend a little time gathering the right materials together, and reflecting on what you have done throughout your project. It is far better to have made notes in a diary on your activities and ideas as you executed your project, but if you have not done this you will need to sift through the bits of paper and jottings that you produced along the way in order to reconstruct a substitute diary.

The way in which people write reports and assignments varies enormously from individual to individual. Some students find the best way is to start at the beginning and plough straight on through to the end of their report, while many others prefer to adopt a top-down approach, where they sketch out a high-level structure for the whole document, add then add detail over one or two iterations until a final version is produced, ready for proofreading. The top-down approach is the one used successfully by most students for large documents, and so is described below in some detail (Figure 11.1).

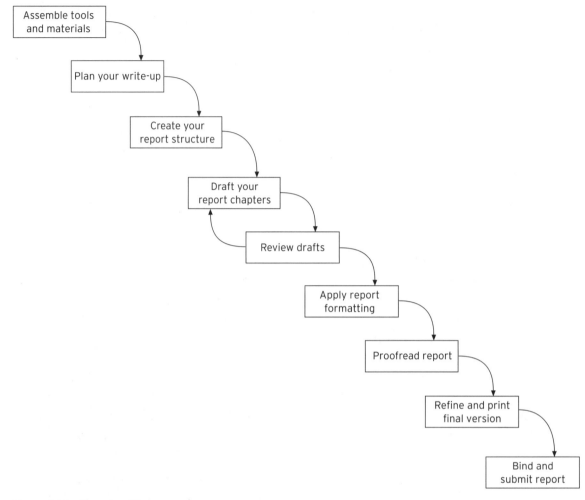

Figure 11.1   Report writing process

Assemble tools and materials

Before starting to write your report it is worth carrying out a little preparation, so that when you do start to work on the content of your report you are not distracted by minor organisational issues. In virtually all universities you will be expected to submit a typewritten report, so the first thing you need to do is select and obtain access to the tools you will be using to produce your report. These tools will normally include a PC, printer and word processor, together with other more project-specific items such as graphics packages, CASE tools, spreadsheets and statistical analysis software.

It is also a good idea to identify a location where you can work on your report without being disturbed and where you can keep all of your project materials ready to hand. Once you have done this you should collect together all of your input material in order to save time later on. Nothing is more disruptive to the writing process than constantly needing to break off to search for a missing piece of information. Input materials for your report might include:

- project diary;
- project plans and project management documents, such as issue logs, meeting minutes and correspondence;
- development products, such as system models, diagrams, test plans, interview notes, Requirements Catalogues and user guides;
- literature search results or early drafts of your review;
- Project Initiation Document;
- software components;
- research data;
- early drafts of any report chapters or sections.

Plan your write-up

Before sitting down to plan how you will assemble and write your report (some of the tips in Table 11.3 below will help in this) you should do a short piece of research into how best to allocate your time, by talking with your supervisor and fellow students (who may be ahead of you in the writing process), and by looking at past reports. This will also help to clarify your ideas on how you want to present your work.

Your plan for writing up your project should always err on the side of caution, as report writing almost always takes longer than you expect, and as your final deadline is immovable you need to plan for any overruns. Remember that if your report is part of your final year project, you will probably be competing with lots of other students for limited resources. So if you are depending on university facilities for tasks such as printing and binding, you should allow plenty of time in your plan for the inevitable delays that will occur while you queue behind other equally deserving students.

Create your report structure

Following discussions with your supervisor, you should have a good idea about what you want to include in your report. Taking this view, you should create an outline of possible report chapters and section headings using pen and paper. You could use the outlining tool in your word processor to do this, but experience shows that once things are inputted into a PC they have a tendency to become 'fixed', and at this stage you will need to experiment with a range of structures. Most universities will have a mandatory framework, within which your report must fit. However, these frameworks usually offer a large degree of flexibility for you to create a structure that fits the needs of your project.

Next to each chapter and section heading you should note an estimate of how many words or pages you would need to present your work to an appropriate level of detail, given a free choice. These estimates should then be double checked against your course requirements, and revised so that they reflect the allocation of marks suggested by the assessment criteria. For example, if you have estimated that your literature review will require three pages (or 5 per cent of the total), but your assessment criteria state that 15 per cent of the marks will be awarded to the review, then you may need to revise your estimate nearer to nine pages. You should not follow assessment criteria blindly, however, as the nature of some sections means that they will take more words or space to present than others, even though they may attract fewer marks.

You should review your potential report structures with your supervisor and rework them until you have a structure that you are both happy with. Once you have done this, you should refine your plan for the rest of your write-up.

Draft your report chapters

Once your report structure is in place you can begin to flesh out each of the sections within it. Often the best way to do this is to import relevant development products or their summaries into each chapter, along with any sections that you have already drafted (such as your literature review). This has the benefit of giving you a feeling of progress, as well as providing a basic flow to your discussions.

There are two basic approaches to drafting the chapters of your report. The first is an incremental approach, where you write a section at a time, finishing each one completely before moving on to the next. The second approach is an iterative one. With the iterative approach you will add detail in a number of cycles to all of your chapters. In the first cycle you might add a set of bullet points or a set of keywords that list the main points that you wish to make in each section. You would then revisit each of these lists and expand the points into rough sentences, before making one final pass through where you ensure that all your sentences make sense and create a logical set of arguments.

In reality, you will probably find a combination of the two approaches is the most successful. Some chapters will be ready to write before others, so you will naturally lean towards an incremental approach. For instance, in most projects you will need to finish the body of your report before you are ready to write your abstract or conclusion sections, as you may not be clear on what you want to say until you have completed your reflections on the execution of your project. Then within each chapter or group of chapters, you will probably find that an iterative approach is the best way to organise your thoughts and to avoid 'writer's block'.

Table 11.2 presents some key guidelines for writing your report. The essential thing to bear in mind when writing your report is that it should act as a demonstration of your academic and practical abilities. Many students will plan to use their final report as evidence for potential employers of their capabilities. So try to put yourself in the place of a professional consultant, and ask yourself how they might present their work. To help you do this, you could search the Internet for case studies and report samples from the websites of consultancy firms.

Table 11.2 Writing guidelines

Guideline	Description
Label every figure and table	In most sections you will need to include tables and figures, such as network diagrams or system models. You must ensure that all of these items are labelled and numbered correctly, and are referred to in the body of your text, even if your reference is little more than a pointer to the figure. A figure that appears without an accompanying reference or explanation may leave the reader wondering what purpose it serves.
Use plain English	Try to avoid overblown or obscure language. It does not impress your assessors, who will appreciate simple straightforward language that aids readability. Pretentious language is all too often used to try to obscure lack of content. You should also avoid unnecessary use of jargon.
Adopt a professional report style	Most professional reports use the passive voice. This is also the preferred style in most universities.
Use a consistent system of referencing	All of the sources that you draw from directly in your report should be referenced using a consistent system, as described in Section 4.8.
Check your grammar and spelling	Poor spelling in particular is indicative of lack of attention to detail. You want to create the impression that you have been conscientious and diligent throughout your project. Sloppy spelling and grammar are very effective in undermining any such impression. There is no real excuse for poor grammar or spelling. All modern word processors have spell checkers and most have grammar-checking tools. You should not, however, rely on these tools, as they have no sense of context or meaning, so can give highly unpredictable results. For this reason, you should always ensure that your report has been proofread by a competent individual (especially if English is not your first language).
Do not use humour and slang	Humour and slang have no place in a formal report.
Avoid use of 'I' and 'we'	Your report is not a personal memoir or diary, so try not to use the first person (I and we), unless it is unavoidable or would make the sentence difficult to read.
Write short paragraphs	Long paragraphs are difficult and tiring to read. So keep them concise and to the point. On the other hand, do not feel tempted to write your report in bullet point format, as it is difficult to construct meaningful arguments using lists alone.
Do not overuse jargon or acronyms	Some acronyms are so much part of common speech that to use anything else would appear awkward, e.g. using personal computer instead of PC, or International Business Machines instead of IBM. In most cases, however, acronyms do nothing to aid readability and can give the impression of laziness. In cases where you are using a long phrase repeatedly, it is quite acceptable to use an acronym as it becomes irritating to read the same words over and over again. You should never use a two-letter acronym if you can possibly help it, and must always spell any acronyms out in full the first time you refer to them or after a long break since they were last used. Remember also that your report is not a chance to impress anyone with your grasp of technical jargon. Your aim should be to help readers understand what you have done. Both jargon and acronyms will stand in the way of this aim.
Avoid abbreviations	Abbreviations, such as 'don't' or 'isn't', are too informal for a project report, so you should always spell them out in full (for example as 'do not' and 'is not').
Be careful with your punctuation	In particular, beware of using the apostrophe improperly. For example, 'the views of the manager' may be written as 'the manager's view', but not as 'the managers views' or 'the managers' views'. If in doubt, avoid apostrophes; after all, what is wrong with 'the views of the manager'? Another common issue with punctuation is overuse of the exclamation mark. In a professional report there is no need to use it at all.
Avoid sexist language	In order to avoid sexist language many students use the rather awkward construct s/he. This does not scan very well, so use 'he or she' or the plural 'they' in its (no apostrophe, please note) place.

Review drafts

Once you have completed a first draft of your entire report it is a good idea to put it to one side for a week or so (no longer, or you run the risk of losing your threads of thought), and then to re-read it. You will find that many of the sections and paragraphs are not quite as you would like. This is entirely expected, so do not worry if you find yourself making quite significant amendments while producing your second draft.

There are no hard and fast rules regarding the number of drafts you should produce, but the constraints of time will probably restrict you to a maximum of three. After your second draft you should review its contents with your supervisor (in some universities this is a formal requirement), and possibly with a fellow student. At this stage I, and many other supervisors, do not expect my students to have produced an immaculately formatted report, so these reviews will focus on content rather than presentation. Nevertheless, any pointers regarding the formatting of your draft should be taken on board, as it will save you some work later on. Fellow students can also be helpful reviewers, as they may know little of the details of your project, so will be able to provide feedback on whether your report is successful in describing its contents and getting across the main points that you wish to make.

Apply report formatting

It is a matter of personal preference as to when you apply proper formatting to your report. Some students like to format their work as they go along, whereas others like to type their work up in a rough format and then format it all at the end, once the content is stable. The latter approach is the most efficient in terms of maximising your use of time. However, you may find that formatting your work as you write gives you a feeling of making progress, or is useful for filling in small gaps in your write-up sessions when you have insufficient time to start anything substantial.

Whichever approach you take, it will still be necessary to spend some time checking that your report is consistently presented, is clear, legible and numbered correctly, and that it conforms to the requirements of your university. If your university does not provide formatting guidelines, you may want to apply the advice given in Table 11.3.

While a well-formatted report is easier to read than a poorly formatted one, it is important to remember that your report is not a showcase for your desktop publishing skills (unless of course that is one of your project objectives). No amount of window dressing will disguise a poorly executed project; indeed, over-elaborate styles of presentation will tend to obscure the real content of your report. In the rare situation where you have some spare time at the end of your project, you would be far better advised to spend it on refining the content of your project, for example by adding some more depth to your critical review, than to waste it on presentational perfectionism.

Table 11.3 Report format guidelines

Guideline	Description
Avoid fancy or comic fonts	Most professional reports use a serif font (such as Times Roman) in 11 or 12 point for main text, and a sans-serif font (such as Arial) in varying sizes for headings. Try to limit yourself to just two fonts, and use italics, underlining and bold text sparingly.
Use double line spacing	Most universities prefer to see a blank line between each line of text, and two or three blank lines between paragraphs or after headings. This provides your assessors with space in which to write comments and questions.
Avoid clutter	Try to create a clean layout that avoids both clutter and too much empty space. Clear headings and a 2.5 cm margin all round will help in this.
Use colour wisely and sparingly	Never use colour in text, and make sure that you use it consistently and sensitively (e.g. by using muted colours) in charts and tables. If you include too much colour it will create a comic book impression.
Ensure all tables and figures are readable	If necessary, you may need to print an A3 version of particularly complex diagrams for inclusion as a fold-out attachment in your appendices.
Always use single-sided A4 white paper	Anything else will only distract from the content of your report. Also, do not use a heavy grade of paper in an attempt to make your report look more substantial than it really is.

Proofread your report

Once you have reached your final draft, complete with proper formatting, you should give it to someone else to proofread. If English is not your first language, then you should choose someone who is a native speaker. You are trying to ensure that your final report is written in a grammatically correct manner, and that it is easy to follow the flow of your arguments. It is more important at this stage that you choose a proofreader who has an eye for detail, than it is to find an expert in your project topic.

Refine and submit your final report

Once you have made any final changes to your report following its proofreading, you can print, bind and finally submit it.

It is likely that your project report is the largest piece of written work that you have produced. It is quite easy therefore to be daunted by its sheer scale, and consequently to suffer from 'writer's block'. Table 11.4 provides some tips for overcoming this problem and for helping you to plan your write-up.

Table 11.4   Tips for getting through your write-up

Tip	Description
Start early	You do not need to wait until you have competed your development to begin writing your report. As soon as you have completed a stage of your project, you can start to write it up.
Identify when you work best	Most people work best at particular times of the day, such as early in the morning or late afternoon. Schedule your writing to coincide with these times.
Break your work down	It is a good idea to break your write-up into small 'chunks' that you can plan individually. This will give a series of smaller milestones that you will have the satisfaction of being able to tick-off regularly. Do not get dejected if you miss one or two, and remember to reward yourself as you pass each milestone.
Do not leave big gaps in your schedule	Try to schedule your work so that you do not have big time gaps between writing sessions. It is all too easy to lose track of what you were trying to say before the gap.
Hide yourself away	You will need to let friends and family know that you will be less free to socialise during the write-up of your report. If necessary, find somewhere to work where you will be less easy to contact (and switch off your mobile phone).
Work little and often, or in big blocks	Some people work more effectively in large blocks of time, where they dedicate themselves to one task. Others (like myself) prefer to work for shorter, more frequent periods of time.
Make notes	If you get stuck for words on occasion, then do not panic as it happens to everyone. Instead, move on to another section and make some notes or jot down some bullet points, and come back to the task of filling out your arguments at another time. Alternatively, just write any old nonsense (the first thing that comes into your head). In many cases, you will then be able to use this as the basis of a well-written section with little revision.
Walk away	If you find yourself staring at your PC with little activity, it is probably time to take a small break. Walk away from your work area and do something trivial, like making a cup of tea, then return five or ten minutes later.
Try to leave complete sections	If you leave sections or tasks in an unfinished state, then it can be difficult to pick up where you left off, as you will all too easily forget what was in your mind at the time. If you have no choice but to leave something half finished, then quickly jot down some keywords to remind yourself of what you were planning to say next.
Write in rough	Do not get obsessed with formatting issues, as it can disrupt your thought processes if you are constantly tinkering with the appearance of your work. This can be a real problem with diagrams. It is possible to move pictures, charts and text endlessly around in a diagram, and to constantly improve upon its visual appeal. It is rarely time well spent, however.
Print out your work	It can be helpful to print your work on a regular basis, and then review it on paper, while having a cup of coffee or travelling into university, for example.
Be cautious in planning	When you plan for your write-up you should take a pessimistic view of how long it will take to format, print and bind your report, as these tasks invariably take longer than you envisage.

11.5 Plagiarism

All materials from outside sources that you have used in your report *must* be fully referenced (as described in Section 4.8). If you fail to do this, you will be guilty of plagiarism. All universities have strict policies to protect against plagiarism, and you should have little difficulty in obtaining a copy of the policy in place at your own university. The University of Westminster (2001), for example, defines plagiarism as:

> Submission of material (written, visual or oral) originally produced by another person or persons, without acknowledgement, such that the work could be assumed to be the student's own.

The presentation of material created by others without proper acknowledgement is a form of theft, and the consequences of plagiarism are invariably severe. The University of Westminster (2001) is fairly typical of universities in general in its penalties for plagiarism:

> It is acceptable to quote from books and journals provided these are correctly referenced. It is also acceptable to allow an author's ideas to inform your own thoughts provided this is acknowledged in a bibliography. However, it is not acceptable to pass off the ideas or words of another as your own. The university regulations on plagiarism are stringent and will be invoked. As the project is 25% of the final degree classification, serious disciplinary action will be taken in the event of proof of plagiarism. Normally this is exclusion from the university.

> The most straightforward form of plagiarism is to pretend that the precise words, diagrams or data of others are your own work. However, this is not the only form of plagiarism. It is equally wrong to paraphrase the work, or to lift the ideas, of others and present them as your own. Nor does this have to be intentional to be viewed as plagiarism. If your record-keeping has been poor during your project, you may unintentionally include material that you have recorded in your notes, but have not referenced at the time, as if it were your own work. This is still a form of plagiarism, and your assessors will not accept ignorance as a defence; after all, how can you prove to them that its inclusion was unintentional?

11.6 Software demonstrations

In many universities you will be expected to demonstrate your software to your assessors. This can take the form of a lengthy and relatively formal demonstration lasting anything up to half an hour. Alternatively, it may form a small part of a viva voce examination, and be limited to five minutes or to specific demonstrations of one or two key features (usually prompted by questions from your assessors).

The advice given below assumes that you have some element of choice in how you present your software, and that you will have the opportunity to demonstrate a significant proportion of its full capabilities. However, even if you are not in this position and are restricted in what you can control, many of the points covered will still be highly relevant. Nothing is more guaranteed to undermine the view your assessors have of your project than an inadequately prepared demonstration, so you should think carefully before ignoring the advice that follows.

The objectives of your demonstration

A software demonstration is your chance to show off the best features of your software, so it is imperative to decide what you want to focus on. For example:

- Do you want to emphasise particular external design features, such as innovative data input interfaces?
- Have you developed some complex algorithms that you will need to explore in detail?
- Do you need to prove that you have fully solved a particular business problem?
- Have you experimented with alternative software solutions, all of which you would like to present?
- Are there some system integration routines that you would like to highlight?
- Have you created a complete business solution that you need to cover all of, at least at a high level?
- Does your software include innovative support for a complex business process that needs to be emphasised?

As part of deciding on your objectives you need to consider who your audience are and what they would like to see. There may be some mandatory course requirements that you need to satisfy, although these are relatively rare. It is a good idea to talk through the expectations of your audience with your supervisor before putting too much effort into preparing for your demonstration.

The two main views of your software that you are likely to want to demonstrate are the user or business view and the academic or technical view. The business view will focus on the functionality of your software and the extent to which it meets its requirements, whereas the academic view will concentrate on how you have constructed your software and focus on specific technical aspects. In many cases you will want to cover both views, but usually with one or other of them as the primary objective for the session.

Preparing for your demonstration

One certain way to make a mess of your software demonstration is to make it up as you go along. Demonstrations are notorious for going wrong, and an under-prepared demonstration is 'an accident waiting to happen'. The key to a successful demonstration is to construct a carefully prepared series of scripts. These will be similar to the scripts you should have used as part of your system testing, but instead of being designed to expose flaws in your software, they will be designed to show off certain features in a way that is easy for your audience to understand.

Using your objectives as a guide, you should produce a list of features, screens and algorithms that you would like to include in your demonstration. If you know your software well, then it should be relatively straightforward to sketch out on paper a series of flowcharts that will demonstrate all the relevant features. Try to create scenarios that demonstrate more than one of your chosen features, but that also create a logical flow, as this will be far easier for your audience to follow than a succession of isolated 'highlights'.

For each of your scenarios you must ensure that you have set up appropriate data for the demonstration to flow smoothly. So, if you need reference data or partially completed transaction data to be in place in order to demonstrate a particular feature, do this in advance. Do not force your audience to sit through repetitions of the same data input routines if you can help it. They will need to see your data set-up programs only once. It is useful to choose easily memorable data, so that you do not have to fumble through your notes during the demonstration in order to find the right codes for data input. You should also have more than one set of data for each scenario, in case of system failure or a request from your audience to see a scenario repeated.

If you are proposing to demonstrate different routes through a particular business process you may be able to start from the beginning with one transaction, and have other partially completed transactions ready to demonstrate (possibly in another operating system session) when needed. This is far more interesting and time efficient than going all the way through the same process from the start for each of the different routes. Again, your audience only need to see the complete process once.

You must ask your supervisor for details of the venue for your demonstration. It may take place in a room with networked computer facilities, in which case you will need to check that the correct software and hardware is in place if you propose to use those facilities. If necessary, you may need to request that some system software is installed or updated prior to your demonstration. You will also need to install your software and test thoroughly that it works properly *before your demonstration*. It will not be acceptable to claim that the network is at fault, if your software subsequently fails.

In some cases you will be expected to use stand-alone computers for your demonstration, which may mean that you will need to create a special version of your software that will run locally in a single tier configuration. It may be advisable to ensure that your software will run in a stand-alone mode in any case, as a back-up in the event of network failure. The safest option in selecting how to demonstrate your software is probably to bring your own computer to the demonstration, assuming you have access to a suitable laptop or desktop machine.

In order to support your demonstration, and to create a positive and professional impression you should consider preparing some handouts for your audience. They will not have time to look at large quantities of material, so you should limit this to a few pages that reflect the content of your demonstration. The sort of thing that you might include would be copies of your flowcharts, together with a few screen shots.

Once you have prepared your demonstration you should practise it a number of times. You will probably find that your first rehearsals will either be far too long or far too short. Try to anticipate the pace at which you will need to deliver your demonstration, and do not attempt to adjust the overall timings by speeding up or slowing down your delivery. The only solution if your demonstration is not the right length is to adjust its content.

You will not be expected to deliver your demonstration entirely from memory. Conversely, you should not be seen to be stumbling through a lengthy and unfamiliar script. In order to strike a balance, you should assemble some prompt cards and flowcharts to help you if you lose your place under questioning, or forget a particular input string. Software demonstrations are somewhat different from presentations as the interaction between you and your software means that timings cannot be fine tuned to the same degree. It is also vital that you give centre stage to your application and not yourself.

Delivering your demonstration

You should begin your demonstration by giving a *brief* introduction to the objectives for the session and to the scope of your software. Do not waste time by talking about the history of your development or project. The focus of the demonstration should be on your software, and not on other project deliverables, such as research results. Your introduction should include descriptions of which features within your software are fully operational, and which are not. There may also be some limitations to the demonstration that are due, for example, to hardware or software constraints within the demonstration environment. Finally, you should tell your audience about the format you are adopting for the demonstration, and in particular how you would like to handle their questions. For example, you may prefer to handle questions at predefined points within your demonstration (although in most demonstrations your audience will tend to interrupt at any point, with questions that are relevant to what you have just shown them).

Ideally you will have been able to set your software up in advance, either on a laptop computer or by gaining prior access to the demonstration environment. If, however, you need to load, set up or start your software at the beginning of your demonstration, you should prepare some material to keep your audience occupied and interested while you do it. If set-up is quite a simple matter, you may be able to deliver your introduction while you configure your software. While this not an ideal way to introduce your session, it is far more important to set up and demonstrate your software than to use valuable time presenting the perfect introduction. Alternatively, you could give your audience something brief and easy to read, such as some bullet points covering the main features of your software or network diagrams of your target production environment.

During your demonstration be aware that your audience is not familiar with your software. So try to explain everything that you do, as you do it. This may appear to you to interrupt the flow of your demonstration, but without an adequate commentary you will leave your audience feeling lost. If there are areas with known problems, then make it clear that the software you are about to demonstrate is still under development. Do not try to hide these areas, but do not go out of your way to point them out. If you have developed your software in a sensible fashion, none of the problem areas will be in core parts of your application, and so should not create a negative impression, unless they are widespread and it appears that you are unaware of them.

If you are demonstrating technically complex areas of your system, you may need to hand out some flowcharts or system models to back up your verbal explanations of how the software has been constructed. You should not overwhelm your audience with handouts, but a few strategically issued papers will help to create the impression that you have prepared thoroughly for your demonstration and are indicative of a rigorous approach in general.

If things go wrong during your demonstration, as they can occasionally do, however well you have prepared, you should have some sort of back-up plan ready. If your software has been installed in an environment that you have been unable to test properly, it is possible that some features will behave unexpectedly. If this occurs, then you should stay calm and explain the issue to your audience and move on to other features in the software. If problems persist, you may need to request another demonstration session, and offer a storyboard presentation or screenshots in the interim. Never try to bluff your way out of a difficult situation, as you will convince no one.

Formal presentations

In addition to demonstrating your software, you may also be required to give a formal presentation of the execution and results of your project. The basic steps in setting up your presentation are similar to those for software demonstration, namely:

1. Identify the audience and course requirements for your presentation.
2. Decide on the objectives for your presentation.
3. List the items that you will need to include to meet your objectives.
4. Create a script for your presentation.
5. Assemble the materials.
6. Rehearse your presentation several times, making any adjustments necessary to ensure that you keep within the time limits (most students have a tendency to overrun).
7. Check that suitable facilities are available in the presentation room, and set them up if not.

Materials and delivery

Most students create presentations that follow the life cycle of their project, but some (especially those who have undertaken complex programming projects) will structure their presentations around key results or deliverables. When

Table 11.5   Tips for effective presentations

Tip	Description
Chose a clear font	You must check that the font you use is clearly visible to your audience. The best choice is usually a 18–20 point sans serif font, such as Arial.
Plain backgrounds	Plain background work much better than graphical backgrounds. They are more readable and present a professional image.
Be careful with colour	Many colours, while easy to read on a monitor, are difficult to read when projected. If in doubt, stick to bold and contrasting colours, with black and white as the dominant colour scheme.
Limit animation	Animation can be useful in building an argument, especially if you use it to add progressively to an on-screen diagram. However, if you litter your presentation with pointless effects you will distract your audience.
Ensure diagrams are readable	If you are presenting a diagram from your report, it may be necessary to edit it so that your audience can read it.
Limit the number of words and points	Each slide should be limited to a maximum of nine bullet points and around 40 words. The best approach is to list keywords or phrases that will act as prompts for you during your presentation.
Summarise tables	Some of your most effective slides will present material that is difficult to describe verbally, such as diagrams, charts and tables of numbers. However, this effectiveness will be undermined if too much information is on show.
Create a consistent style	All of your slides should have a consistent style, with the same basic layout, colours and logos.
Avoid handwritten slides	Handwritten slides do not look at all professional.
Avoid reading from a script	If you recite or read from a prepared script your presentation will not flow naturally and many of your key points will fall flat. Instead, you should use your slides as prompts, or take in some prompt cards (although this is rarely as effective as slides as you tend to get out of step with cards).
Pace yourself	Keep an eye on the time. If you have rehearsed well you should not overrun unless you get a lot of questions. However, the tension of the occasion may lead you to speed up.
Have a back-up plan	If you do fall behind schedule, you should have one or two optional slides that you can drop in order to finish on time.
Speak clearly	Try not to mumble. Your voice needs to be audible right at the back of your audience. This can appear quite unnatural, so try to rehearse at least once in the presentation venue, preferably with a friend in the back row to give you some feedback.
Address the whole audience	Remember to talk to all your audience, and not just one or two familiar faces.
Have a whiteboard handy	It can be useful to keep a whiteboard or flipchart nearby, so that you can sketch out answers to questions if needed.

delivering your presentation, you should also provide a brief introduction that lists what you plan to cover, and a conclusion that summarises your key points and conclusions.

In most cases you will deliver your presentation using slides, either on acetates or more often by using a computer-based presentation package. Whatever format you use, there are a number of tips that will applicable to virtually any presentation, as summarised in Table 11.5.

11.7 Viva voce examinations

A viva voce examination is an oral examination conducted after you have submitted your report. In some universities all students will be required to attend a viva voce examination, while in others just a sample or selection of students will be interviewed. For postgraduate projects a viva voce examination may be attended by a panel of interviewers, which will often include an external examiner; while for undergraduate projects a viva voce examination is normally attended by the project supervisor and one other member of the academic staff.

The purpose of a viva voce examination is to explore the contents of your project and final report in detail. The length of the examination will vary widely from university to university, and between individual students. Most viva examinations will open with general questions regarding your project as a whole, such as 'Can you give us an overview of your project?' or 'What would you do differently next time?' before drilling down into more detail.

Detailed questions may focus on specific technical aspects or concerns within your project, but may equally well be designed to fulfil the following objectives:

- Verify the report and project are your own work.
- Clarify details that are not well described in your report.
- Confirm detailed results and outcomes.
- Dig into your depth of knowledge.
- Supplement the content of your report by drawing out missing information.
- Provide the opportunity for you to demonstrate your software.
- Explore the wider implications of your project.
- Challenge the validity of your findings and conclusions.
- Identify opportunities for further work.

Attending a viva voce examination

Before attending your viva voce examination you should talk to your project supervisor about how and where it will be conducted, and the types of questions you might be asked. As most examinations will open with a short description of your project, you should think in advance about what things you wish to include in your overview. Try to pick out the key milestones, deliverables and achievements of your project, rather than repeating your report's abstract or running through a highly condensed version of your entire report.

The other main part of your preparation should be to read through your report, preferably more than once, on the day before your examination. While you may feel that you have lived and breathed your report for such a long period of time that this is unnecessary, you will be surprised at how much detail has slipped your mind between its submission and your examination.

If your examination includes a software demonstration, then you should prepare for this as described in Section 11.6. As well as your software (and laptop computer if needed), you should also take a copy of your report and any products that you did not include in your report, but that may prove useful if asked in detail about your development, such as a full set of interview transcripts. You should also take some blank paper with you, in case you need to make notes or draw a diagram in order to clarify your answers to questions.

It is important to arrive at your examination in plenty of time. You should look upon a viva voce examination in the same way as you would an interview. Some universities have an expectation that you will dress smartly for the examination, so find out whether this is the case for yourself, and dress accordingly.

During the examination you should listen carefully to all questions, and if you are in any doubt about what is being asked you should say so. None of your examiners will be offended or concerned if you ask for clarification of a question. Your answers should be short and to the point. If you cannot answer a question, you should admit it. Do not be tempted to waffle in an attempt to hide your inability to provide an answer. Conversely, try to avoid one-word answers, unless you are asked a genuinely closed question.

If you find yourself being pressed on a point of detail or being challenged on the validity of your answers, do not get heated and try to resist adopting a defensive attitude. High-pressure questioning is rarely an attempt to catch you out. It is usually intended to dig into an area that was not clear in your report, or to explore further a point of particular interest. So if you feel under pressure, you should not get heated and start to argue your point aggressively. Instead, you should remain polite at all times, and try to explain and justify your views in a calm and professional manner.

11.8   Summary

1. Interim reports are usually around 1000–1500 words in length, and often include a summary of the following: the objectives of your project, high-level literature review, progress and achievements to date, interim deliverables, results and conclusions, and up-to-date project plan.

2. Poster presentations are similar in form to public exhibitions. Each student prepares a 'poster', which provides an overview of their project. The posters are then displayed around the walls of a room, for viewing and comment by members of the academic staff and fellow students. Most poster presentations take place at a similar time to the interim report, so their contents need to be consistent with each other.

3. The purpose of a final report is to present the content, execution and results of your work. Its main function is to show what you have done, not to impress assessors with your desktop publishing skills or your ability to regurgitate lecture material. It is important therefore to produce a report that presents your deliverables in a concise, coherent and readable form.

4. Most students adopt a top-down approach to writing their report, where they sketch out a high-level structure for the whole document, add then add detail over one or two iterations until a final version is produced, ready for proofreading.

5. All materials from outside sources that you have used in your report *must* be fully referenced, otherwise you will be guilty of plagiarism.

6. The two main views of your software that you are likely to want to demonstrate are the user or business view and the academic or technical view. The business view will focus on the functionality of your software and the extent to which it meets its requirements, while the academic view will concentrate on how you have constructed your software and focus on specific technical aspects.

7. One certain way to make a mess of your software demonstration is to make it up as you go along. Demonstrations are notorious for going wrong, and an under-prepared demonstration is 'an accident waiting to happen'.

8. A viva voce examination is an oral examination conducted after you have submitted your report. The purpose of a viva voce examination is to explore the contents of your project in detail.

Bibliography

Projects and project management

Bell, J. (1999) *Doing Your Research Project* (3rd edition), Buckingham, Open University Press.

Casey, C. (1999) *Department of Computing Project Handbook*, University of Central Lancaster Website. Available from http://www.uclan.ac.uk/facs/destech/compute/staff/casey/project/newhandb.htm (accessed 14 June 2002).

Dawson, C. (2000) *The Essence of Computing Projects, A Student's Guide*, Harlow, FT Prentice Hall.

Maylor, H. (1999) *Project Management* (2nd edition), Harlow, FT Prentice Hall.

The University of Westminster (2001) *Student Guide to the Major Project*, Harrow, Middlesex, Harrow Business School.

Yeates, D. and Cadle, J. (2001) *Project Management for Information Systems* (3rd edition), Harlow, FT Prentice Hall.

System development

Bennett, S., McRobb, S. and Farmer, R. (2001) *Object-oriented Systems Analysis and Design using UML* (2nd edition), London, McGraw-Hill.

Bocij, P., Chaffey, D., Greasley, A. and Hickie, S. (2003) *Business Information Systems, Technology, Development and Management for the e-Business* (2nd edition), Harlow, FT Prentice Hall.

Boehm, B. (1988) 'A spiral model of software development and enhancement', *IEEE Computer*, **21**, 5, May, 61–72.

Booch, G. (1991) *Object-oriented Analysis and Design with Applications*, Menlo Park, Benjamin/Cummins.

Booch, G., Jacobson, I. and Rumbaugh, J. (1999) *Unified Modeling Language User Guide*, Reading, Addison-Wesley, ACM Press.

Bray, I. (2002) *An Introduction to Requirements Engineering*, Harlow, FT Prentice Hall.

Coad, P. and Yourdon, E. (1990) *Object-oriented Analysis* (2nd edition), Englewood Cliffs, Prentice Hall.

Coad, P. and Yourdon, E. (1991) *Object-oriented Design*, Englewood Cliffs, Prentice Hall.

Cockburn, A. (2001) *Writing Effective Use Cases*, Boston, Addison-Wesley.

Dennis, A., Wixom, B. and Tegarden, D. (2002) *Systems Analysis and Design, An Object-oriented Approach with UML*, New York, Wiley.

DSDM Consortium (2002) *The Underlying Principles*, DSDM Website. Available from http://www.dsdm.org/en/about/principle.asp (accessed 7 January 2003).

DSDM Consortium (2003) *Frequently Asked Questions*, DSDM website. Available from http://www.dsdm.org/en/resources/faqs.asp (accessed 7 January 2003).

Jacobson, I., Christerson, M., Jonsson, P. and Overgaard, G. (1992) *Object-oriented Software Engineering: A Use Case Driven Approach*, Wokingham, Addison-Wesley, ACM Press.

Jacobson, I., Booch, G. and Rumbaugh, J. (1999) *The Unified Software Development Process*, Reading, Addison-Wesley, ACM Press.

Rumbaugh, J., Blaha, M., Premerlani, W., Eddy, F. and Lorensen, W. (1991) *Object-oriented Modeling and Design*, Englewood Cliffs, Prentice Hall.

Stapleton, J. (1997) *Dynamic Systems Development Method, The Method in Practice*, Harlow, Addison-Wesley.

Weaver, P., Lambrou, N. and Walkley, M. (2003) *Practical Business Systems Development Using SSADM, A Complete Tutorial Guide* (3rd edition), Harlow, FT Prentice Hall.

User interface design

Galitz, W. (2002) *The Essential Guide to User Interface Design: An Introduction to GUI Design Principles*, New York, Wiley.

Mandel, T. (1997) *The Elements of User Interface Design*, New York, Wiley.

Report writing

Cottrell, S. (1999) *The Study Skills Handbook*, Basingstoke, Palgrave.

Riley, M., Wood, R., Clark, M., Wilkie, E. and Szivas, E. (2000) *Researching and Writing Dissertations in Business and Management*, London, Thomson Learning.

Research

Coombes, H. (2001) *Research using IT*, Basingstoke, Palgrave.

Cornford, T. and Smithson, S. (1996) *Project Research in Information Systems, A Student's Guide*, Basingstoke, Palgrave.

Creswell, J. (2002) *Research Design: Qualitative, Quantitative and Mixed Method Approaches*, London, Sage Publications.

Oakshott, L. (2001) *Essential Quantitative Methods for Business, Management and Finance*, Basingstoke, Palgrave.

Saunders, M., Lewis, P. and Thornhill, A. (2003) *Research Methods for Business Students* (3rd edition), Harlow, FT Prentice Hall.

Change management

Burnes, B. (2000) *Managing Change*, Harlow, FT Prentice Hall.

McCalman, J. and Paton, R. (2000) *Change Management: A Guide to Effective Implementation*, London, Sage Publications.

Index